Microsoft®
Expression® Web
FOR
DUMMIES®

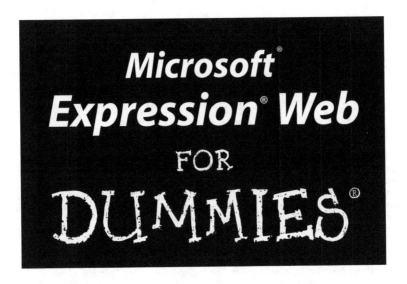

Microsoft® Expression® Web FOR DUMMIES®

by Linda Hefferman and Asha Dornfest

BICENTENNIAL
1807
WILEY
2007
BICENTENNIAL

Wiley Publishing, Inc.

Microsoft® Expression® Web For Dummies®

Published by
Wiley Publishing, Inc.
111 River Street
Hoboken, NJ 07030-5774
www.wiley.com

Copyright © 2007 by Wiley Publishing, Inc., Indianapolis, Indiana

Published by Wiley Publishing, Inc., Indianapolis, Indiana

Published simultaneously in Canada

For general information on our other products and services, please contact our Customer Care Department within the U.S. at 800-762-2974, outside the U.S. at 317-572-3993, or fax 317-572-4002.

For technical support, please visit www.wiley.com/techsupport.

Wiley also publishes its books in a variety of electronic formats. Some content that appears in print may not be available in electronic books.

Library of Congress Control Number: 2007920017

ISBN: 978-0-470-11509-1

10 9 8 7 6 5 4 3 2

WILEY

About the Authors

Since 1989, **Linda Hefferman** has been explaining technical stuff to everyday people who use technology but are not exactly best buddies with their computers.

Her first computer manual taught people how to make pretty graphs and charts from project management data using a software program written for the first version of Microsoft Windows. Since then she has written help systems and user manuals on such diverse products as Web stores, Flash-based educational Web sites, and customer management software for cosmetic salespeople.

This is her first title for the *For Dummies* series, and she's thrilled to combine her passion for writing with her technical skills to do what she loves best: help the average Joe and Jane feel comfortable and confident on computers. Visit Linda on the Web at www.lindahefferman.com.

On her first day of college, **Asha Dornfest** took a bold step: She replaced her broken typewriter with a PC.

Asha didn't consider herself a geek; her computer was simply a tool to help her write papers and reports. But by her senior year, she came to regard her computer with a sense of kinship.

In 1994, Asha discovered the Internet. Soon after, she and her husband Rael started a Web design business in their dining room and began hawking their electronic wares. Mind you, this venture began during the Web-publishing Stone Age, when many people had never even heard of the World Wide Web. Rael quipped that *For Dummies* books about Web publishing may one day hit the shelves. Asha scoffed.

Rael obviously had more foresight than Asha did; Asha went on to write several books and articles on the topic, including *Microsoft FrontPage For Dummies*. She now spends an inordinate amount of time online — she's the founder and editor of the popular parenting Weblog Parent Hacks (www.parenthacks.com) and still maintains her personal site at www.ashaland.com.

Dedications

To my amazing co-author, Asha Dornfest. We truly are the A Team. And to my parents, Doris and Dave Ohde, who taught me from a young age the importance of a well-crafted sentence.

Authors' Acknowledgments

We'd like to thank all the people who made *Microsoft Expression Web For Dummies* run so smoothly. Special thanks to Project Editor Becky Huehls, Acquisitions Editor Steve Hayes, Technical Editor Mike Lerch, and Copy Editor Rebecca Whitney.

The Microsoft Expression Web development team put together an excellent beta program and software product. We are especially grateful to Wayne Smith, for making sure we had the latest information when we needed it, and Devindra Chaini, for timely answers to our nitpicky questions.

Cheryl D. Wise offered much guidance on many of the niggling techie subtleties of moving from FrontPage to Expression Web.

To our family and friends . . . thanks for tolerating near neglect and chaos on the road to getting this book done, and still loving us anyway.

The wisdom of many professional Web designers graces our Part of Tens chapters, especially Jim 'G' Davidson, Holly Brewer, Emma McCreary, and Kevan Alan Embleton.

And, last but not least, I, Linda Hefferman, owe my sanity to David Bowie, Jason Webley, The Dresden Dolls, Modest Mouse, Jack White, Johann Sebastian Bach, and the folks at KNRK 94.7 FM for keeping my foot tapping while my typing digits were working overtime.

Publisher's Acknowledgments

We're proud of this book; please send us your comments through our online registration form located at www.dummies.com/register/.

Some of the people who helped bring this book to market include the following:

Acquisitions, Editorial, and Media Development

Project Editor: Rebecca Huehls

Sr. Acquisitions Editor: Steve Hayes

Copy Editor: Rebecca Whitney

Technical Editor: Michael Lerch

Editorial Manager: Leah P. Cameron

Media Development Specialists: Angela Denny, Kate Jenkins, Steven Kudirka, Kit Malone

Media Project Supervisor: Laura Moss

Media Development Manager: Laura VanWinkle

Editorial Assistant: Amanda Foxworth

Sr. Editorial Assistant: Cherie Case

Cartoons: Rich Tennant (www.the5thwave.com)

Composition Services

Project Coordinator: Jennifer Theriot

Layout and Graphics: Claudia Bell, Jonelle Burns, Carl Byers, Joyce Haughey, Barbara Moore, Heather Ryan, Alicia B. South, Erin Zeltner

Proofreaders: Aptara, Melanie Hoffman

Indexer: Aptara

Anniversary Logo Design: Richard Pacifico

Publishing and Editorial for Technology Dummies

> **Richard Swadley,** Vice President and Executive Group Publisher
>
> **Andy Cummings,** Vice President and Publisher
>
> **Mary Bednarek,** Executive Acquisitions Director
>
> **Mary C. Corder,** Editorial Director

Publishing for Consumer Dummies

> **Diane Graves Steele,** Vice President and Publisher
>
> **Joyce Pepple,** Acquisitions Director

Composition Services

> **Gerry Fahey,** Vice President of Production Services
>
> **Debbie Stailey,** Director of Composition Services

Contents at a Glance

Table of Contents

Introduction

*W*eb publishing has changed dramatically in the years since the first sites appeared on the Internet cyberfrontier. Like anything else new and experimental, the Web has had its high-tech equivalent of strange fashions, bad hair days, and utter lawlessness. If you're just getting into Web publishing now, you may feel as though you've missed the boat. In fact, you've missed a lot of hassle — browser wars, shifty HTML code, and creaky, hard-to-use Web publishing software. Now is as good a time as any to stake your claim on the Web.

What's more, you're already a step ahead: You chose Expression Web. The Microsoft development team who birthed this baby adopted a just-say-no-to-nonstandard-Web-site-building approach when designing Expression Web. They've incorporated the latest and best in Web building practices and technologies to help you, the Web designer, build Web sites that not only look and work great but also hum with the precision of a German luxury vehicle.

Yet if you've never built a Web site, or even if you have but don't have a clue what Microsoft means by those buzzwords on the Expression Web box — standards-driven, Cascading Style Sheets, and the like — you're not alone. *Microsoft Expression Web For Dummies* is here to help.

About This Book

Expression Web is a hefty piece of software capable of building Web sites that range from a few basic pages to immense, data-driven powerhouses. We assume that you fall somewhere in the middle: You want to use Expression Web to build a well-designed, easy-to-navigate Web site, not become an expert on databases. In this book, we focus on the information you need to know: how to fill your site with text and graphics and how to link pages, build forms, and do even more — and have it all look good.

We believe that you'll find Web site building easier and more enjoyable if you understand and feel comfortable with how your site is put together. So, throughout this book, we introduce you to the code that works behind the scenes. And because we give the code to you in little bits, you may not even notice that you're getting up to speed on HTML and CSS.

If you're a complete Web-building newbie, you may want to skim this book to get a sense of what building a Web site entails, and then read the stuff that looks useful. If you need a little help with the code terminology, give the first part of Chapter 14 a read-through. If you've already tried your hand at site building, you can use *Microsoft Expression Web For Dummies* as a reference manual. Skip around and read the parts that interest you.

Foolish Assumptions

This book helps you jump right into using Expression Web. We therefore make a few assumptions about who you are and what you already know how to do:

- ✔ **You're on good terms with your computer and its associates: the mouse, keyboard, monitor, and modem or network connection.** You ask the computer nicely to do things by pressing keys and clicking the mouse, and it usually complies. You're comfortable with the basic workings of Windows, such as using the Start menu, double-clicking items, getting around the Windows desktop, clicking buttons on toolbars, and choosing commands from menu bars.

- ✔ **You have an Internet connection through your workplace, school, Internet service provider (ISP), or online service, and you've spent some time surfing the Web.** You may not understand how the Internet works, but you can find your way around and have someone you can call — a techie friend, neighbor, or work colleague — when you have a problem.

- ✔ **You have Expression Web sitting on your desk, and you may have already installed it on your computer.**

- ✔ **You're new to Expression Web, and you're likely also new to Web publishing.** If you've tried Web publishing, you've never done it with Expression Web. If you have worked with Expression Web, you were perplexed after fiddling with the program, rushed to the bookstore, and are reading this book right now.

How This Book Is Organized

In this book, we include all the information you need to get started creating great-looking Web sites with Expression Web. Expression Web is no small topic, so we divide the subject into easily chewable parts.

Part I: Getting Started with Expression Web introduces you to Expression Web and helps you become comfortable with how the program's menus, commands, task panes, and workspace look and act. We show you how to set up a new Web site and open an existing one. Chapter 2 covers everything you need to know about individual Web pages.

Part II: Coaxing Content onto the Page covers how to work with the triumvirate of Web page content: text, hyperlinks, and pictures. We also introduce you to creating forms for interacting with your visitors.

Part III: Great Design Doesn't Have to Be Difficult familiarizes you with the fundamentals of formatting and layout. It dives into using Cascading Style Sheet (CSS) styles to control how your pages look, and how to arrange stuff on your pages by using both CSS and tables. You also find out how to create tables for tabular data and templates to streamline site building and updating.

Part IV: Going Live and Keeping House covers everything you need to know to publish your Web site on the Internet, as well as how to keep your sites and their files tidy and organized. You find out about different reports you can run on your Web site, how to back up and move a Web site, and how to import and export to and from Expression Web. Finally, we ease you into working with the Expression Web code tools, and we present basic HTML concepts that make working in Expression Web easier.

For **Part V: The Part of Tens,** we compiled some cool gizmos that you can add to your pages. We also asked a bunch of professional Web designers to share their favorite design resources.

For more Part of Tens goodies, go to www.dummies.com, use the search box to navigate to this book's Web page, and then click the Bonus Chapters link. There you'll find bonus Chapters 17 and 18, full of professional Web designers' secrets and techniques for planning a new Web site and updating a horribly outdated one.

Conventions Used in This Book

We use a few text conventions throughout this book:

- ✔ A notation like "Choose File➪Open" is a condensed version of "From the File menu, choose the Open command."

- ✔ When we say, "Press Ctrl+N," we mean, "While holding down the Ctrl key on your keyboard, press the N key."

- ✔ E-mail address and Web site addresses appear in this computerese font, as do certain terms and symbols lifted right out of the code, like these: class, id, <h1>. If a Web address is really long, or if we want to show you a chunk of code, it appears on its own line, like this:

```
This is a line of code.
```

Expression Web often gives you more than one way to tackle a task. For example, choosing a menu item, clicking a toolbar button, and pressing a keyboard shortcut might all accomplish the same task. In this book, we generally tell you the easiest way to carry out a particular task. If you prefer to use an alternative method, by all means, go ahead.

Icons Used in This Book

Icon-studded paragraphs and sidebars highlight special information.

Here, you find a timesaving Expression Web shortcut. Or, you may receive a design tip that you can use to add oomph to your Web site. Or, perhaps you get a pointer to relevant information on the Web.

This icon points out important details you don't want to forget.

The information flagged with this icon is for those of you who want to dig a little deeper into the technical aspects of Web publishing.

Your computer doesn't explode when you see this icon. But it does alert you to a potential Expression Web or Web publishing sticky spot.

Watch for these sections throughout this book to help you understand what's happening in your page's code, by which we mean HTML (or its newest incarnation, XHTML) or CSS (Cascading Style Sheets) or both.

Where to Go from Here

Enough preamble — it's time to get that Web site started!

Our hope is that this book helps you develop the confidence and skills to create whatever Web site you envision. Onward, ho!

Part I

Getting Started with Expression Web

The 5th Wave   By Rich Tennant

"Just how accurately should my Web site reflect my place of business?"

In this part . . .

Allow us to introduce you to Expression Web. We'll break the ice during that awkward getting-to-know-each-other period. In Chapter 1, we walk you around the Expression Web workspace and show you how to create your first Web site. In Chapter 2, we familiarize you with the basics of creating Web pages.

Chapter 1

Creating a Web Site with Expression Web

*I*n this chapter, you get started with Expression Web: You get familiar with the workspace and find out how to create and save Web sites. Before you hang your shingle as a Web publisher, though, you should understand what you're really doing when you create and publish a Web site. No doubt you've already seen a Web site. Web sites are the places you visit as you make your way around the World Wide Web. In the same way as a book is made up of individual pages, a Web site is made up of individual files called Web pages. *Web pages* contain the text, pictures, and other content you see when you visit a Web site.

As you construct a Web site, you create Web pages and then string the pages together by using hyperlinks. *Hyperlinks* are the highlighted words and pictures inside the page that visitors can click to jump to a different location, page, or Web site. Hyperlinks can also initiate a download or pop open an e-mail window.

After your site is complete, you *publish* it. In other words, you make the site visible to the rest of the world on the World Wide Web (or, if you're working on an internal company site, on the company's intranet). This process isn't automatic. For a Web site to be live, you must transfer the site's files from your computer to a *Web server,* a host computer that runs special Web server software and is connected to the Internet 24 hours per day.

If you're working on an intranet site, the publishing process is similar, except that only people with a password to access the intranet can view your site. An *intranet* is an internal company network based on the same type of technology as the Internet, with access restricted to people within that company. Intranet sites generally contain information useful to company insiders, such as policies, collaborative tools, and department announcements.

Many people gain access to a host Web server by signing up for an account with an Internet service provider (or *ISP*) that makes Web server space available to its users. Others use a Web server maintained by their workplaces or schools. Another option is to sign up with one of the many hosting companies that offer server space for free.

Starting Expression Web for the First Time

The first time you start Expression Web, you need to jump through a few basic setup hoops before you can get down to building your site.

To get started, on the Windows taskbar, choose Start➪All Programs➪ Microsoft Expression➪Microsoft Expression Web. Expression Web opens. What happens next varies. Here are some dialog boxes you may encounter and instructions for how to handle them:

✔ A dialog box may prompt you to enter your name and initials. Expression Web uses these details to identify the Web sites and pages you create and modify. If necessary, in the Name and Initials text boxes, enter your name and initials, and click OK.

✔ A message box prompts you to make Expression Web the default Web page editor for HTML documents, which is another way of saying "Expression Web wants to become the go-to program whenever you want to create or update a Web page. Okay?" If you want to make Expression Web your default HTML editor (and we suggest that you do), click the Yes button.

If you click No, this message continues to pester you each time you launch Expression Web unless you turn it off by deselecting the Always Perform This Check When Starting Expression Web option.

✔ The Privacy Options dialog box appears, prompting you to select options for tracking how Expression Web performs on your system and reporting information back to Microsoft. We suggest that you select both options. The Expression Web development team uses this information to make future versions of Expression Web better.

✔ A dialog box appears, prompting you to sign up for the Microsoft Update service. This service offers automatic updates for Expression Web and other Microsoft programs installed on your system. We suggest that you choose to download and install updates when they are available.

Your screen should look like the one shown in Figure 1-1. If it doesn't look like it, close the program and restart it.

Expression Web has found the My Documents folder on your hard drive and, inside it, has created a new folder named My Web Sites in which to store all the Web sites you build.

Although Expression Web appears to be ready for you to start adding content to the blank page that appears, please don't. You must first *create a Web site*, which is a specially designated folder in which Expression Web stores all pages associated with the site. We tell you how to create a site in the section "Creating and Saving a New Web Site," a little later in this chapter.

Menu bar   Toolbar

Figure 1-1:
Expression
Web as it
appears
the first
time you
launch the
program.

Task panes   Editing window   Status bar

Task panes

Touring the Expression Web Screen

Now that you're here, allow us to show you around the Expression Web workspace so that you can start getting comfortable.

As you get used to working with Expression Web, you may want to customize the workspace so that everything you need is visible on the screen and the features you don't use are tucked away from view. You can begin with the simple tour that follows, but when you're ready, feel free to experiment with the layout of the Expression Web workspace.

To start the tour, step right this way. . . .

Workspace

The *workspace* is where you build your Web site and all its Expression Web parts (refer to Figure 1-1). If you have more than one Web site open at the same time, each Web site appears in its own Expression Web workspace window (see Figure 1-2).

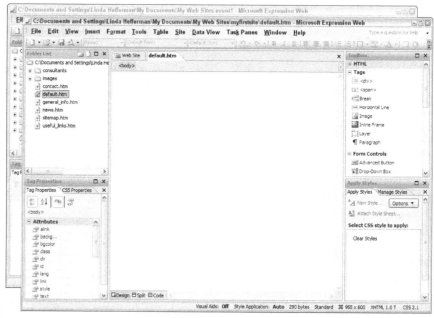

Figure 1-2:
Each
separate
Web site
has its own
workspace
window
with the
path and
title of the
Web site.

Menu bar and toolbars

Like most other Windows programs, the *menu bar* at the top of the workspace contains all the Expression Web commands. You find buttons for the most commonly used commands on the Common *toolbar*, located just below the menu. (Expression Web has many more toolbars, which contain buttons for commands specific to a particular function. To show other toolbars, choose View⇨Toolbars and then click the name of the toolbar you want to see.)

The Standard toolbar deserves special mention. It contains a handful of useful buttons not found on the Common toolbar — such as Spelling, Print, Cut, Copy, and Paste and the Format Painter — but doesn't have as many text formatting options. We suggest using the Common toolbar most of the time, and then popping open the Standard toolbar if you find that you need quick access to its buttons.

Because the Common toolbar contains a lot of buttons, not all of them show up if your screen resolution is set to 1024 x 768 or lower. Click the down arrow at the far-right end of the toolbar to see all the buttons.

You can customize Expression Web toolbars by adding or removing commands. To add a command to a toolbar, follow these steps:

1. **On the right side of the toolbar you want to customize, click the down arrow.**

2. **Choose Add or Remove Buttons⇨Customize.**

   The Customize dialog box appears.

3. **If the Commands tab isn't already showing, click it.**

4. **In the Categories list box, select the menu containing the command you want to add.**

5. **In the Commands list box, click and drag the command onto the toolbar.**

   As you drag, the cursor turns into an arrow pointing to a button.

   As soon as you arrive at the toolbar with your command in tow, an insertion point — it looks like a capital *I* — shows you where the button for the command would appear if you were to release the mouse button.

6. **Move the cursor along the toolbar until the insertion point arrives at the spot on the toolbar where you want the button to live, and then release the mouse button.**

   Voilà! The button appears on the toolbar.

7. **If you want to add more buttons to the toolbar, repeat Steps 4 through 6 for each button addition. When you finish, click Close in the Customize dialog box.**

To remove a button from a toolbar, drag it down and off the toolbar. Expression Web is picky about certain toolbar buttons. If you try to remove a toolbar button and it doesn't budge, you can't remove it. Expression Web always lets you remove a button you added, though.

The Expression Web menu bar and all its toolbars can be dragged around the screen as free agents or fixed in various locations (called *docking*). When you first launch Expression Web, the menu bar and Common toolbar are docked at the top of the screen.

To move a docked toolbar, follow these steps:

1. **Move your cursor over the left edge of the menu or toolbar until the cursor turns into a four-pointed arrow.**

2. **Drag the toolbar away from its original location toward the center of the screen.**

   The menu bar or toolbar pops away from its location, and its title bar appears.

   When you let go of the mouse button, the toolbar stays where you left it. You can move it somewhere else by dragging its title bar.

You can redock the menu bar or a toolbar on any of the four sides of the workspace window. To do so, drag the menu bar or toolbar where you want it and, when it pops into its new spot, release the mouse button.

Expression Web Help tells you more about customizing the menus and toolbars. To launch Help, choose Help⇨Microsoft Expression Web Help or press F1.

Editing window

The editing window takes up the majority of the Expression Web workspace. That's where you add text, pictures, hyperlinks, and other goodies to your Web pages. The filename of each open Web page appears on its own tab. Figure 1-3 shows a Web site with two Web pages open in the editing window. You can flip between pages by clicking the pages' tabs or by pressing Ctrl+Tab or Ctrl+Shift+Tab. Expression Web points out pages that contain unsaved changes by placing an asterisk next to the filename, like this: default.htm*.

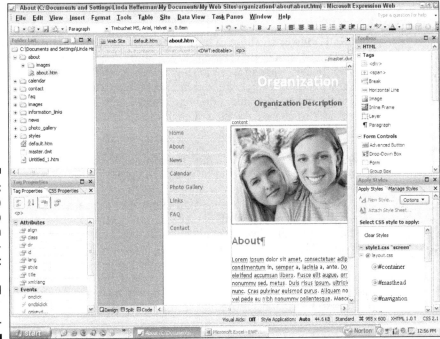

When you open a Web site, a Web Site tab also appears in the editing window. This tab shows you the site's list of files and folders or the contents of the folder selected in the Folder List task pane. Chapter 13 gives you detailed information about this tab. (In Chapter 2, we cover how to add and organize Web pages). To close an open Web page, click the X button in the right-hand corner of the editing window.

The editing window contains three different views: Design, Code, and Split:

- ✔ **Design view** shows you a rough idea of what your Web page will look like to your visitors, and you're likely to spend much of your time here.

  Design view only *approximates* how your pages will look when viewed with a Web browser, such as Internet Explorer, Mozilla Firefox, or Netscape. How your page looks to your visitors depends on their individual browser settings, which can vary from person to person. We tell you how to pre-view your pages in different browsers in Chapter 2.

- ✔ **Code view** displays the page's underlying HTML code. No matter whether you know HTML, you can rest assured that the Expression Web code tools are superb. (The same could not be said of its predecessor, Microsoft FrontPage.)

✔ **Split view** is the best of both worlds. A moveable bar divides the editing window, with Code view on the top and Design view on the bottom. Using Split view, you can work in the comfort of Design view while watching the page's underlying code change in real time. (And vice versa: If you make changes to the code, you can press F5 to see the results in Design view.) To change the size of each view, click the divider bar and drag it up or down.

Switch between views by clicking the buttons at the bottom of the editing window or by pressing Ctrl+PgUp or Ctrl+PgDn.

Split view might indeed be one of the strongest Expression Web features, especially if you're an HTML newbie. Expression Web writes such clean, by-the-book code that if you pay attention as you build your Web pages, you pick up HTML almost painlessly. Why learn to use HTML? As powerful a program as Expression Web is, as you become experienced with Web design, you find that it's often easier to tinker with code than to wade through commands and dialog boxes. We gently introduce you to bits of code so that your introduction to HTML feels more like stepping into a kiddie pool than plunging headlong into the icy deep end.

Quick Tag Selector bar

Look beneath the tabs in the editing window: That's the Quick Tag Selector bar. Click anywhere on your Web page, and the Quick Tag Selector bar shows you all the HTML tags that apply to the item you clicked. You can click a tag to select the element. For example, click <p> to select the whole paragraph in Design view or Code view (or in both if you're in Split view). Click the down arrow next to a selected tag for more options. We cover using the Quick Tag Selector bar in more detail in Chapter 14.

Task panes

Surrounding the editing window on either side are *task panes* for working in detail with various aspects of your Web pages. They become useful as you begin building and refining your site. When you launch Expression Web, the Folder List task pane appears in the upper-left corner; the Tag Properties and CSS Properties task panes are located below it, in the lower-left corner. On the other side of the editing window, the Toolbox is in the upper-right corner, with the Apply Styles and Manage Styles task panes in the lower-right corner.

Expression Web has many other task panes for working with other controls. All are listed on the Task Panes menu. Depending on what kind of Web site you're building, you use some task panes more than others, but you will find the Folder List task pane invaluable for managing your site's folders and files. And the style-related task panes (Apply Styles, Manage Styles, and CSS Properties) become your best friends as you format your pages to look the way you want. (We get into detail about styles in Chapter 7.)

As with the menu bar and the toolbars, you can move and dock task panes. For example, if you want more screen real estate for the editing window, move all your task panes to one side or close the ones you aren't using.

To move a task pane, follow these steps:

1. **Move your cursor over the task pane's title bar until the cursor turns into a four-pointed arrow.**

   You can also right-click and, from the pop-up menu that appears, choose Float.

2. **Drag the task pane away from its original location toward the center of the screen.**

   The task pane pops away from its location.

3. **Keep the mouse button down (and don't let go) until the task pane is where you want it (and *then* let go).**

   If the task pane ends up in entirely the wrong place, don't worry. Simply grab hold of its title bar and drag it again.

Task panes are friendly screen elements that like to hang out with other task panes more than they like floating around the screen by themselves. This characteristic can be frustrating when you first start moving the task panes around the workspace window.

You might notice this behavior. If you move a task pane on top of another task pane, they join together into one big task pane family. Although this behavior can be aggravating if that isn't what you want, it's actually a feature. In Figure 1-4, we dragged the Tag Properties (with CSS Properties in tow) into the Apply (and Manage) Styles task pane. (We made it a little bigger so that you can see all the tabs.)

In a task pane group, click the right and left arrows to scroll through the different task panes. Each task pane's name appears on a tab. The active task pane's tab sits on top of the other tabs, and its name appears on the group's title bar.

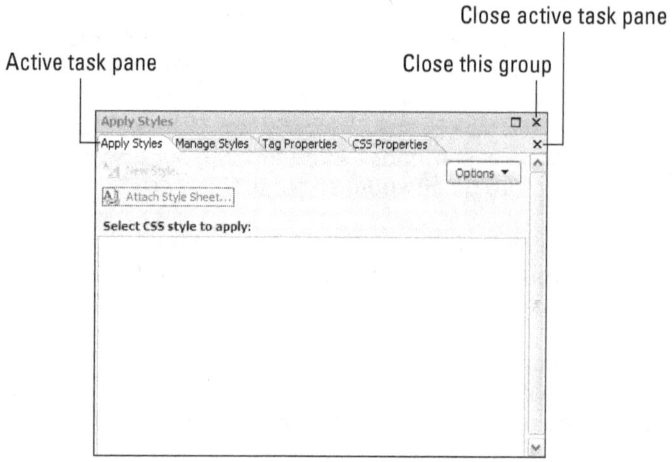

Close active task pane

Active task pane   Close this group

Figure 1-4:
Task panes
can be
combined
into groups.

To make a task pane active, click its tab. To close the active task pane, click the X on the tab bar. To close a whole group of task panes, click the X on the group's title bar.

If you don't like your new task pane arrangement and you want to go back to the way Expression Web placed them, choose Task Panes⇨Reset Workspace Layout.

Status bar

The bottom edge of the workspace window contains a few more useful goodies, such as the page size dimensions now displayed in Design view and which version of HTML Expression Web is using to write your Web page's code. (The default is XHMTL 1.0 Transitional.) This may not mean much to you now, but you find out more about setting the Design view dimensions in Chapter 8, and we talk about HTML versions in a sidebar in Chapter 14.

Creating and Saving a New Web Site

If you already read the first part of this chapter and did enough idling, it's time to rev the engines and create your first Web site.

Here's how to create and save a Web site with one page: the default home page.

The care and naming of Web sites

Because you most likely will create and save more than one Web site, you should think about how you want to organize your sites' files and folders now, when you're just getting started. If you don't have any other Web sites in your My Documents folder, Expression Web saves your first Web site's files in the folder My Documents\My Web Sites\mysite. When you create another new Web site, Expression Web adds another Web site folder inside My Documents\My Web Sites, named mysite2, and places your new site's files there. The next folder is named mysite3, and so on. Left to its own devices, Expression Web creates a folder-and-file structure for each new site inside the My Web Sites folder.

Although this method does keep everything nice and tidy and separate, the problem is that it doesn't scale well if you create more than a few sites. Is the site you created for Aunt Martha's knitting club mysite6 or mysite16? We suggest that you choose intuitive names for your Web sites that indicate what the sites are about (like knitclub or marthaknit). We also suggest that you store all your Web sites inside the My Web Sites folder, which keeps them separate from the morass of files in My Documents, sequestered in their own little Web site world.

To create and save your first Web site, follow these steps:

1. **With Expression Web running, choose File⇨New⇨Web Site.**

   You can also click the drop-down arrow to the right of the New Document button on the Common (or Standard) toolbar and choose Web Site.

   The New dialog box appears with the Web Site tab displayed, as shown in Figure 1-5. The General and One Page Web Site options are selected. The Description box displays a helpful little blurb about what the selected options do.

   The Specify the Location of the New Web Site text box displays the full path and default folder name of the Web site. If you have no other Web sites in My Documents, Expression Web assumes that you want to create a unique folder for your Web site within the My Web Sites folder. In this case, the path probably looks something like this: C:\Documents and Settings\your user name\My Documents\My Web Sites\mysite (or mysite2 or mysite3, for example).

   Note: If you share a computer with other people and use the Windows system of users and passwords to maintain separate settings, the My Documents folder is located inside the Documents and Settings folder, in a subfolder identified by your username.

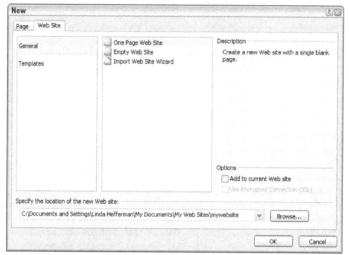

Figure 1-5:
The New
dialog box.

2. **Type over the default folder name that Expression Web has assigned for the Web site, and enter your own, unique folder name.**

   The easiest way to do this is to click twice at the end of the path shown in the Specify the Location of the New Web Site text box and press the Backspace key to erase the default folder name (leave the \ in place). Then type a name for your Web site folder.

   When naming folders, try to use only lowercase letters and underscores (_) rather than spaces. Current standards require that filenames and pathnames be in all lowercase; whenever you are working with anything Web related, it just makes good sense to follow this simple rule. Also, try keeping your folder names short. See the earlier sidebar "The Care and naming of Web sites" for more information.

   The full path should now look something like this: `C:\Documents and Settings\your name\My Documents\My Web Sites\folder_name`, where `folder_name` is your Web site name.

3. **Click OK.**

   The dialog box closes, and Expression Web opens a new workspace with your Web site and its `default.htm` home page (if you chose to create a one-page Web site).

To create additional Web sites, follow these steps again. Each new site opens in its own workspace window.

When you launch Expression Web, it opens the last Web site you were working on, to the last page you had open.

Congratulations — you created your first Web site! You're now ready to take the next step, which could be in any number of directions:

- ✔ If you want to get to work adding content to your new home page, go to Chapter 3, which talks about text, that most fundamental element of most Web pages.
- ✔ To add more Web pages to your Web site, go to Chapter 2.
- ✔ If you're not sure where to go from here, read on.

Creating a New Web Site from a Template

Templates are a good place to start if you need to throw together a Web site quickly, or if the prospect of building a site from scratch seems daunting. Expression Web comes with templates for several types of sites. Use the template that most closely approximates the site you want, and then tweak it to your heart's content:

- ✔ **Organization:** Use one of these templates to design a Web site for your professional organization or club. Visitors can read news, look at photos, view an FAQ (frequently asked questions) page and find out how to contact you.
- ✔ **Personal:** Use one of these templates as a springboard for designing your own, personal Web site. You can add your résumé and contact information, as well as a photo gallery of your work or a page listing downloadable documents or links.
- ✔ **Small Business:** These types of templates are ideal for quickly building a Web site for your small business. They contain predesigned pages for news posts, press releases, products, services, and promotions; a links page for more information; a site map; and contact information.

Even if you don't end up using a template as the basis for your Web site, you may want to take a look at what pages the Expression Web templates contain and how they're organized, to get ideas about how to put together your own site.

All Expression Web site templates use a *Dynamic Web Template (DWT)*. A DWT contains common elements (such as logos and navigation links) that appear on every page in the Web site so that it looks cohesive. A DWT can save you a lot of time because after you build the template and apply it to a new page, all you need to add is the content specific to that page. We talk about Dynamic Web Templates in Chapter 11.

To create a new Web site by using a template, follow these steps:

1. **With Expression Web running, choose File⇨New⇨Web Site.**

2. **Click Templates.**

   A list box appears, showing variations on the different types of templates. When you click a template name, Expression Web shows you a picture of what the Web site template looks like in the Preview area.

3. **In the list box, click the template you want to use.**

4. **In the Specify the Location of the New Web Site text box, enter the name of the new Web site folder or accept the default given by Expression Web.**

   We describe how to change the Web site folder name earlier in this chapter.

   If you want Expression Web to store the Web site's files in another location, click the Browse button and, in the New Web Site Location dialog box, navigate to the folder you want and click the Open button. The dialog box closes, and you return to the New dialog box. The path you chose appears in the Specify the Location of the New Web Site text box.

   If you want Expression Web to place the template in the Web site you have open, select the Add to Current Web Site check box in the Options area of the New dialog box.

5. **In the New dialog box, click OK.**

   If another Web site is already open in Expression Web when you create a Web site from a template, the Web site you just created appears in a new workspace window.

After Expression Web creates the new Web site, a bunch of folders unfurl in the Folder List task pane and on the Web Site tab. You see a file named `default.htm` marked with a little house icon — that's the site's home page. (We talk more about home page filenames in Chapter 2.) You also see a file named `master.dwt`, which is the site's Dynamic Web Template. It contains the design elements common to all the pages in the site.

Building your site from one of these templates can be confusing if you're new to using CSS styles to format and position page elements, or if you've never worked with Dynamic Web Templates. But the templates are great examples of how these technologies work together to build a Web site. (In Chapter 9, we walk you through a template's code step by step.) If tinkering with actual changes seems too daunting, just create a site from a template and have a look around. At the very least, you will probably come away with some ideas.

Opening an Existing Web Site in Expression Web

You can open most Web sites regardless of whether they were created in Expression Web. Use the Open Site command to open Web sites whose files are stored on your computer's hard drive or on a network drive.

To open a Web site located on your hard drive or on a network drive, follow these steps:

1. **With Expression Web running, choose File⇨Open Site.**

   You can also click the arrow next to the Open button on the Common toolbar and choose Open Site.

   The Open Site dialog box appears, with the Web Sites location listed in the Look In text box.

What about ASP.NET?

As we're sure you've already discovered, Expression Web is a complex program, full of features that the beginning-to-intermediate Web designer (that's you!) are likely never to use. For example, in Expression Web you can create two types of Web pages: regular Web pages, also known as *HTML pages,* and *ASP.NET* pages.

An ASP.NET page looks, to the casual Web surfer, like any other Web page. But from the Web designer's perspective, ASP.NET pages are vastly more powerful and complicated to build. ASP.NET pages can interact with Web server-based databases and other sources of live data and have specific hosting requirements. (They must eventually be published on a Web server that supports ASP.NET 2.0.) As such, they fall into the intermediate-to-advanced category, which is outside the scope of this book.

That isn't to say that you shouldn't try your hand at creating ASP.NET pages. If your Web hosting provider supports ASP.NET 2.0 and you're feeling

adventurous, go ahead and experiment with the Expression Web ASP.NET tools. The nice thing is that the features are there if you need them but don't get in your way if you don't.

If you think that you want to give ASP.NET a spin, here are a few resources for finding out more:

✔ Wikipedia, at `http://en.wikipedia. org/wiki/Asp.net`, clearly describes what ASP.NET is all about.

✔ Expression Web Help covers the basics of creating ASP.NET pages in Expression Web, as well as how to use the different ASP.NET task panes and tools. The Help feature also explains the different ASP.NET controls and how to add them to `.aspx` pages. Choose Help⇨Microsoft Expression Web Help and then click ASP.NET.

✔ Visit the Microsoft ASP.NET Developer Center at `http://msdn.microsoft. com/asp.net` to find out about ASP.NET and the tools that use it.

The Web Sites location is sort of a virtual bookmarking list for Web sites that have been opened in Expression Web, regardless of whether they were originally created in Expression Web. For example, if you open a site created in Dreamweaver or FrontPage in Expression Web, it appears in this list.

If you delete or move a Web site in Windows Explorer, the reference to it still appears in the Web Sites list. It doesn't mean that the site is still there; it just means that Expression Web remembers that the site *was* there once upon a time in recent memory. If you try to open the site and the location is out of date, you get an error message. For this reason, you should always delete a Web site from within Expression Web. (We tell you how, later in this chapter.) To remove an outdated Web site pointer from the list, right-click and choose Remove.

If you don't see the Web site you want to open, find it by using the short-cuts on the left side of the dialog box.

2. **Double-click the Web site, or click to select it and then click Open.**

   The Web site opens in a new workspace window.

Adding Existing Files to a Web Site

Let us compare a Web site to a manila file folder for a minute — any container that can hold a bunch of stuff related to a particular project. If you're redesigning your son's bedroom, for example, your file folder might contain a random assortment of bits and pieces: fabric swatches, paint chips, pages torn from magazines, and rough sketches of the furniture layout.

Think of your Web site folder in a similar way. It should contain all the random files you will use for your Web site, regardless of whether you include them in their final form. For example, you may have written some brainstorming notes about the text for certain Web pages in Microsoft Word. (We talk about pasting text into Web pages in Chapter 3.) Or, you might have created some PDF files that you will make available for download. You also might have created a logo and some icons and cropped and sized a collection of photos in your graphics program. (We cover including pictures in a Web site in Chapter 5.)

All these files can and should go into your Web site folder, by either dragging them directly into your Web site's Folder List task pane or importing them. There are two reasons for this:

✔ If you're going to use the file in its final form (such as a picture file or a downloadable PDF), Expression Web needs to have the file in the Web site so that it can create and maintain working links to that file. This ensures that when you publish your site on the Internet, all the files for the Web site get copied to the host server correctly. (You can exclude files you don't need in their final form, such as text documents, when you publish your Web site. We show you how in Chapter 12).

✔ Keep everything in one place so that you don't have to remember where all your stuff is.

You can open documents and work on them in their original programs from within Expression Web. For example, if you import a Microsoft Excel spread-sheet into your Web site, double-click the file's icon in the Folder List task pane to open it in Microsoft Excel.

If you have one or two files to bring into your Web folder, it's a snap to drag them from a folder on your computer or network into your Web site's Folder List task pane directly into a specific folder, as shown in Figure 1-6.

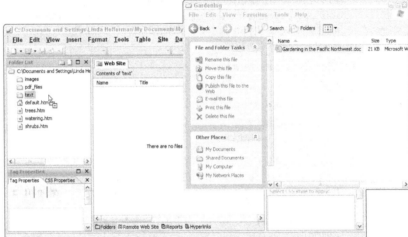

Figure 1-6: Drag files from your computer into the Expression Web Folder List task pane.

If you have several files in different locations, or if you want to bring in entire folders, you can load everything into the Import dialog box and import every-thing in one fell swoop. When you import a file, Expression Web places a copy of the file inside the open Web site and leaves the original file and its location unchanged.

In this section, we show you how to add, or import, existing files into the Web site that's open in Expression Web. If you want to import an entire Web site into Expression Web and you have access to the source files, no fancy importing is necessary; simply open it in Expression Web. (We tell you how earlier in this chapter.)

In the following steps, we show you how to import single files from your com-puter or local network into the Web site that's open in Expression Web. At the end of this set of steps, we tell you how to import entire folders.

1. **With a Web site open in Expression Web, choose File➪Import.**

   (If the File➪Import menu item is grayed out, in the Folder List task pane, click the Web site's top-level folder to select it, and then choose File➪ Import again.)

   The Import dialog box appears.

2. **In the dialog box, click the Add File button.**

   The Add File to Import List dialog box appears. You use this dialog box to poke around your hard drive or local network to find the files you want to import.

3. **Navigate to your hard drive or local network and select the files you want to import.**

   To select multiple files, press and hold down the Ctrl key while clicking file icons in the Add File to Import List dialog box. To select a range of files, press and hold down the Shift key while clicking the first and last file icons. If you don't see the file you want to import, from the Files of Type list box, choose All Files (*.*).

4. **Click the Open button.**

   The Add File to Import List dialog box closes, and the file appears in the import list in the Import dialog box.

5. **To add another file to the import list, repeat Steps 2 through 4. When you're finished, click OK to close the dialog box and import the files.**

   If you would rather put off importing the files, click the Close button in the Import dialog box. Expression Web saves the import list and closes the dialog box, which you can later access by choosing File➪Import.

To import a folder into your Web site, in Step 2 of the preceding list, click the Add Folder button. The File Open dialog box appears, enabling you to choose the folder you want to import. Click the folder and then click the OK button. The File Open dialog box closes, and the folder's contents appear in the import list.

Deleting a Web Site

If you have old Web sites lying around on your computer or network and taking up precious storage space, feel free to get rid of them. May we suggest, however, that you take a good look around *first?* You might have used a particularly nice combination of colors or a page layout that you want to hang on to for future reference.

Although you *can* delete a Web site by using Windows Explorer, we recommend doing all your Web site file cleanup from inside Expression Web. This way, Expression Web stays in the loop about your site's whereabouts.

Okay, there's *one* advantage to using Windows Explorer to delete a Web site: The site's files get thrown into Recycle Bin, giving you a chance to retrieve them if you have a change of heart. But Expression Web gives you another option, which we explain in the following instructions.

To delete a Web site that's open in Expression Web, follow these steps:

1. **In the Folder List task pane, click the Web site's top-level folder and then press the Delete key.**

   Alternatively, in the Folder List task pane, right-click the Web site's top-level folder and, from the pop-up menu, choose Delete.

   The Confirm Delete dialog box appears and warns you that deleting a Web site is a permanent action. It also gives you two options:

   • *Delete only hidden metadata files from this Web site, preserving all other files and folders.* This option tells Expression Web to pretend that the Web site doesn't exist when listing Web sites in the Open Site dialog box, but doesn't delete the files and folders. This choice is a good one if you think that the Web site contains some elements that you might want to use in the future.

   • *Delete this Web site entirely.* This option is a one-way street. After you select it and click OK, the Web site is toast.

2. **In the dialog box, select the Delete This Web Site Entirely option and then click OK.**

   The dialog box closes, and Expression Web deletes the Web site.

Closing a Web Site and Closing Expression Web

Closing a Web site is easy. You can use either one of these methods:

✔ Click the X in the right-hand corner of the workspace window. If you have only one Web site open, this method also closes Expression Web.

✔ Choose File➪Close Site. Use this option if you want to close the current Web site but keep Expression Web running.

To close Expression Web, close the last open Web site or choose File➪Exit.

If you haven't saved your files yet, Expression Web prompts you with a friendly reminder to do so before closing.

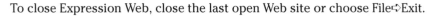

Chapter 2

Working with Web Pages

*N*o matter how big your Web site becomes, the basics for putting it together are the same: Create a Web site (we tell you how in Chapter 1) and fill it with Web pages. At its simplest, a Web site contains a single home page. After that, the sky's the limit; you may end up with a handful of pages, or hundreds.

In this chapter, we go over the different ways to create, open, and save pages. By the end of this chapter, you'll be comfortable with all the basics of Web pages and ready to launch into the real fun of Web site building: adding content (which we introduce you to in Chapter 3).

Creating and Saving Pages

Web pages are the canvases onto which you paint your brilliant ideas. Creating a new page in Expression Web is simple: A few clicks of the mouse and you've got a blank page ready for action.

To create a new, blank page in an existing Web site, follow these steps:

1. **Launch Expression Web, and open the Web site you want to work with.**

   Chapter 1 explains how to create and open Web sites.

2. **Choose File⇨New⇨Page.**

Or, on the Common (or Standard) toolbar, click the down arrow next to the New Document button. You can also press Ctrl+N.

The New dialog box appears, with the Page tab selected. The options General and HTML are selected.

3. **Click OK.**

The New dialog box closes, and a new, blank page appears in your view of choice (Design, Split, or Code view). The cursor blinks patiently on and off in the editing window, waiting for your content. The default filename for the new page, `Untitled_x.htm`, appears on its tab. Until you save your Web page and give it a name, this is the default name Expression Web has assigned to it. That's it. You're ready to add content and then save your page.

If you were to close Expression Web right now without saving the page you just created, Expression Web would simply discard the page. When you next open the site, your page will have vanished into cyber-obscurity. This isn't a big deal because as soon as you type even a single character, Expression Web notices the content and prompts you to save your changes before closing the page. But it's worth keeping in mind.

Note: Although we only cover adding HTML pages here, you follow the same basic process outlined in this section to add other types of pages to your Web site. We tell you how to add style sheets in Chapter 9. We cover Dynamic Web Templates in Chapter 11.

The care and naming of Web pages

Here are a few tips to keep in mind as you consider what to name your Web pages:

✔ **Filename:** Keep your filenames short and intuitive. Your best bet is to stick to one-word names that use only lowercase letters. If you must use more than one word, fill the spaces with underscores, like this: `fall_catalog`.

✔ **Home page filename:** The host Web server, on which you will eventually publish your finished Web site, determines your home page filename. Most Web servers recognize either *index* or *default* as the home page filename, with the extension `.htm` or

`.html` (or `.aspx` for ASP.NET sites). Before you publish your Web site, ask your system administrator or a helpful person at your hosting provider which home page filename you should use.

✔ **Filename extension:** It's up to you whether to use the `htm` or `html` filename extension — they're interchangeable. Expression Web automatically appends the `.htm` extension to whichever filename you choose; if you prefer to use `html`, when you save the file, add `.html` to the file name you specify.

Saving a Web page in the current site

If there's one thing we've discovered as writers, it's to obsessively save our work. In fact, pressing Ctrl+S has become almost as automatic as ending a sentence with a period. We recommend that you adopt this habit as well. That way, when you accidentally step on your surge protector's power button or a truck plows into the power pole down the street and your computer monitor goes sickeningly black, you're covered.

To save a Web page, follow these steps:

1. **With Expression Web running and the Web site open that you want to save the page in, choose File⇨Save As.**

   The Save As dialog box appears. The Save In text box displays the location of the Web site folder.

2. **In the File Name text box, enter the filename you want to give the Web page.**

   The nearby sidebar "The care and naming of Web pages" contains tips for choosing filenames.

3. **To change the page title, click the Change Title button.**

   The Set Page Title dialog box appears.

   When you view a Web page in a Web browser, the title appears on the browser's *title bar* — the colorful strip at the top of the browser window. Page titles also appear in search indexes (such as Yahoo! and Google) and in visitors' lists of browser bookmarks (although your visitors can rename their browser bookmarks if they want). A good title for your Web page should sum up the page's content in a way that's meaningful to visitors. For example, whereas the title My Home Page or Home could apply to millions of different pages all over the World Wide Web, a more specific title, such as Tips and Tricks for Northwest Gardeners, tells the visitor exactly what to expect on that page.

4. **In the Page Title text box, enter a title.**

5. **Click OK to close the Set Page Title dialog box.**

   You return to the Save As dialog box.

6. **Click the Save button.**

   The Save As dialog box closes. If pictures appear on the page, the Save Embedded Files dialog box appears. See the sidebar "Saving pages containing pictures," a little later in this section, for tips on dealing with pictures. When Expression Web is done saving, the Folder List task pane lists your new, saved page.

Saving pages containing pictures

If you save a page that was originally opened from a location outside the current Web site and that page contains pictures, or if you added pictures to your page, Expression Web prompts you to save the associated picture files too. (You discover lots more about Web pictures in Chapter 5.)

When you save a page containing pictures, in addition to saving the page, Expression Web pops open the Save Embedded Files dialog box. It enables you to save the picture files and to change the filenames and specify the folder in which the pictures are stored. You can also click the Picture Options button in the dialog box to specify details about the picture file's format details. After you specify your preferences, click OK to save the pictures.

After you save a page and give it a name, click the Save button on the Common or Standard toolbar or press Ctrl+S to resave it. Expression Web tells you when a page needs saving because an asterisk appears next to the page's filename on the tab, like this: pagename.htm*. If you made changes to several pages in your Web site, you can save all pages and files at one time by choosing File⇨Save All.

Add the Save All command to your favorite toolbar so that it's right there where you need it. We tell you how to add commands to a toolbar in Chapter 1. (You find the Save All command on the File menu.)

We suggest dropping the Save All command to the right of the Save button, as shown in Figure 2-1.

Figure 2-1:
Add the
Save All
command to
the Common
toolbar.

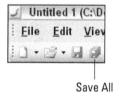

Save All

Adding new pages and folders in the Folder List

If you're the big-picture type, you may prefer to begin by setting up all your site's Web pages first and then filling them with content and linking them. (We show you how to build hyperlinks in Chapter 4.) This is how our friend the professional Web designer does it: She builds the site's basic framework to make sure that she doesn't forget any important pages, such as a contact information page or a site map. You can always add or delete pages later on, but this method gives you a good place to start. The easiest way to do it is to add new Web pages by using the Folder List task pane.

To add a new Web page in the Folder List task pane, follow these steps:

1. **With Expression Web running, open the Web site you want to add pages to.**

2. **In the Folder List task pane, select the folder that will contain the new page.**

    If you want to add the page to the main Web site folder or you do not yet have subfolders, select the top-level folder of the Web site. (We show you how to add subfolders at the end of these instructions.)

3. **On the Folder List task pane title bar, click the New Page button, as shown in Figure 2-2.**

Figure 2-2:
Add new pages to your Web site quickly in the Folder List task pane.

A new page icon appears, with the default title `Untitled_x.htm`.

4. **To rename the file, right-click it and, from the pop-up menu, choose Rename. Then type the filename.**

    Do not delete the file extension `htm`. If you do, Expression Web doesn't recognize the file as a Web page and can't open it.

    To add a page title to the new page, right-click the page's icon and then, from the pop-up menu that appears, choose Properties. In the General tab Title text box, type the page title and then click OK to save.

Adding *subfolders* in the Folder List task pane is simple. Follow the same steps as for adding a page, except click the New Folder icon. To rename the subfolder, right-click it and, from the pop-up menu, choose Rename and type the name. After you create a folder, you can drag and drop files into it just like in Windows.

The Folder List task pane shows you the full file and folder structure of the open Web site. You will come to love this handy task pane as you use it to navigate in your Web site. As you can in Windows, you can press the + and – buttons to collapse and expand the contents of a folder, and you can double-click an icon to open a file.

Creating a page based on an existing page

Expression Web knows how to use an existing page as the basis for another page — a major timesaver when you want to create a bunch of standard pages with slightly different content. This is also useful if you want to see how changing a few page elements will look but keep everything else the same (for example, if you're wondering what red headings would look like).

If you expect to create similarly laid-out pages regularly, consider creating a page template. Expression Web gives you several ways to work with templates, depending on your needs. See "Creating and Using Page Templates," later in this chapter, for how to create a template from an existing page and use it as a basis for creating new pages. After you experience the timesaving power of page templates, you may want to consider using a template as the foundation for your entire site. We explain how in Chapter 11.

To create a new page based on an existing page, follow these steps:

1. **Open the Web site to which you want to add the new page.**

2. **In the Folder List task pane, right-click the file you want to use as the base page, and then, from the pop-up menu that appears, choose New from Existing Page.**

   A new page, named `Untitled_x.htm`, with the same content appears in the editing window.

3. **Choose File⇨Save As and, in the Save As dialog box, navigate to where you want to save the file.**

4. **In the File Name text box, type the new page's filename.**

5. **Click the Change Title button, and, in the Set Page Title dialog box, type the new page's title then click OK.**

6. **In the Save As dialog box, click Save.**

Expression Web keeps track of your Web site's folder and file structure and the links between pages. At this point, you might not yet have created any links; we cover hyperlinks in Chapter 4.) When you add, rename, or delete a page or change its location within your Web site by moving it to a new folder, Expression Web updates any affected page links. For this reason, always make changes to your Web site file and folder structure inside Expression Web rather than use Windows Explorer. If you move files and folders outside the safe confines of Expression Web, you end up wrestling with error messages and, potentially, broken hyperlinks.

Opening Web Pages

You can easily open any Web page in Expression Web. It also knows how to open non-Web page files that are part of your Web site (such as picture files or Microsoft Office documents) by launching the appropriate program for that type of file.

Opening a page that's part of the current Web site

Expression Web gives you several ways to open pages and files that make up your Web site. Here are the easiest methods:

✔ First, open the Web site that contains the page you want to open. (If you're not sure how to open a Web site, see Chapter 1.) Next, double-click a page or file icon in the Folder List task pane or in the Web Site tab in the editing window.

✔ You can open one page at a time, or you can open several pages and move between them by clicking their tabs in the editing window.

✔ To open a non-Web page contained in your Web site (such as a Microsoft Word document), double-click it in the Folder List task pane. Expression Web launches the appropriate program and opens the file in that program.

Opening a page stored on your computer or network

You may want to open a page that's part of an Expression Web site, but not the Web site that's *already open* in Expression Web. No problem. You can even open a Web page that *isn't* part of a Web site created with Expression Web.

To do so, follow these steps:

1. **On the Common or Standard toolbar, click the arrow next to the Open button and click Open.**

   You can also choose File➪Open or press Ctrl+O.

The Open File dialog box appears, displaying a list of files and folders contained in the Web site that's open in Expression Web. If no Web site is open, the dialog box displays the contents of the last folder you viewed.

   2. In the dialog box, navigate to the location of the file you want to open.

   The page can be stored anywhere on your computer or network.

   3. In the dialog box's file list, click the file and then click the Open button.

   The Open File dialog box closes, and the page opens.

   If the page is part of a Web site, regardless of whether it was created with Expression Web, the Web site opens in a new workspace window with the selected page open in the editing window. The Web site's files and folders appear in the Folder List task pane.

Closing Web Pages

Closing a single Web page or a whole Web site full of open pages is easy:

   ✔ **To close the page that's open and displayed in the editing window,** choose File⇨Close or click the X in the upper-right corner of the editing window. (If you haven't saved yet, don't worry. Expression Web prompts you to save your changes before it closes the page.)

   ✔ **If you want to close an open page that isn't the active page,** click its tab and then close it. You can also right-click a page's tab then choose Close from the pop-up menu.

   ✔ **To close all pages in a Web site** (which closes the entire Web site), choose File⇨Close Site; or click the X in the upper-right corner of the Expression Web workspace.

Taking a Peek at a Page in a Web Browser

As you create pages in the Expression Web Design view, the pages look *kind of like* how they appear when viewed with a Web browser. In technospeak, this similarity is called *WYSIWYG* (pronounced "wizzy wig"), which stands for *What You See Is What You Get.*

Monitors and windows: Size does matter

In the world of print design, readers don't get to determine the page sizes of the books or reports they read. Barring differences in visual acuity, what one reader of a print document sees is pretty much identical to what every other reader sees. Not so in Web design. The size of the "page" (if you can call an electronic Web document a page) is determined by two factors: the visitor's monitor resolution (how many pixels a monitor can display) and the size of the visitor's browser window.

Both these factors vary from user to user. Therefore, you can never be sure what "size" your Web page will be when it appears on your visitors' screens. You can, however, by using a handful of different tools, get a sense of what your page looks like in different situations:

✔ The Preview In Browser feature helps in this regard, by enabling you to see how your page looks in several different browsers without ever leaving Expression Web.

✔ Using the built-in ruler, you can design your page with an eye toward keeping the page width narrow enough to fit within standard browser window sizes without the need for pesky horizontal scroll bars. Choose View➪Ruler and Grid➪Show Ruler to make the ruler appear.

✔ Expression Web has another tiny feature you may not have even noticed yet. In the lower-right corner of the Expression Web workspace window, you see two numbers separated by an X. Click those numbers to reveal a menu containing a range of pixel values that simulate, in Design view, several resolutions and browser window sizes that visitors commonly use. For example, the menu item 760 x 420 (800 x 600, Maximized) shows how a page would look if viewed in a maximized browser window on a monitor with 800 x 600 resolution.

As you design your pages, keep an eye on this feature to be sure that your pages look good to a wide range of visitors.

We say "kind of like" because, although the folks at Microsoft have done a great job of making Expression Web Design view as close to WYSIWYG as possible, it's no substitute for looking at your pages in a real Web browser, such as Internet Explorer or Mozilla Firefox. Previewing your pages in a Web browser gives you a more accurate representation of how your pages will appear to your visitors after the site has been published. Expression Web enables you to quickly preview your pages in several browsers.

Trying to keep track of which browsers are the most popular with Web surfers is like trying to make the waves in the ocean stand still. For this reason, we recommend previewing your pages with the latest versions of the most popular browsers, which at this moment are Microsoft Internet Explorer 6 (and version 7) and Mozilla Firefox (although Opera and Netscape are popular enough to warrant giving them a glance). The insight you gain about how different pages might look in different browsers is worth the extra bit of effort that installing the extra browsers requires. (Of course, you can see how your pages look inside Windows-based browsers only; keep in mind that pesky display variations occur across operating system platforms as well. After you publish your finished site, ask your Mac- and Unix-using friends to give the site a once-over to be sure that everything's kosher.)

If you want to find out which browsers are winning the popularity contest this month, check out this link at W3Schools: `www.w3schools.com/browsers/browsers_stats.asp`. Or simply type **browser statistics** in your favorite search engine. You end up with a plethora of sites that track browser use, monitor resolutions, and many other handy stats. You can download different Web browsers from Download.com at `www.download.com`.

 To preview your page in a Web browser, click the Preview in Browser button on the Common or Standard toolbar. Or press the F12 key.

To pick a specific browser to view your page, follow these steps:

1. **Choose File⇨Preview in Browser.**

   The Preview in Browser menu expands to display a range of preview options and monitor resolutions, as shown in Figure 2-3.

   A monitor's *resolution* refers to the number of pixels the monitor can display on-screen. The larger the number, the higher the resolution of the picture and the more "real estate" a monitor can display.

2. **From the menu, choose the name of the browser and the resolution size you want to use.**

   If the browser you want isn't listed on the drop-down menu, choose More Browsers (at the bottom of the list). In the Preview in Browser dialog box that appears, select the browser from the list, and click the Preview button.

   If you haven't yet saved your page, a Microsoft Expression Web dialog box pops up, prompting you to do so. In the dialog box, click Yes to save the page. After saving the Web page, Expression Web opens your page in the browser and window size of your choice.

To edit the page, return to Expression Web by clicking the Expression Web button on the Windows taskbar (or press Alt+Tab to switch between open windows). Make any changes you want, and then save the page. To view changes, click the Preview in Browser button again or switch back to your browser and click the browser's Reload or Refresh button.

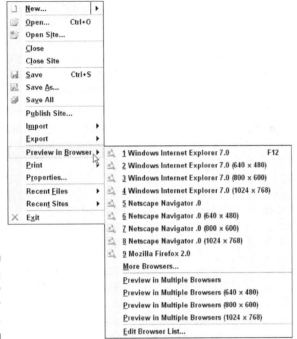

Figure 2-3:
The Preview
in Browser
menu.

The first time you click the Preview button or press F12, Expression Web picks your default Web browser. The next time you use these shortcuts, it chooses the last browser (or browsers) you picked.

Adding a browser to the list

If you don't see the browser you want in the list, that's no problem. As long as you already installed a browser on your computer, you can add it to the list of preview options. To do so, follow these steps:

1. **Choose File⇨Preview in Browser⇨Edit Browser List.**

   The Edit Browser List dialog box appears.

2. **Click the Add button.**

   The Add Browser dialog box appears.

3. **In the Name text box, type the browser name as you want it to appear in the list.**

It's useful to include the version number (such as Internet Explorer 7, Opera 9), especially if you're adding multiple versions of the same browser.

To add the browser, find its program file (also called an *executable file*), which is the name of the browser plus the extension .exe (opera.exe, firefox.exe, or iexplore.exe, for example).

4. Next to the Command text box, click the Browse button.

5. Navigate to the location of the browser's program file by using the selections in the Add Browser dialog box.

A browser is usually installed in the Program Files folder, in a subfolder with its name (for example, C:/Program Files/Opera). For example, to locate Opera, go to the Program Files folder, find and open the Opera folder, and then click Opera.exe, as shown in Figure 2-4.

Note: Your version of Windows may be set to hide the .exe extension. If this is the case, click the main program icon.

If you can't find the browser program file you're looking for, use Windows Search to look for it on your computer (for example, search for the file opera.exe).

Figure 2-4:
Click to select the browser you want to add.

6. Click the Open button.

You end up back at the Add Browser dialog box, where the full path of the browser appears in the Command text box.

7. Click OK.

Previewing by using more than one browser

Expression Web lets you preview your page in a bunch of browsers at one time so that you can compare what your page looks like in each one. And you get to choose which browsers you want to use.

To tell Expression Web which browsers to open, follow these steps:

1. **Choose File➪Preview in Browser➪Edit Browser List.**

   The Edit Browser List dialog box appears.

2. **In the Browsers section, check or uncheck the browsers you want to use by clicking in the little box to the left of the browser name.**

3. **In the Additional Window Sizes area, select or deselect the window sizes you want to use.**

4. **Click the OK button.**

To preview your page in these browsers, choose File➪Preview in Browser➪ Preview in Multiple Browsers. Your page opens in all the browsers you told Expression Web to use.

Creating and Using Page Templates

If you created a page containing a standard layout that you want to use for a number of different pages, you can save it as a template. This feature is especially useful if you're working with a team of designers and you all want to use a set of shared templates. For example, if you're creating a Web site for a consulting business, you may want to create a separate Web page for each consultant where all consultant pages have the same basic layout, introductory text, and headings. You would create a consultant page template and then use it as the basis for creating each individual page.

After you create a page from a template, the relationship between the page and the template ends. They meet, they create the page, they go their separate ways. If you then *change* the template and resave it, the pages you created based on the template aren't affected. For example, you may want to change the main picture for your consultant pages, but you already created several consultant Web pages. You have to not only change the picture on the template itself but also on each existing consultant page. (Any new pages made from the template *do* include the change.)

What goes into a template?

When considering what your page template should contain, think about which kinds of information will stay exactly the same on all pages and which pieces of information will vary. For example, if a block of text will always be in the same place and say the same thing, you should put it on the template. But if the text block will *look* the same but *say* something different, you can add a placeholder text block to the template, such as "Replace this text with consultant's bio" or, in a heading, "Consultant name goes here". Then, on the actual Web page, the person responsible for writing the text knows where to put it. In general, for everything that will vary on each page but appear in the same

place and in the same format, create a placeholder for it. For every element that is exactly the same on all pages, add it to the template in its final form. Here are a few more examples of elements you may want to put on the template:

- ✔ A picture (for example, a company logo or icon)
- ✔ A main heading (for example, Meet Our Consultants)
- ✔ An introductory paragraph that's the same on all pages using the template (for example, an overview of qualifications for all consultants)

If you think you'll be using templates extensively, consider using Dynamic Web Templates rather than the page templates described in this section. Dynamic Web Templates stay linked to the pages created from them so that you can change the template and have Expression Web update specific pages or all pages in the Web site. We cover Dynamic Web Templates in detail in Chapter 11.

To create a template from a Web page, follow these steps:

1. **With the page you want to save as a template open in Expression Web, choose File⇨Save As.**

   The Save As dialog box appears.

2. **In the Save as Type list box, choose Page Template (it's at the bottom of the list) and then click Save.**

   The Save As dialog box closes, and the Save As Template dialog box appears.

3. **In the Save As Template dialog box, type a descriptive title in the Title text box.**

4. **In the Name text box, type a filename.**

   Just type a short word. Remember to keep filenames in all lowercase, and use underscores rather than spaces. Expression Web automatically applies the appropriate extension (.tem) to the filename you enter.

5. **In the Description text box, type a short description of the template's function.**

6. **To create a shared template that other site authors can use when they're working on the Web site, select the Save Template in Current Web Site check box.**

7. **Click OK.**

   The dialog box closes, and Expression Web saves the page as a template. (The page visible in Expression Web is a regular Web page, so any additional changes you make aren't saved as part of the template.)

   If the page you're saving contains pictures, the Save Embedded Files dialog box appears. We explain how to use this dialog box in the sidebar "Saving pages containing pictures," earlier in this chapter.

After you create a template and save it, it's a snap to create a new page based on that template. Just follow these steps:

1. **Choose File⇨New⇨Page.**

   The New dialog box appears, with the Page tab displayed.

2. **Click My Page Templates and then click the title of the page template you want to use.**

   The list displays the titles you gave your template files when you saved them, and the description box shows your description. Expression Web even shows you a visual preview of what the selected template looks like so that you know you're picking the right one.

3. **Click OK.**

   A new page appears in the editing window, with the elements from your template included on it.

4. **Save the page as you would any other Web page, by giving it a unique filename and page title.**

Here are a few more tips for working with page templates:

✔ Give your page templates meaningful titles and descriptions. This advice is especially important if you're working in a team.

✔ If you find you need to make a lot of changes to a template after you already made several pages based on the template, you may find it easier to create new pages based on the *changed* template and then copy any page-specific information from the existing pages to the new ones. When working with an evolving Web site, you always have to balance which method is the most efficient.

✔ If you find page templates too limiting, you can easily convert a regular page template into a Dynamic Web Template (DWT). See Chapter 11 for everything you need to know about Dynamic Web Templates.

✔ You cannot attach an Expression Web page template to an already existing page (although you *can* attach a DWT to an existing page). You must use the template as the starting point.

Part II

Coaxing Content
onto the Page

The 5th Wave   By Rich Tennant

"I can't really explain it, but every time
I animate someone swinging a golf club,
a little divot of code comes up missing
on the home page."

In this part . . .

A Web site is only as good as its content. In this part, we show you how to add stuff to your pages and start making them look good. Chapter 3 covers text; Chapter 4, hyperlinks; and Chapter 5, pictures. Chapter 6 shows you how to add an interactive form. Throughout these chapters, we ease you into getting to know the code that works quietly behind the scenes to make the magic happen.

Chapter 3

Just the Text, Ma'am

*A*fter you find out how to set up a Web site and then create and organize pages, it's time to get down to the business of putting stuff on those pages. What better place to start than with text — words, letters, numbers, and characters? Text may seem rather prosaic alongside the World Wide Web's flashy graphics and interactive effects, yet text is the most important part of each page you create, because the text makes up the majority of the content. You can dazzle your visitors with cutting-edge visuals and multimedia tricks, but the content — fresh, interesting, useful information — is what keeps people coming back for more. In this chapter, you discover everything you need to know about putting text on a Web page. And while you're at it, you see the behind-the-scenes code that makes everything look the way you want.

Tools for Text

Look at the top of the Expression Web workspace. The Common toolbar contains an array of buttons for applying styles, selecting fonts and sizes, and changing the appearance of words and paragraphs. Figure 3-1 shows the text formatting buttons on the Common toolbar.

Figure 3-1:
Text
formatting
buttons.

This collection of buttons contains the text tools you're likely to use most often — those tools for bold, italic, indenting, and lists, to name just a few. If you don't see what you're looking for on the Common toolbar, check the various dialog boxes that are accessible from the Format menu. They contain many more commands for precise text formatting. For example, if you want to customize the bullets in your bulleted list, choose Format➪Bullets & Numbering. (We cover these in more detail later in this chapter.)

The Formatting toolbar contains a few more text editing buttons that aren't on the Common toolbar. Display the Formatting toolbar by choosing View➪ Toolbars➪Formatting.

You can add and remove toolbar buttons and commands, so if you find yourself always digging for a text tool that's buried in a dialog box, go ahead and add it to the toolbar of your choice. We tell you how in Chapter 1.

Expression Web also includes a number of handy tools for working with words on the page:

- ✔ **Spell checking:** Click anywhere in your Web page and then choose Tools➪Spelling➪Spelling (or press the F7 key), and Expression Web spell checks the whole page. Choose the command while the Web Site tab or Folder List task pane is displayed, and Expression Web gives you the option of spell checking a selected page (or pages) or the entire site.

- ✔ When the Standard toolbar is showing (choose View➪Toolbars➪ Standard), click the Spelling button.

- ✔ **Thesaurus:** Got writer's block? Select a word, and then choose Tools➪ Thesaurus, and the built-in Expression Web Thesaurus suggests some alternatives.

- ✔ **Find and Replace:** The Edit➪Find command allows you to find a bit of text — a character, a whole word or phrase, or basically any string of characters you throw at it — in a single page, in open pages, or throughout the whole Web site. Choosing Edit➪Replace gives you the option of replacing that text with something else. These functions can even sift through the pages' HTML tags, which is a useful feature if you have to make sitewide changes to your HTML code, such as bringing an old page or site up to current standards. (We talk about this topic in Chapter 18, which is a downloadable bonus chapter on this book's page at www.dummies.com.)

Adding Text to a Page in Design View

The beauty of working in Design view is that you can forget, for the most part, that you're working in a Web design program and just focus on getting words on the page. And because that view feels a lot like word processing, you can change the text at any time. As writers, we often find that it's hard to get going on a new project, but if we just start typing, words appear miraculously on the page. (Sometimes, they even sound good!) So, enough procrastinating! Let's get started.

Entering text from scratch

If you're starting with a blank page, entering text in Design view is simple. Just follow these steps:

1. **Open the page to which you want to add text. (We show you how in Chapter 2.)**

   If you're not already in Design view, click the Design button in the lower-left corner of the editing window.

   You should see a blinking cursor, waiting patiently, in the editing window.

2. **Start typing, as shown in Figure 3-2.**

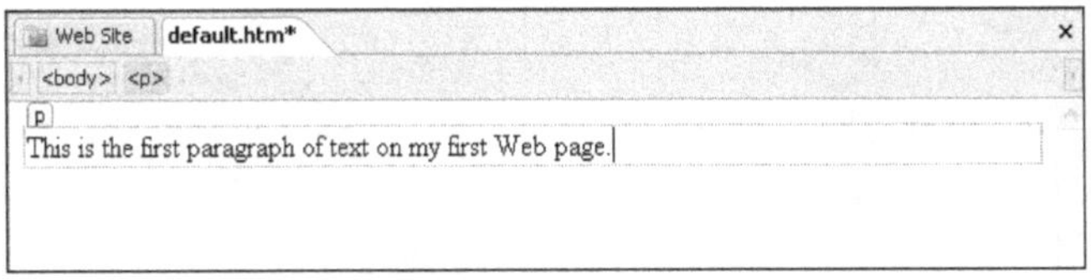

Figure 3-2:
Enter text in the editing window.

> Web Site   default.htm*   ✕
> <body> <p>
> p
> This is the first paragraph of text on my first Web page.

3. **When you reach the end of your first text chunk — whether it's a word, a single line, or a complete paragraph — press the Enter key.**

Every time you reach the end of a word, line, or paragraph and then press the Enter key, Expression Web assumes you want a break between what you just typed and what you will type next. Each of these text blocks, whether they contain one word, one character, or one hundred words, is treated as a separate paragraph. Expression Web automatically puts some white space between your paragraphs (every time you press the Enter key). You find out more about paragraphs and paragraph formatting later in this chapter.

If you want to format a line of text as a heading, see "Handling headings," later in this chapter.

Pasting existing text into a Web page

Maybe you have chunks of text already written that you want to add to your Web pages. You can paste text that's copied to the Windows Clipboard directly into the Expression Web Design view from another document, such as a text-only document file (a file with the extension `.txt`), a word processing document, or even another Web page.

Text you paste into a Web page from another document can bring excess baggage along with it, in the form of formatting codes that can seriously clutter your page's HTML code. Then, after you start formatting the text in Expression Web, you end up with a rat's nest of messy code. In this section, we show you the safest method for getting just the words and nothing else onto the page when you paste text from other sources.

To paste text from another document, follow these steps:

1. **In the original document, select the text that you want to paste into your Web page and choose Edit➪Cut or Edit➪Copy.**

   Or, follow the program's instructions for copying or cutting text.

2. **With the Web page into which you want to paste your text open, click in Design view where you want the text to be placed.**

3. **Choose Edit➪Paste.**

   Or, click the Paste button on the Standard toolbar. (Choose View➪ Toolbars➪Standard if you don't see it.)

   Expression Web pastes the text in the Web page, and the Paste Options button appears next to the pasted text. (It looks just like the Paste button.)

4. **Click the down arrow on the Paste Options button to display the Paste Options menu.**

   The contents of this menu change depending on the program from which the text came and how the pasted text is formatted.

5. **Click the Paste Text option.**

   The Paste Text dialog box appears, giving you several options for controlling paragraphs and line breaks within the text.

6. **Click the Normal Paragraphs Without Line Breaks option and click OK.**

If you're pasting a lot of formatted text and you want to preserve *some* formatting, search for the Microsoft Expression Web Help topic **how to paste text** (in the "Text" section) for more information about pasting text from other programs. You may be able to save yourself some work by using some of the other selections on the Paste Option menu or the Paste Text dialog box. Be sure to take a look at the text in Code view (or the code portion of Split view) after you make your selections, though, to make sure that no odd code remnants are lurking in the text.

Fonts and Font Tools

After you enter some text, you probably want to dress it up by applying a little font formatting.

In addition to changing the font itself (such as Times, Helvetica, Palatino, Garamond, or Courier), you can find tools for applying familiar character treatments, such as bold, italic, text size, and color. Although you have many other options, these are the most common tools in your arsenal of font formatting, and you'll use them often. Buttons for most of these options are conveniently located on the Common and Formatting toolbars.

The Font dialog box contains every tool you need to control your characters. The options in this dialog box contain the options found on the Common and Formatting toolbars, as well as many others for precise control over your characters. To open the Font dialog box, choose Format⇨Font.

Using font tools

You can use font tools in either of the following ways:

- ✔ Type a bunch of text, select the text that you want to format, and then turn on the appropriate tool, by either choosing an option in the Font dialog box or clicking a button on the Formatting toolbar.

- ✔ Turn on the tool first, type the formatted text, and then turn off the tool when you're done.

You can also use the Format Painter button on the Standard toolbar (choose View⇨Toolbars⇨Standard) to copy formatting from one piece of text and then apply that formatting elsewhere. To do so, follow these steps:

1. **Select the text that contains the formatting you want to copy.**

2. **Click the Format Painter button.**

   If you want to apply the formatting to more than one chunk of text, *double-click* the Format Painter button.

3. **Select the text to which you want to apply the formatting.**

   If you're applying formatting to more than one chunk of text, repeat this step until you apply the formatting to all desired text. Then click the Format Painter button to deselect the tool when you're finished.

To remove all font styles from a selected chunk of text, choose Format⇨ Remove Formatting.

Serifs and such

When you start messing around with fonts, sooner or later you run across some strange terms that describe fonts. Here's what they all mean:

Fixed-width: Doles out the same amount of space to every letter, regardless of whether it's skinny, like *i* and *l,* or fat, like *m* and *w.* These fonts are also called *monospace* fonts. Courier (or New Courier) is the most common fixed-width font. Use it whenever you want your text to look like it was typed on your grandmother's old Smith Corona manual typewriter. In Web sites, this font is often used to indicate code. (In fact, we use it for that purpose in this book!)

Proportional: Allots more room on a line to fat letters than to their skinny cousins. Books are printed in proportional fonts, and designers now have at their disposal, because of the desktop publishing revolution, a dizzying array of proportional fonts to choose from. Proportional fonts come in two flavors: serif and sans serif.

Serif: The backbone of body text, with little feet and fancy dots *(serifs)* on the letters that dress them up beyond mere stick figures. The main body text in this book, as in most books, is in a serif font, and typographers (artists who make text formatting their art) say that large blocks of text are more readable in a serif font. Garamond, Georgia, Palatino, Times, and Times New Roman are serif fonts. If your Web site contains more than a few lines of text, consider using a serif font for your main body text.

Sans: Plain-dotted and footless (hence the French *sans,* which means *without*). Sans serif fonts are often used for headings, although they can be used to set off certain blocks of text (like this sidebar). Arial and Helvetica are two common sans serif fonts.

Bold, italic, and beyond

Bold and italic text makes up the foundation of the font-formatting team. You pull these formats out like a trusty hammer every time you build a page.

 Try these shortcuts for turning on bold and italic: Press Ctrl+B to turn on bold; if you have text selected, the bold text effect is applied to it; if no text is selected, any text you type from the cursor's location forward is bold. To turn off bold, press Ctrl+B again. Do the same with italic, but press Ctrl+I.

In addition to the indispensable bold-and-italic team, you have a bunch of other text effects at your disposal, such as subscript, superscript, strikethrough, underline, and small caps. Use these effects sparingly. Having too many text treatments on a Web page detracts from your text's readability.

To apply a font effect, select some text and do one of the following things:

✔ Click the appropriate button on either the Common or Formatting toolbar.

✔ Choose Format➪Font to open the Font dialog box. Choose a style from the Font Style list, or select the check box next to the effect you want (if any). If you're not sure how a particular effect looks, select the check box to see a preview of the effect in the Preview area of the dialog box. When you're done, click OK.

Before you get too far along, take a little break and peek at the code that creates text effects. Click Split in the lower-left corner of the editing window, and you now see Code view at the top of the editing window and Design view at the bottom. Because this may be your first look at your page's code, it's a good time to give Split view a spin. Take a look at some font effects and the code that Expression Web uses to make them look that way. We start with bold and italic. In Design view, find some bold text (or make a chunk of text bold). Here's an example, using the sentence "Does a kid exist who does not like **ice cream**?"

Now look at the code for this sentence:

```
<p>Does a kid exist who does not like <strong>ice
        cream</strong>?</p>
```

Add italic to the words *ice cream* and look at the code again:

```
<p>Does a kid exist who does not like <strong><em>ice
        cream</em></strong>?</p>
```

The thingies between the angle brackets are HTML *tags*. The tag `<strong>` (strong text) turns on bold, and the tag `<em>` (emphasis) turns on italics. (You also see a set of `<p>` tags, telling you that the bit of text is a paragraph; we talk about paragraph tags a little later in this chapter.) Notice that the tags turn on the effect with an opening tag (`<strong>` — anything from here on out is bold) and turn off the effect with a closing tag, indicated by a forward slash (`</strong>` — bye-bye, bold!). If two effects are applied to the same text chunk — like in our italic-and-bold example — they open and close in a nested manner, like matching bookends within matching bookends. The following HTML code is incorrect because the tags close in the wrong order:

```
<strong><em>ice cream</strong></em>
```

Now look at the top of the editing window. As you apply font effects, Expression Web adds the tags to the *Quick Tag Selector* bar, as shown in Figure 3-3. This bar gives you quick access to the HTML tags for a particular element (in this case, a bit of text) without having to go into Code view. We talk more about the Quick Tag Selector bar in Chapter 14.

Quick Tag Selector bar ⎯⎯⎯⎯⎯⎯⎯⎯⎯⎯ Code for text

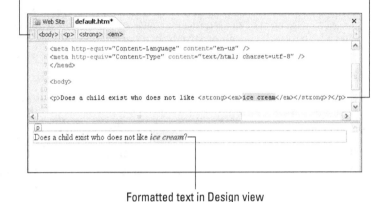

Figure 3-3:
The Quick
Tag Selector
bar shows
the tags for
the element
selected in
Design
view.

Formatted text in Design view

Expression Web uses the HTML tags `<strong></strong>` to create bold
text and `<em></em>` for italic. For all other text formatting — for example,
underline, font color, subscript, small caps, and font names — Expression
Web uses styles, or CSS. CSS code works a little differently from HTML code;
we take a look at the code for styles a little later in this chapter.

You may run across the tags `<b>` for bold and `<i>` for italic in older Web sites,
and browsers interpret them just fine. But these tags have fallen out of favor
by the Web powers that be. We recommend that you stick with `<strong>`
and `<em>`. If for some reason you're getting `<b>` and `<i>` in your code rather
than `<strong>` and `<em>`, choose Tools➪Page Editor Options and, on the
General tab, select the Use `<strong>` and `<em>` When Using Bold and Italic
Toolbar Buttons check box.

Changing fonts

Usually, someone who talks about a document's font actually means its *type-
face,* or the style and shape of the characters. The right choice of font helps
set the visual tone for your document and makes the text easy to read. Although
you can choose any fonts you want for your Web pages, follow good design
sense and stick with only a few fonts: one for the main body text and another
for headings. Better yet, choose a font family for each of these elements. The
reason is explained in the nearby sidebar "Text for the Web: Fonts and font
families."

To change the font, follow these steps:

1. **Select the chunk of text whose font you want to change.**

2. **On the Common or Formatting toolbar, choose a font or a font family from the Font list box.**

   Or, choose Format⇨Font and, in the Font dialog box that appears, choose a font or font family from the Font list box.

Text for the Web: Fonts and font families

You have probably already used a word processor to write a report or letter, and you may have printed it on your printer. And you probably fiddled around with the fonts to make it look the way you want. When you create a document for print, you get to decide exactly how your text looks on the page. If you select a fancy font, like Matisse, for your headings (and your printer supports it), that's what you get on your hard copy — end of story.

Not so with Web pages. Whether your Matisse headings show up on your visitors' computer screens is beyond your control. Unlike a printed page, your Web page is being viewed by any number of different browsers on any number of different computer monitors. It may even be viewed on a portable device, such as a PDA or mobile phone, and these devices have special Web browsers of their own. Here's what this means for Web page text: For a font (Matisse, for example) to display in a browser, the font has to be installed on the computer or device that's viewing the Web page. If the Web browser doesn't find the font on the visitor's system, it substitutes the default font specified by the browser (usually Times or Times New Roman). You have a couple of ways to gain more control over which fonts get displayed:

✔ **Assign a font family rather than a specific font:** A *font family* lists several fonts in order of preference. For example, this font family (Matisse, Garamond, Times New Roman, Times, serif) tells the Web browser to do this: "For this text, use Matisse; if you don't find Matisse, use Garamond; if you can't find Garamond, try Times New Roman; if you don't have Times New Roman, Times will do. What? You can't find any of these? That's okay, just use a serif font." We cover how to create a font family later in this chapter.

✔ **Include your text as an image:** Say you have your heart set on Matisse and no other font will do. In that case, create the text in a graphics program and save it as an image, such as a GIF file. (We cover how to add images to Web pages in Chapter 5.) If you do this, the text is treated as an image and is displayed exactly as you created it. Keep in mind, however, that some Web visitors may have their browsers set to not show images (especially on mobile devices). Images also slow down a page's load time. For foreign-language visitors, text as images doesn't translate correctly. So if the chunk of text contains information vital to understanding your page, you're better off using font families. You just have to live with the fact that your lovely Matisse font will be substituted sometimes for something less glamorous!

Expression Web comes with three predefined font families, listed at the top of the Font list box:

- *Sans serif:* Arial, Helvetica, sans-serif
- *Serif:* Times New Roman, Times, serif
- *Monospace:* Courier New, Courier, monospace

Or, you can make your own font family. (We explain how in the next section.)

Creating a new font family

The saying goes that you can pick your friends but not your family. Not so with font families. If the basic Expression Web font families don't excite you, you can easily make your own family and fill it with the font family members you like best. Just follow these steps:

1. **On the Common or Formatting toolbar, click the arrow on the Font list box.**

   The Font list box appears, with the predefined font families listed at the top.

2. **In the list box, click Customize Font Family.**

   The Page Editor Options dialog box appears, with the Font Families tab open.

   You can also get to this dialog box by choosing Tools⇨Page Editor Options. Then click the Font Families tab.

3. **In the Select Font Family list box, click the (New Font Family) line.**

4. **In the Add Font list box, click the name of the first font you want to add to the family.**

   The font name appears in the Add Font text box.

5. **Click the Add button.**

   The font name appears in the Select Font Family list box, at the bottom of the list. Fonts are selected in the order they appear in the font family. We explain this arrangement in the earlier sidebar "Text for the Web: Fonts and font families."

6. **Repeat Steps 4 and 5 until you add all the named fonts that you want the font family to contain.**

7. **For the last selection, choose a font type (such as sans-serif, serif, or monospace), as shown in Figure 3-4.**

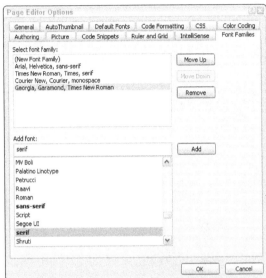

Figure 3-4: Choose the type of font as your last selection in a new font family.

You can change the order the font families appear in the Font list box by selecting a font family in the Select Font Family list box and clicking either the Move Up or Move Down button.

To remove a font family, select it and click the Remove button.

8. **Click OK to close the dialog box.**

Although you can modify a predefined font family (or one you created), Expression Web doesn't give you the option of reordering the fonts *within* the family. The only thing you can do is add new fonts, which Expression Web sticks at the end of the list. You could end up with a font family that looks something like this: Times New Roman, Times, serif, Georgia. Because the Web browser stops looking for specific fonts when it gets to serif, adding another font at the end of the list doesn't do much good. So, if you need to change a font family, you're better off creating a new one.

Earlier in this chapter, we mention that, for all text decoration with the exception of bold and italics, Expression Web uses CSS code, also known as *styles*. Take a look at the code that Expression Web creates when you assign a font family to some text, as shown in Figure 3-5. We assigned the Arial, Helvetica, sans-serif font family to the second sentence.

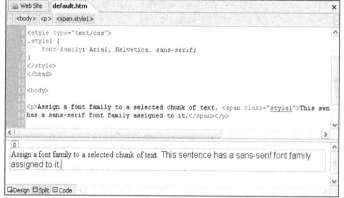

Figure 3-5:
Split view
shows a
font family
applied to a
sentence.

Open Split view (click Split at the bottom of the editing window) and take a
look at the code:

```
<p>Assign a font family to a selected chunk of text. <span
        class="style1">This sentence has a sans-serif
        font family assigned to it.</span></p>
```

Expression Web uses the opening <span> and closing </span> tags to identify the chunk of text we styled. In the opening <span> tag, Expression Web
inserts more code that indicates which style applies to this text (in this case,
style1), like this:

```
class="style1"
```

The word class is a *selector.* We talk more about selectors and how they're
used in Chapter 7, but for now just look at the style that Expression Web created. Scroll up in Code view until you see the style code for style1 that
looks like this:

```
.style1 {
        font-family: Arial, Helvetica, sans-serif;
}
```

This *style rule,* or *style definition,* tells the browser: "On this page, find the
stuff between the <span> tags with the class selector style1, and give the
stuff the font family Arial, Helvetica, sans-serif."

Style rules are always written in this format, starting with the thing being
styled (in this case, a class identified with style1), a curly bracket to start
the style rule, a style *property* (in this case, font-family), and a *value* for

that property (the font family Arial, Helvetica, sans-serif). Properties and their values are separated by colons; each property/value pair ends with a semicolon. This punctuation comes in handy when a style rule contains multiple property/value pairs. At the end of the style rule comes another curly bracket that ends the style rule.

If this style stuff seems a little confusing at first, don't fret: Chapter 7 covers styles in depth. At this point, we just want you to start getting comfortable peeking into the code and paying attention to how Expression Web writes style rules as you format your text.

Changing text size

Text size in print documents is measured in absolute units called *points,* or *picas.* When you create a new print document, you set the text size for headings and body text and then print the document, and everything is hunky-dory.

Because of the way HTML works, text size in Web pages is based on a relative system of *increments.* As with font typefaces (see the earlier sidebar "Text for the Web: Fonts and font families"), the default text size is determined by the viewer's Web browser, which they can adjust to make the text larger or smaller. For example, a vision-impaired person may make the text on your page huge for maximum readability, or a software developer may shrink the text to cram as much content as possible onto a large monitor. (By the way, most Web browsers let you set text size by using the View➪Text Size command).

To give you control over the size of text on your pages, *and* to allow your visitors maximum control over how text appears in their browsers, most Web designers use relative text sizes rather than fixed point sizes. Relative text sizes range from xx-small (roughly 8 points when viewed on a browser with the text size set to medium) to xx-large (about 36 points when viewed on a browser with the text size set to medium). When a viewer increases the text size in the browser, xx-small text gets a little larger, as does x-small, medium, and so on. However, if you assign an exact point size rather than a relative size, the text remains that size, no matter what the text size of the browser is set to. That means that 6-point type in the Web page remains 6-point type on the screen, no matter how much the text size is increased in the browser. Have you ever tried to read 6-point type in a Web browser?

To change text size, on the Formatting toolbar, choose a size from the Font Size list box, or click the Increase Font Size or Decrease Font Size button until you're happy with what you see.

If you must set an exact (or *absolute*) text size for a selected chunk of text, follow these steps:

1. **Choose Format➪Font.**

   The Font dialog box appears.

2. **In the Size text box, type the text size followed immediately by the letters** pt **(for points).**

   For example, to make the text exactly 72 points, type **72pt**.

3. **Click OK.**

Changing text color

You can dress your text in any color of the rainbow (plus a few fluorescent shades that don't appear in nature). Color gives your text panache, calls attention to important words, and, if it's coordinated with the colors of the page's graphics, unifies design.

To change the color of selected text, click the down arrow attached to the Font Color button to display a list box of standard colors, as shown in Figure 3-6. Click the desired color swatch to apply that color to your text.

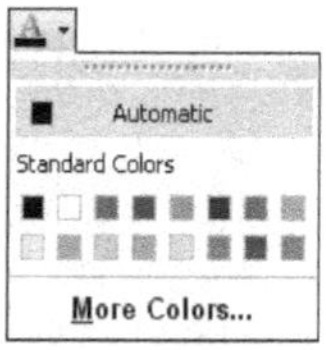

Figure 3-6:
Choosing a
font color.

If you don't see a standard color you like, you can choose from a palette of 135 browser-safe colors. (We explain what *browser-safe* colors are in Chapter 5.) You can even grab colors from any object on your screen, such as a graphic or an icon. To do so, follow these steps:

1. **On the Common or Formatting toolbar, click the down arrow next to the Font Color button and then click More Colors.**

   The More Colors dialog box appears, as shown in Figure 3-7.

2. **In the dialog box's color palette, click the color you like.**

   Or, if you would rather grab a color from an existing object, click the Select button. The cursor turns into a little eyedropper. Move the eyedropper over an object on your screen that contains the color you want to use (the active color appears in the New box), and then click to select the color.

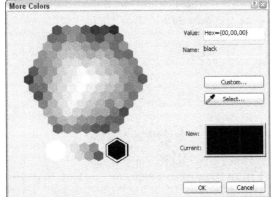

Figure 3-7:
The More
Colors
dialog box.

3. **Click OK.**

   The More Colors dialog box closes, and Expression Web applies the selected color to your text.

Each time you apply a color to your page, Expression Web adds that color to the Document Colors section in all color-related list boxes. You run into these list boxes whenever you add or change an element's color in your page, such as hyperlinks (covered in Chapter 4) or table borders (covered in Chapter 10). This thoughtful "extra" makes applying colors elsewhere in your page easy, and it helps you keep an eye on your page's overall color scheme.

To change the body text color for the entire page, follow these steps:

1. **Choose Format⇨Background.**

   The Page Properties dialog box appears, with the Formatting tab open.

2. **In the Colors section, from the Text list box, select the color swatch you like and then click OK.**

Take a look at the code that Expression Web creates when you change the color of some text. In the following example, we changed the text color in the phrase this text is gray to gray by selecting it from the Font Color palette of standard colors. Here's the code for the text:

```
<p>In this paragraph, the phrase <span class="stylex">this
         text is gray</span> has been made gray.</p>
```

As in the example earlier in this chapter for applying a font family to a bit of text, Expression Web uses the opening <span> and closing </span> tags to identify the chunk of text we styled. In the opening <span> tag, Expression Web inserts the selector for this style rule: class=stylex. (Expression Web numbers incrementally the styles it creates on a page, so if this is the second style you apply, it's `style2`.) Now look at the style that Expression Web created:

```
.stylex {
        color: #808080;
}
```

This style rule tells the browser, "On this page, find the stuff between the `<span>` tags with the class selector `stylex`, and color it #808080." The number 808080 is the hexadecimal number for gray.

Don't worry: You don't have to memorize any hexadecimal numbers for colors. Just pick your colors from the dialog boxes and toolbars that show them. Or visit one of the many color charts on the Web. (A few of our favorites are at `www.lynda.com/hex.asp#` and `www.webmonkey.com/webmonkey/ reference/color_codes`.) We recommend that you get used to hexadecimal color numbers because they're the common currency when working with color in Web pages. We talk more about color for Web pages in a sidebar in Chapter 7.

Changing character spacing

Expression Web makes it easy to change the amount of blank space between letters or characters (known in typography circles as *kerning*). To change the space between selected characters, follow these steps:

1. **Choose Format⇨Font to display the Font dialog box.**

2. **In the dialog box, click the Character Spacing tab to make the options visible.**

3. **From the Spacing list box, choose Expanded or Condensed.**

4. **In the accompanying By box, enter the number of pixels by which Expression Web will expand or contract the selected text.**

   Note: The Position options in this dialog box enable you to control the amount of space between regular text and superscript or subscript text.

5. **Click Apply to see how the spacing change looks before closing the dialog box, or click OK to close the dialog box and apply the character spacing.**

Creating Stylish Paragraphs

Unlike font effects, which you apply to individual letters and words, paragraph styles apply to entire paragraphs. A paragraph in a Web page differs from the paragraph you had to write in second grade about your summer vacation. In Expression Web, every time you press the Enter key, you create a new paragraph. Even if you type only one word and then press Enter, Expression Web considers the word a paragraph.

If you simply want to create a new line without creating a new paragraph, use a line break instead. To create a line break, press Shift+Enter.

In this section, we cover the paragraph types that you use for the majority of text on your Web pages:

- **Paragraph:** This type is the default style for paragraphs. It's nothing fancy — just regular old left-aligned paragraphs with a proportional font. (The Times font appears in most Web browsers.) Every time you press Enter, Expression Web creates a new paragraph and surrounds it with the HTML code <p></p>. We cover all the different ways to customize paragraphs in this section.

- **Headings:** Headings are bits of text that help identify clumps of information inside a page. Large headings, usually located at the top of the page, identify what the page is all about, and smaller headings, sprinkled throughout, divide the page's information into manageable chunks. Headings in Web pages come in six sizes, or levels. Heading 1 (<h1></h1>) is the largest size and Heading 6 (<h6></h6>) is the smallest. We discuss headings in more detail in "Handling headings," later in this chapter.

- **Lists:** Lists group related bits of information by using bullets, numbers, or special text formatting. There are two types of lists: "ordered" for sequential lists with numbered items, and "unordered" for lists of bulleted items. Ordered lists use the HTML tag <ol></ol>, and unordered lists use <ul></ul>. We cover lists in detail later in this section.

Expression Web can create other types of paragraphs, although you use these paragraph types rarely, if at all:

- **Preformatted:** Creates paragraphs with a fixed-width font (Courier for most browsers). Use this paragraph style if you want your paragraph to look like it was typed on a typewriter. The HTML tag for this type of paragraph is <pre></pre>.

- **Address:** A holdover from the olden days of Web design (around 1993). Back then, the Address style was used to designate the page creator's e-mail address so that visitors could get in touch. Now, folks format their contact information in any number of ways, so the Address style has, for the most part, become obsolete. Besides, the style creates italic text just as the italic font style does, so why use the old clunker? The HTML tag for this type of paragraph style is <address></address>.

✔ **Defined Term/Definition:** Formats terms and definitions in a dictionary look-alike manner. The tags for these paragraph types are `<dt></dt>` for defined term and `<dd></dd>` for definition.

✔ **Blockquote:** Indents a block of text on both the left and right sides to set it off from surrounding text. The HTML tag for this paragraph type is `<blockquote></blockquote>`.

To change the style of a paragraph, follow these steps:

1. **Place the cursor inside the paragraph you want to change, or select more than one paragraph.**

2. **On the Common or Formatting toolbar, choose the paragraph type you want from the Style list box, as shown in Figure 3-8.**

   This list box is called the Style list box because it refers to the different "styles" of paragraphs.

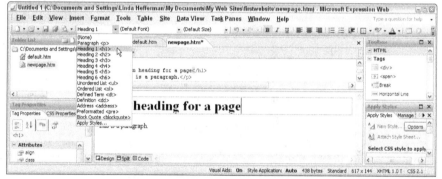

Figure 3-8: Paragraph styles.

Take a peek in Code view and notice how Expression Web has formatted your paragraphs with opening and closing HTML tags for each type of paragraph type, like this:

```
<h1>Main heading for a page</h1>
<p>This is a paragraph.</p>
```

Adjusting paragraph alignment, indenting, and spacing

By default, basic Expression Web paragraphs (with the exceptions of headings and lists) are single-spaced; they line up with the page's left margin; and they contain no indentation (that is, no extra space exists between the margin and the paragraph). Also, a little bit of space precedes and follows each paragraph. You can change these default paragraph settings in a few different ways. First, here's the quick methods:

✔ **Quick way to change a paragraph's alignment:** Click inside the paragraph (or select multiple paragraphs) and, on the Formatting toolbar, click the Align Text Left, Center, Align Text Right, or Justify button.

✔ **Quick way to change paragraph indentation:** Click inside the paragraph (or select multiple paragraphs) and, on the Formatting toolbar, click the Increase Indent Position button. Click the button as many times as you want to achieve the desired effect. To decrease the level of an indented paragraph, click the Decrease Indent Position button.

If you're the precision-minded type, you can change paragraph alignment, indentation, and spacing by following these steps:

1. **Click inside the paragraph (or select multiple paragraphs).**

2. **Choose Format⇨Paragraph.**

   The Paragraph dialog box appears.

3. **From the Alignment list box, choose the alignment option you want.**

4. **From the list boxes in the Indentation section, specify the amount of indentation (in pixels) you want.**

   The Left Side list box controls indentation along the left margin, and the Right Side list box controls indentation along the right margin. The Indent First Line list box enables you to apply a different indentation setting to the first line of the paragraph.

5. **From the list boxes in the Spacing section, specify the amount of spacing (in pixels) you want.**

   The Before list box controls the amount of space before the paragraph; the After list box controls the amount of space after the paragraph; the Word list box controls the amount of space between words in the paragraph; and the Line spacing list box controls (you guessed it) the space between the lines in the paragraph.

6. **Click OK.**

   The Paragraph dialog box closes, and Expression Web applies the formatting to the selected paragraphs.

Whether you click the buttons on the Formatting toolbar or use the options in the Paragraph dialog box, Expression Web uses styles to control paragraph alignment, indentation, and spacing. Take a look at the style rule that Expression Web created for a paragraph indented with one click of the Increase Indent Position button:

```
.stylex {
          margin-left: 40px;
}
```

For each time you click the Increase Indent Position button, Expression Web indents another 40 pixels from the left. If you use the Paragraph dialog box to set the indent, you can specify an exact number of pixels.

Here's a style rule for a center-aligned paragraph:

```
.stylex {
          text-align: center;
}
```

In case you want more control over the placement of your paragraphs than the Paragraph dialog box can give you, we cover using styles for positioning in Chapter 8.

Adding borders and shading

Want to surround the selected paragraph with a box? Or give the paragraph a colorful background so that it visually jumps off the page? These effects and more await you in the Borders and Shading dialog box.

Adding a border

To quickly add a border to the selected paragraph, click the down arrow next to the Outside Borders button and choose a border style you like. For a little more control, do this:

1. **Click inside the paragraph (or select multiple paragraphs) and then choose Format⇨Borders and Shading.**

   The Borders and Shading dialog box appears, as shown in Figure 3-9.

2. **In the Setting area of the dialog box, click the option that corresponds to the type of border you want.**

3. **In the Style box, click the name of the border style you want.**

4. **Choose a border color from the Color list box.**

   If you choose More Colors, the More Colors dialog box appears. We explain how to use the More Colors dialog box in the previous section "Changing text color."

5. **Enter a border width (in pixels) in the Width box.**

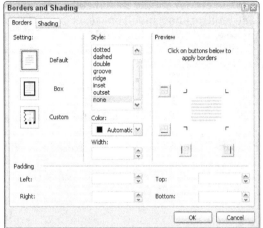

Figure 3-9:
The Borders
and Shading
dialog box.

6. **To turn on or off individual borders, in the Preview area, click the button that corresponds to the border you want to change.**

7. **To add empty space between the paragraph text and its surrounding border, enter pixel values in boxes in the Padding area of the dialog box.**

8. **Click OK to close the dialog box and apply the border settings.**

As with other text formatting, borders are controlled by styles. Here's the style for a paragraph with an outside border around all sides applied by clicking the Outside Border button and selecting the Outside Border option (in the upper-left corner of the drop-down menu):

```
.stylex {
        border-style: solid;
        border-width: 1px;
        padding: 1px 4px;
}
```

As you can see, a few goodies are associated with borders, all of which you can set individually in the Borders and Shading dialog box. Because you have so many options for adding borders, Expression Web sometimes abbreviates style definitions, using standard CSS shorthand. Here's an example of a style rule for a paragraph with a 4-pixel-wide, dotted, fuchsia border around all sides:

```
.stylex {
        border: 4px dotted #FF00FF;
        padding: 1px 4px;
}
```

The first line states that the border should be 4 pixels wide, dotted, and fuschia. The second line controls how much space, or *padding*, is inserted between the paragraph text and the border. In this case, there's 1 pixel on the top and bottom and 4 pixels on the left and right sides. (We discuss padding around page elements in more detail in Chapter 8.)

Adding shading

In Expression Web, *shading* refers to the paragraph's foreground and background attributes. The paragraph's foreground is its text color, and its background refers to the color or picture that sits behind the selected paragraph's text.

To quickly apply a background color to selected text, click the Highlight button. To add more complex shading, do this:

1. **Select the paragraph (or select multiple paragraphs), and then choose Format⇨Borders and Shading.**

   The Borders and Shading dialog box appears.

2. **In the dialog box, click the Shading tab to make those options visible.**

3. **To change the paragraph's background color, choose an option from the Background Color list box.**

4. **To change the paragraph's foreground (text) color, choose an option from the Foreground Color list box.**

5. **Click OK to close the dialog box and apply the shading settings.**

After you start positioning elements on your Web pages, the real fun with borders and backgrounds begins. We talk more about using borders and backgrounds effectively in Chapter 8. We show you how to add a background picture in Chapter 5.

All options in the Borders and Shading dialog box and the Highlight effect are controlled by styles. Here's the style rule for a paragraph with a red background:

```
.stylex {
        background-color: #FF0000;
}
```

Handling headings

Headings break up text on your Web pages into meaningful chunks. Well-constructed headings can also give your visitors a sense of the page's content at a glance. Web pages can contain six levels of headings: Heading 1 is the largest, and Heading 6 is the smallest. (Trust us — Heading 6 is so small that you never use it.)

Expression Web automatically makes all headings bold and sets relative text sizes for them. Just as with any chunk of text on your Web page, however, you're in control. You can make all your headings hot pink if you want!

To make a line of text a heading, follow these steps:

1. **Click inside the text you want to format as a heading.**

2. **On the Common toolbar or Formatting toolbar, click the arrow next to the Style list box (refer to Figure 3-8) and click the desired heading level.**

   Notice that Expression Web nicely displays the HTML tags for the different heading levels.

   For example, to create a first-level heading, click Heading 1 <h1>.

The HTML code for headings works simply. Notice that Expression Web has replaced the paragraph <p></p> tags with heading tags:

```
<h1>This is a first-level heading</h1>
```

Notice also that when you click inside a heading, the <h1> tag appears in the Quick Tag Selector bar (we cover using the Quick Tag Selector bar in Chapter 14) and on a little tab above the heading text in the editing window. And, if you change any aspect of a heading, such as its color or font size, Expression Web writes a style rule. For example, the style rule for a heading in small caps with red text looks like this:

```
.stylex {
        color: #FF0000;
        font-variant: small-caps;
}
```

If you decide that you want all first-level headings colored red and in small caps throughout your entire page, you can create a style rule that uses the <h1> HTML tag as the selector. We tell you how in Chapter 7.

Creating bulleted and numbered lists

Whether you're a list lover or hater, you're likely to eventually be in a situation where a list is the best tool for organizing your page's information.

Lists come in two basic flavors:

- *Bulleted lists* are groups of items, each of which is preceded by a solid dot, or *bullet*. The Web design term for this list flavor is *unordered list* (a list with items in nonsequential order).

- A *numbered list* looks like a bulleted list, except that numbers stand in for the bullets. In the world of Web, this flavor is an *ordered list*. Ordered lists are useful if you need to present a series of sequential steps.

To create an ordered or unordered list, follow these steps:

1. **Place the cursor in the page where you want the list to begin.**

2. **Click the Numbering button or the Bullets button.**

   A number or a bullet appears at the beginning of the first line.

3. **Type the first list item and then press Enter.**

   A number or bullet appears on the next line.

4. **Type your second list item (and so on).**

5. **After you're done adding items to your list, press Enter twice to end the list.**

You can convert existing paragraphs into bulleted or numbered lists by selecting the paragraphs that you want included in the list and then clicking the Numbering button or the Bullets button.

To split a long list into two separate lists, click at the end of a list item and press Enter twice. The list splits into two lists and, in the case of numbered lists, renumbers itself automatically.

If the plain dots or numbers sitting in your lists don't thrill you, you can change them. The List Properties dialog box enables you to change the shape of your bullets or replace the dreary black spots with pictures. If you want to give a numbered list a makeover, you can use the List Properties dialog box to apply Roman numerals or change the list's starting number.

To access the List Properties dialog box, click within the list you want to format, and then choose Format⇨Bullets and Numbering. Or, right-click the list and, from the pop-up menu that appears, choose List Properties.

Nesting a list in a list

Sometimes a simple list doesn't cut it. Suppose that you need something more sophisticated, such as a multilevel outline or a numbered list with bullets following certain items (similar to the one shown in Figure 3-10). No problem!

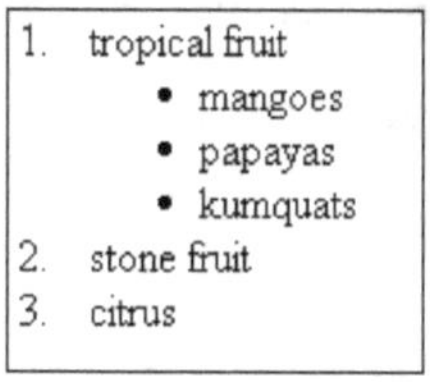

Figure 3-10:
A number-
bullet
combo list.

1. tropical fruit
      • mangoes
      • papayas
      • kumquats
2. stone fruit
3. citrus

To create this type of fancy-shmancy combo list, follow these steps:

1. **Create a bulleted or numbered list.**

   The list should contain every item, regardless of level.

2. **Highlight the item or items you want to put in the second level of the list, and then click the Increase Indent button.**

   The list items move to the right.

3. **To change the items' numbering or bullet style, with the items still highlighted, right-click and choose List Properties from the pop-up menu.**

4. **Choose the numbering or bullet style you want from the List Properties dialog box, and then click OK.**

   Note: Use the Decrease Indent button to demote list items. It's basically the preceding process in reverse!

Take a look at the Quick Tag Selector bar: The HTML tags are really building up. In Split or Code view, the code for a default bulleted list with three items looks like this:

```
<ul>
        <li>mangoes</li>
        <li>papayas</li>
        <li>kumquats</li>
</ul>
```

First on the scene is the HTML tag that tells the browser, "Hey, get ready for an unordered list" <ul>. Then the <li> and </li> tags enclose each *list item*. After the last item, the </ul> tag tells the browser, "Okay, that's it for the list."

If you change the bullet style for this list to squares, Expression Web adds a class selector to the <ul> tag:

```
<ul class="stylex">
        <li>mangoes</li>
        <li>papayas</li>
        <li>kumquats</li>
</ul>
```

Practicing safe styles

You may remember when word processors first appeared on the scene. Some people, seduced by the millions of text styles at their disposal, started churning out documents that looked more like cut-and-paste ransom notes that you might see in old private-eye movies than in professionally designed documents. Although the text was readable, it was a gaudy mess.

We relate this example only to illustrate how the moderate use of font and paragraph styles enhances a page's readability and visual appeal, whereas overuse sends your readers screaming to a new Web destination.

As with most things in life, moderation is the key. Choose a single font for headings, and perhaps one more font for body text. Keep your hyperlinks a single color so that visitors can easily identify clickable bits of text. (We show you how to change hyperlink colors in Chapter 4.)

Here's the style rule:

```
.stylex {
        list-style-type: square;
}
```

Play around with creating lists and changing bullet and numbering styles, and look at the code. Aren't you glad that Expression Web keeps track of all those tags for you and all you have to do is click a few buttons and type in your items?

Chapter 4

Getting Around with Hyperlinks

. . . .

In This Chapter

▶ Creating hyperlinks

▶ Linking to downloadable files and e-mail addresses

▶ Editing hyperlinks

▶ Fixing broken hyperlinks

▶ Removing hyperlinks from your page

▶ Using bookmarks to jump to a specific place inside a page

▶ Using text hyperlinks for navigation bars

▶ Inserting interactive buttons

▶ Using Dynamic HTML behaviors with hyperlinks

▶ Embedding hyperlinks in a picture

. . . .

*I*f Web sites were individual islands of text and graphics, they would be little more than glorified digital billboards. *Hyperlinks* are the waves that propel Web surfers around the globe in a few deft clicks. Links are where the action is; they're what turns a pile of disconnected Web pages into a useful, usable Web destination.

Adding Hyperlinks to Your Site: The What and the Where

A hyperlink can be anything — a word, a phrase, a single character, or an image — that acts as a springboard from somewhere on a Web page to another location. In the magical world of Harry Potter, you could compare hyperlinks to port keys: Touch an object (which, on a Web page, means that you click an object) and you're whisked off to someplace else.

Hyperlinks between pages and files in a Web site *(internal hyperlinks)* transform the site from a jumble of separate pages into a cohesive unit. Hyperlinks to locations outside the Web site *(external hyperlinks)* connect the site to the rest of the World Wide Web.

Here are the basic steps to create a hyperlink (the rest of this chapter fills in the details):

1. **In the page, select the "thingy" you want to transform into a hyperlink.**

   We call this thingy the *hyperlink source.* The hyperlink source is the object that people click.

2. **Connect the hyperlink source to the place you want visitors to end up after they click the hyperlink.**

   From now on, we call this location the *hyperlink destination.* A hyperlink destination can be a spot in the same page, another page or file inside the same Web site, or a different site on the World Wide Web. A hyperlink destination can also point to an e-mail address or initiate a file download, such as a PDF document.

Linking to a Web page or file

Most often, when you create a hyperlink, you already have the link's destination in mind. As long as you know that destination's location — whether it's a page inside the same Web site or a different Web site altogether — you're ready to roll.

To link to an existing page or file, follow these steps:

1. **In the page, select the object you want to turn into a hyperlink (the hyperlink source).**

   Highlight a bit of text, click a picture, double-click a word — whatever. (We cover how to add a picture to a Web site in Chapter 5.)

2. **On the Common or Standard toolbar, click the Insert Hyperlink button.**

   The Insert Hyperlink dialog box appears, as shown in Figure 4-1.

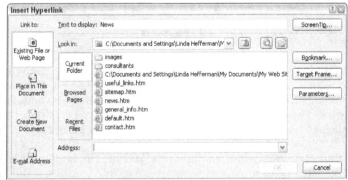

Figure 4-1:
The Insert
Hyperlink
dialog box.

3. **Click the Existing File or Web Page icon in the dialog box's Link To section (if it's not already selected) to make those options visible.**

4. **Depending on the location of the page or file to which you want the hyperlink to lead, specify the hyperlink destination:**

- *If the destination file is part of the open Web site, in the dialog box's file list, click the file.*

When a page is open in Design view, *two* instances of that page appear in the dialog box's file list. You can click either icon in this step.

- *If the destination file is located on the World Wide Web, type its address (also known as its* URL*) in the Address box.*

You need to include the full address, including the `http` and any slashes, periods, or other characters, as in these examples:

```
http://www.server.com
http://www.server.com/filename.htm
http://www.server.com/foldername/filename.htm
```

If you can't remember the URL, in the dialog box, click the Browse the Web button (it looks like a globe with a magnifying glass on top) to launch your Web browser. Surf to your destination and switch back to Expression Web by clicking the Expression Web button on the Windows taskbar (or press Alt+Tab). The URL should appear in the Address text box.

Expression Web is a little temperamental when it comes to copying URLs. If the URL doesn't magically appear for you, you have to copy it from the Web browser and paste it into the Address text box manually.

- *If the page or file is elsewhere on your hard drive or network, be aware of the potential problems with this type of hyperlink.* If you're sure that you want to create the link, in the dialog box, navigate to the location of the file and then click it.

The problem is that when you publish your finished Web site on a host Web server, the link no longer works because the location of the hyperlink destination file is specific to your computer's file system, not to the Web server's.

Sometimes this feature comes in handy, such as when you're creating a local Web presentation to be displayed only on your computer or local network (not on the World Wide Web). If you decide to use this option, proceed with care, and double-check the link after you publish your site, to be sure that the link works properly.

5. **Click OK.**

The dialog box closes, and a hyperlink is born.

If the hyperlink source is text, that text now displays the proud markings of a link: underlining and color.

You can still apply the same font and paragraph styles (bold and italic, for example) to text hyperlinks as you can to regular text. You can also get rid of the default underlining that appears when you transform regular text into a hyperlink. To do so, click inside the link, and then click the Underline button on the Formatting toolbar. As with regular text and paragraphs, formatting changes are applied to hyperlinks by using CSS styles. The cool thing about using styles is that you can monkey around with a single hyperlink until you get it looking the way you want. You then apply the hyperlink style to all links to give them a consistent look and behavior throughout the site. We talk about styles in detail in Chapter 7.

If the hyperlink source is a picture, the image itself looks no different than before its transformation. Trust us: The image is now a *graphic hyperlink.* If you want proof, pass your cursor over any text or graphic hyperlink, and the link destination appears in the lower-left corner of the Expression Web status bar.

When your visitors are viewing your page in their Web browser, passing their cursor over a graphic hyperlink changes the cursor into its "This thing is clickable" shape, usually a hand icon with a pointing index finger. This cursor behavior has been in practice for so long — in Web pages, e-mail, software, and even documents — that it's probably not necessary to make graphic hyperlinks stand out in any other way (unless you really want to).

Here are a couple more tips and shortcuts for creating hyperlinks:

- ✔ **Open the page that you want to add a hyperlink to in Design view, and then drag an icon for a file or Web page from the Folder List task pane to the open page.** (If the Folder List task pane isn't visible, choose Task Panes➪Folder List.) The file or Web page that you drag becomes the destination, and the destination page's filename is the hyperlink text. This is a great shortcut if you have a whole bunch of document files (such as PDFs) you want to create links to.

- ✔ **Type a URL or an e-mail address inside the body of your page and then press the spacebar or Enter.** Expression Web automatically turns the URL or address text into a hyperlink to that location or address.

The steps in this section apply to links leading to *any* type of file, not just to Web pages. For example, you may want to create a hyperlink that, when clicked, enables visitors to download a file. No problem. Simply add the item (in this case, the file you want to make available for downloading) into your Web site (see Chapter 1 for details on adding files), and then create a hyperlink leading to that item. When a visitor clicks that link, if the visitor's Web browser doesn't know how to open that file type, the browser automatically prompts the visitor to download the file. (Try it and see.)

Take a look at the HTML code for hyperlinks. If it's not already selected, click Split at the bottom of the editing window to turn on Split view, and find a few hyperlinks.

Here's what an external link to a Web site address outside the current Web site looks like:

```
<a href="http://www.google.com">Google</a>
```

Notice that the full Web address, including the `http://`, appears inside the HTML code for a hyperlink. This is an *absolute* link because absolutely every bit of the Web address is included. There can be no question about its location.

In HTML, a link appears inside the tag pair `<a></a>`, which stands for *anchor*. When a Web browser sees the `<a>` tag, it looks for the two parts: the hyperlink destination and the hyperlink source. The `href="http://www.google.com"` part tells the Web browser, "This place inside the quotation marks is the hyperlink destination." Notice that the hyperlink destination is inside the opening tag angle brackets, like this: `<a href="http://www.google.com">`. The next part, inserted between the opening and closing tags, is the hyperlink source. In this example, clicking the text `Google` takes the visitor to the Web address, `http://www.google.com`.

Here's a link to another Web page inside the same Web site, located in the same folder as the page containing the link. The link takes the visitor to the site's home page when the word `Home` is clicked:

```
<a href="default.htm">Home</a>
```

Here's an internal link to a page located in a subfolder in the same Web site:

```
<a href="/bigplants/trees.htm">Trees for small gardens</a>
```

Choosing worthy hyperlink words

Many beginning Web designers (and even some seasoned professionals), create links that include the phrase "Click here," such as "Click here for a list of trees suitable for small yards." Pretty soon their Web pages are peppered with underlined Click here commands, which visually shout at visitors but give them little information — like obnoxious car dealers on television commercials.

Instead, choose text that describes what visitors will see when they click the hyperlink. In the preceding example, "Trees suitable for small yards" is a good phrase for the hyperlink text because it describes exactly what visitors see after clicking the link.

These links are *relative* links because they point to a location relative to the current page. As long as you build your Web page and folder structure and create hyperlinks between pages within Expression Web, the program keeps tabs on where everything is, even if you move things around a bit. When you publish your site to the Web, the links work as advertised (although you should always check them to make sure!).

Here's an internal link to a page inside the same Web site that uses an image rather than text as the clickable thing:

```
<a href="/bigplants/trees.htm"><img alt="Japanese maple"
        src="japanesemaple.jpg" /></a>
```

Images have their own, special HTML tag, `<img>`, which opens and closes with only one set of angle brackets. So, instead of a bit of text sitting between the `<a></a>` hyperlink tags, you see another HTML tag, this one specifying the location and filename of an image file (in this case, `japanesemaple.jpg`). (We talk more about image tags in Chapter 5.)

Linking to an e-mail address

The quickest way to help your visitors get in touch with you is to include a link to your e-mail address inside each page in your site. That way, if visitors have comments (or, heaven forbid, complaints), they can click this link to pop open an e-mail window, preaddressed to you, from their Web browsers. From there, they can fire off messages in seconds.

For e-mail links to work, the visitor's browser must either have a built-in e-mail component or be able to hook up with the visitor's e-mail program. Also, nefarious "scraper" programs sometimes harvest e-mail addresses from Web pages and then use them to spam their owners. Keep this information in mind if you decide to include your e-mail address on your site.

If creating a direct e-mail link doesn't appeal to you, consider creating a form that visitors fill out with their names, e-mail addresses, and comments. Your e-mail address remains hidden from the form-filler-outers, but they still have a way of getting in touch with you. We cover creating forms in Chapter 6.

The quickest approach to creating a link to your e-mail address is to type your e-mail address in the page, followed by pressing the spacebar or the Enter key. Expression Web automatically transforms the address text into a link. Otherwise, do this:

1. **In the page, select the hyperlink source.**

2. **Click the Insert Hyperlink button to open the Insert Hyperlink dialog box.**

3. **In the dialog box's Link To section, click the E-Mail Address icon.**

   The contents of the Insert Hyperlink dialog box change accordingly.

E-mail Address

4. **In the E-Mail Address text box, type an e-mail address.**

   The address should look something like this: name@address.com. When you start typing your address, Expression Web automatically tacks mailto: to the beginning. Don't fret — that's good HTML.

5. **Optionally, in the Subject text box, type a subject line for the e-mail message generated by this link.**

   Not all e-mail programs and Web browsers use the subject heading you enter.

6. **Click OK.**

If you want a link to your e-mail address on every page in your site, place the mailto link in a template. We tell you how to create a page template as the basis for new pages in Chapter 2. In Chapter 11, we tell you how to place elements common to several Web pages in Dynamic Web Templates.

Editing Hyperlinks

You can change your hyperlinks as easily as you can change anything else about your Web page. You can change the text that makes up the link, the destination to which the link leads, the appearance of the link, and even how it behaves.

Changing a hyperlink's text or destination and adding a ScreenTip

A visit to the Edit Hyperlink dialog box enables you to change the text that makes up a hyperlink, change its destination, or add a ScreenTip. A *ScreenTip* is a captionlike label that pops up when a visitor passes the cursor over a link (similar to the ToolTip that appears when you hover your cursor over a toolbar button in Expression Web).

ScreenTips don't show up in all browsers, especially older ones. (For example, Microsoft Internet Explorer before version 4.0 doesn't display them.)

To change a hyperlink's text or destination, or to add a ScreenTip to a hyperlink, follow these steps:

1. **In the page, click the hyperlink that you want to change. If it's text, click anywhere in the hyperlink text.**

2. **Click the Insert Hyperlink button to open the Edit Hyperlink dialog box.**

   You can also right-click the hyperlink and, from the pop-up menu, choose Hyperlink Properties.

3. **To change the hyperlink text visible in the page, type new text in the Text to Display text box.**

4. **To change the link's destination, click a different file in the file list or type a different URL in the Address list box.**

   Refer to the "Linking to a Web page or file" section, earlier in this chapter, for detailed instructions on how to specify a link's destination.

5. **To add a ScreenTip, click the ScreenTip button to display the Set Hyperlink ScreenTip dialog box. Type the ScreenTip text into the appropriate text box and then click OK.**

   The Edit Hyperlink dialog box becomes visible again.

6. **Click OK to close the dialog box.**

Displaying a hyperlink's destination in a new browser window

You may have experienced this trick during your own Web wanderings: You click a link inside a Web page, and, instead of replacing the contents of the current browser window, the hyperlink destination shows up in a new browser window.

This effect comes in handy for several situations. Some Web site creators program all their external links (links that point to locations outside the Web site) to pop open new windows when clicked so that visitors get a clear visual cue when they "leave" the site. Other designers use this effect to display supplementary information without replacing the contents of the original window. (A good example is a product catalog with a link leading to a size chart that appears in its own window.)

Regardless of what *you* want to happen when a visitor clicks a link, in many browsers your visitors control whether the link opens in a new window, a new tab, or in the open tab or window (usually by changing settings in the Options, Internet Options, or Preferences dialog box). Not to worry: A visitor who knows how to change a Web browser's settings also knows how to find her way back to your Web site! To cause the hyperlink destination to appear in a new browser window, do the following:

1. **In the page, click the hyperlink you want to change.**

2. **Click the Insert Hyperlink button to open the Edit Hyperlink dialog box.**

3. **In the dialog box, click the Target Frame button.**

   The Target Frame dialog box appears.

4. **In the dialog box's Common Targets list box, click New Window, and then click OK.**

   The Target Frame dialog box closes, and the Edit Hyperlink dialog box becomes visible again.

5. **Click OK to close the dialog box.**

Take a look at the code for a link that opens a new browser window. In this example, the hyperlink initiates a file download — in this case, a PDF of a user manual:

```
<a target="_blank" href="usermanual.pdf">Download the user
        manual</a>
```

The opening <a> tag contains both the code telling the browser to open a new window (`target="_blank"`) and the hyperlink destination, `href="usermanual.pdf"`.

Another way to control whether a link opens a new browser window is to use JavaScript. Check out *JavaScript For Dummies,* 4th Edition, by Emily A. Vander Veer (Wiley) for details.

Changing hyperlink color

Hyperlinks stand out from regular text because they're often underlined and a different color from surrounding text. The default hyperlink color is blue, but you can change the link's color to coordinate with the site's color scheme.

Hyperlinks have four distinct colors, or *states;* these colors appear when a visitor views the page in a Web browser:

- ✔ **Default color:** The link's color before the visitor clicks it and jumps to the hyperlink destination. When a visitor arrives at your page for the first time, all the page's links appear in the default color because the visitor hasn't yet followed any links.

- ✔ **Active color:** The color the link becomes "mid-click." The appearance of the active color tells visitors, "Fasten your seatbelts; you're going somewhere new."

- ✔ **Visited color:** The color the link changes to after a visitor follows a link and then returns to the page. The visited color lets visitors know which links they have already followed. (Each individual visitor's browser keeps track of which links that person has followed inside each page.)

- ✔ **Hover color:** The color the link changes to when a visitor passes the mouse cursor over the link. The appearance of the hover color tells the visitor, "Click me; I'll take you somewhere."

To select link colors for a page, follow these steps:

1. **With the page open in Design view, choose Format⇨Background.**

   The Page Properties dialog box appears with the Formatting tab visible. The current link color settings appear in the list boxes labeled Hyperlink, Visited Hyperlink, Active Hyperlink, and Hovered Hyperlink, as shown in Figure 4-2.

   Note: If an external style sheet is controlling the formatting for the page, the Background command is unavailable. You have to change hyperlink colors in the style sheet file itself. We tell you how to edit styles in Chapter 7. We cover external style sheets in Chapter 9.

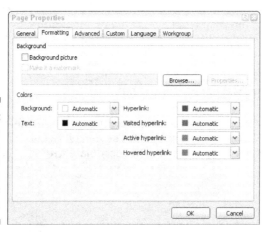

Figure 4-2:
The Formatting tab in the Page Properties dialog box.

2. Choose a new color from one or all of the list boxes corresponding to each hyperlink state.

If you choose More Colors, the More Colors dialog box appears. We explain how to use the More Colors dialog box in Chapter 3.

3. Click OK.

The dialog box closes, and the page's links change color. To see how the active and visited colors look, preview the page in a Web browser. We explain how to preview pages in Web browsers in Chapter 2.

Although you can set different hyperlink colors for each page, keep in mind that Web surfers expect hyperlinks to look the same throughout a Web site. So if you change hyperlink colors and formatting, change them for all pages on your Web site.

When you change the default colors for links, Expression Web writes the new color information as CSS styles. But these styles affect only the current page. After you figure out your link colors on your page, you can save the link color styles to an external CSS style sheet and attach it to the rest of your pages, and — voila! — all your Web pages throughout the site use the same link color scheme. We tell you how to use external style sheets in Chapter 9.

Take a look at the style rules that Expression Web sticks in your code when you change hyperlink colors. In this example, you change default hyperlinks to lime green and change visited links to dark green:

```
a {
        color: #00FF00;
}
a:visited {
        color: #008000;
}
```

The first style rule controls the color of an unvisited hyperlink sitting patiently on a page while waiting to be clicked for the first time. CSS uses a for the <a> (anchor) tag as the selector to tell the browser what's being styled. The second style rule controls the color of the visited link. This style rule also uses a for the selector, but tacks :visited onto it, which tells the browser more specifically which of the four link states the rule applies to.

Making Sure Your Hyperlinks Work

If you spend any time surfing the Web, you probably click a broken link now and then. Whereas the occasional broken link is merely an annoyance, several can damage your site's reputation and send your visitors stalking away in a huff.

A hyperlink breaks if the destination page the link points to becomes unreachable. A link can break because the Web server on which the destination page is stored goes down or because the page's author moves or renames the page. After a visitor clicks a broken hyperlink, rather than deliver the requested page, the destination Web server delivers an error message stating that it can't find the page.

The most common cause of broken hyperlinks — renaming a page in your Web site and then forgetting to update the hyperlinks elsewhere in the Web site that lead to the page — is a moot point in Expression Web. The program automatically updates hyperlinks for you as long as you do all your moving, shuffling, and renaming inside Expression Web. (We describe all the details of maintaining files in Chapter 13.)

Certain situations are beyond Expression Web's control, however, and cause hyperlinks in your Web site to break:

✔ You delete a file that another page in the Web site is linked to.

✔ You import an existing Web site into Expression Web and leave out some files.

✔ You mistype a URL while creating a hyperlink to a site on the Internet.

✔ You create a link to a site on the Internet, and that site changes location or otherwise becomes unreachable.

Fortunately, Expression Web knows how to deal with these pitfalls and can perform the following tricks:

✔ Find all broken or unchecked links in your Web site and list them in the Hyperlinks report

✔ Check links to external Internet sites to make sure they work properly

✔ Enable you to fix individual broken links

✔ Update the corrected links in selected pages or throughout the entire Web site

Verifying hyperlinks

Verifying hyperlinks involves locating broken internal links (links between pages and files that reside inside the Web site) and double-checking external links to make sure they work.

To verify the hyperlinks in your Web site, follow these steps:

1. Activate your Internet connection.

2. Save all open pages, if you haven't already, by choosing File➪Save All.

3. Choose Site➪Reports➪Problems➪Hyperlinks.

Expression Web switches from Design view to the Hyperlinks report in Reports view. The report displays a list of broken internal hyperlinks and as-yet-unverified external hyperlinks, as shown in Figure 4-3. Broken internal links (if any exist) are flagged with the status label Broken and a broken chain-link icon, and unverified external links are flagged with the label Unknown and a question mark icon.

Expression Web may also display a message asking whether you want it to verify the hyperlinks in your Web site.

Figure 4-3:
The
Hyperlinks
report.

4. In the upper-right corner of the Hyperlinks report, click the Verifies Hyperlinks in Current Web button. Or, if the Verify Hyperlinks message appears, select Yes.

The Verify Hyperlinks dialog box appears.

If the report turned up unknown hyperlinks, you have the choice of verifying all hyperlinks or only those that are unknown.

5. In the dialog box, click the Start button.

If your Web site contains lots of external links, the verification process takes awhile. Be sure that you have a few minutes to spare.

After you click the Start button, Expression Web verifies each external link by contacting the destination Web server and then making sure that it can reach the page. As the verification process is going on, a progress message appears on the Expression Web status bar to let you know what's happening. As Expression Web checks each link, its status label in the report changes from a question mark to either a green check mark followed by OK (indicating valid links) or a broken chain link followed by Broken (indicating broken links). When the verification process is complete, Expression Web lists a summary of its findings on the status bar.

To stop the verification process, press the Esc key. To resume verifying hyperlinks, click the Verifies Hyperlinks in the Current Web button again.

Fixing broken hyperlinks

If Expression Web finds any broken links, you need to fix them. To do so, follow these steps:

1. If you haven't already, follow the steps in the preceding section.

2. From the Hyperlinks report, double-click the broken hyperlink you want to fix.

The Edit Hyperlink dialog box appears, as shown in Figure 4-4.

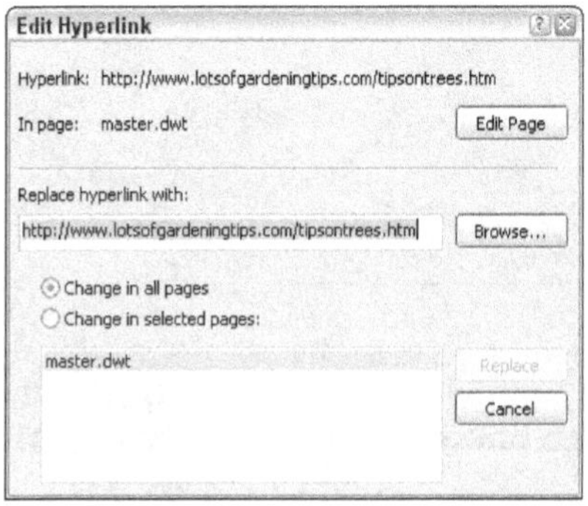

Figure 4-4:
The Edit
Hyperlink
dialog box
shows a
broken
hyperlink.

3. Decide whether you want to edit the page containing the hyperlink or update the hyperlink destination itself; then take the appropriate action:

To edit the page containing the link, click the Edit Page button. The page opens in Design view so that you can fix the ailing link. When you switch back to Reports view, repaired internal links disappear from the list, and the status of repaired external links changes from Broken to OK if they work (if Expression Web can test them via your Internet connection and they check out okay) or to Unknown, if they still don't work.

To edit the link itself, in the Edit Hyperlink dialog box, type a new URL in the Replace Hyperlink With text box. If you can't recall the URL, click the Browse button to launch your Web browser. Browse to the destination, and when you switch back to Expression Web, the destination URL should be visible in the text box. (If it isn't, copy the URL from the browser and paste it into the Replace Hyperlink With text box.) To change the link in selected pages (rather than throughout the entire Web site), select the Change in Selected Pages option button and then click the names of the pages you want to update in the box underneath it. Click the Replace button to fix the hyperlink and close the dialog box.

4. **Continue repairing broken hyperlinks by repeating Steps 2 and 3, and then click the Verifies Hyperlinks in Current Web button again to recheck.**

   Like a carpenter who measures twice before cutting, rechecking your links ensures that all your links work as advertised!

To exit from Reports view, in the editing window, click a Web page tab or click Folders in the lower-left corner of the Web Site tab.

After you publish your finished site, we recommend verifying your site's hyperlinks at least every couple of weeks. Web pages move and change all the time, breaking hyperlinks in your Web site. Expression Web makes checking your links easy — why not make it a regular habit?

Unlinking Hyperlinks

We all know that too much of a good thing is, well, too much. Suppose that you became so intoxicated with the power of hyperlink creation that, looking at your page now, your visitors will barely be able to get through a single sentence without being led astray by all the links beckoning them to click here and there. Perhaps removing a few links so that the others can shine would be wise. To remove a hyperlink (or two or three or four), follow these steps:

1. **Click the link you want to unlink.**

2. **Click the Insert Hyperlink button to open the Edit Hyperlink dialog box.**

3. **In the dialog box, click Remove Link.**

   The dialog box closes, and your link returns to regular text (or, if the link's a picture, to its original state).

Using Bookmarks to Get Somewhere within a Page

A *bookmark* is an invisible spot inside a Web page that can be used as the destination of a link. Bookmarks enable you to better control where visitors end up after they click a hyperlink. A link without the benefit of a bookmark drops visitors off at the top of the destination page. When a visitor clicks a hyperlink that leads to a bookmark inside a page, the visitor jumps straight to the bookmark location.

Bookmarks are like express elevators, especially in long pages that normally require lots of scrolling. For example, your question-and-answer page may have questions at the top and the answers below. Certainly, your visitors can scroll the whole page and read all the answers. Bookmark each answer, though, and link to it from the question, and you give them a much faster way to get to the answer to that single question they want to read. All a visitor has to do is click the question and — answer, ho!

To make a good thing an even better thing, add a bookmark at the top of the question list and link to it from each answer. Then a visitor who has read the answer can jump back to the question list.

As with hyperlinks, creating bookmarks is a two-step process: Add the bookmark (the destination), and then create the hyperlink to it.

Creating bookmarks

A bookmark can be the current location of the cursor or any selected bit of text: a word, a phrase, or even a letter. Text defined as a bookmark looks (and acts) no different from regular text; the text is simply flagged with an invisible marker to which you can point a hyperlink.

To create a bookmark, follow these steps:

1. **In the page, select the text you want to turn into a bookmark.**

   Or place the cursor in the location where you want the bookmark to sit without selecting any text.

   The bookmark eventually becomes the hyperlink destination.

2. **Choose Insert⇨Bookmark.**

   The Bookmark dialog box appears. If you selected text in Step 1, the text is visible in the Bookmark Name text box. (Expression Web wisely assumes that you want to give the bookmark the same name as the text it's made of.) Otherwise, the text box is empty.

3. **If the text box is empty (or if you want to choose a different name), type a brief name in the Bookmark Name text box.**

   A good name describes the bookmark's function or location.

4. **Click OK.**

   The dialog box closes. If the bookmark is made of text, a dotted line appears underneath the selected text in Design view. If the bookmark is a single point, a flag icon appears at the location of the bookmark. (In real life, bookmarks are invisible. Visitors viewing your page with a browser can't distinguish bookmarks from regular text unless they sift through the page's underlying HTML code.)

   If you don't see the bookmark flag in Design view, turn on Show Paragraph Marks. To do so, choose View➪Formatting Marks and then click Show. Make sure Paragraph Marks is selected, as shown in Figure 4-5.

5. **Click Save to save the new bookmark information.**

Figure 4-5:
Viewing
bookmark
flag icons in
Design view.

Linking to a bookmark

Any bookmark on any page in your Web site is an eligible candidate for a link. To forge this link, follow these steps:

1. **In the page, select the hyperlink source.**

   This step is the same as for creating a regular link: Select the word, phrase, or picture you want to turn into a hyperlink.

2. **Click the Insert Hyperlink button to open the Insert Hyperlink dialog box.**

3. **In the dialog box's file list, click the page that contains the bookmark to which you want to link, and then click the Bookmark button.**

   Or, if the bookmark is in the same page as the hyperlink, in the dialog box's Link To area, click the Place in This Document icon.

Depending on which item you click, either the Select Place in Document dialog box appears, or the Insert Hyperlink dialog box changes its options to display essentially the same information — the bookmarks inside the selected page.

4. **From the list of bookmarks, click the bookmark to which you want to link.**

5. **Click OK. (If the Insert Hyperlink dialog box is still open, click OK again to close it.)**

The dialog box closes, and the bookmark and hyperlink live happily ever after. (Trumpets sound.)

Take a minute now to peek at the code for bookmarks. Here's one that considerate Web designers often include in long Web pages. Tucked into the top of a Web page, it gives visitors a way to quickly jump back to the beginning of the page:

```
<a name="top"></a>
```

Notice that the bookmark also uses the <a></a> (anchor) tag pair. The opening tag contains the bookmark name (in this case, top), referring to the top of the Web page. Here's what a link to this bookmark looks like elsewhere on this page:

```
<a href="#top">Back to top</a>
```

Notice that the hyperlink destination consists of the # symbol followed by the bookmark name. The # symbol tells the browser that this hyperlink destination is on the same page. The hyperlink source, the magic bit of text the visitor clicks to get to the bookmark, is the text Back to top.

Dismantling bookmarks

Get rid of any bookmarks that outlive their usefulness. The procedure is quick and painless (for both you and the bookmark). If the bookmark is made up of text, right-click inside the bookmark you want to dismantle, and from the pop-up menu that appears, choose Bookmark Properties. In the Bookmark dialog box that appears, click Clear. If the bookmark is marked with a flag icon, place the cursor to the right of the flag icon and then press the Delete key.

Nifty Text-Based Navigation Bars

Imagine trying to navigate your way through a city without street signs. And in really big cities, like New York or Paris, even street signs can't help you figure out where you are or where to go if you don't know what part of the city you're in, because the whole city wouldn't possibly fit on one readable map.

Navigation for your Web site is just as important. Your visitors need to be able to find their way around (and get back to where they started) easily and quickly. Good navigation to a Web site is like excellent signage to a city: If it works well, most people don't notice it. But if it doesn't, they complain — loudly (or they simply click away from your site and never return).

Many Web designers build a Web site's navigation by grouping hyperlinks into navigation bars (often known by their nickname, nav bars). A *navigation bar* at its simplest is nothing more than a series of text hyperlinks arranged in a horizontal row or vertical column somewhere near the top of a Web page (although the bar can be anywhere on the Web page). Or it can be an elaborate graphical affair with fancy drop-down submenus. Complicated navigation systems often require scripting and graphics skills beyond the reach of the beginning Web site builder (and beyond the scope of this book; we show you some cool tricks to jazz up buttons later in this chapter). No matter how fancy or plain a site's navigation, its most important job is to provide Web surfers with a graceful road map through the site's different locations. A simple collection of text hyperlinks can accomplish this task quite nicely.

In Expression Web, you can build a simple text navigation bar in a matter of minutes. With a little more time and some tinkering with CSS styles, you can dress it up with font formatting, borders, and background colors so that it becomes an attractive design element on a Web page. Take a look at the navigation bars used in the Expression Web templates to get ideas for your own site. All navigation bars in the templates are text hyperlinks that put CSS styling to work to make them look pretty.

Creating attractive text-based navigation

Many Web designers use common text treatments to make a line of text hyperlinks look interesting. Customize hyperlink colors and remove the underline, and pretty soon your plain text hyperlinks start looking downright classy.

But what about link bars?

If you used Microsoft FrontPage to generate link bars for your site's navigation, you may be lamenting the loss of a favorite feature. But according to the Web powers that be, FrontPage link bars weren't quite kosher when it came to by-the-book code generation. Expression Web is a lean, mean, clean-code-generating machine, so the link bars had to go. If you have a FrontPage Web site you're trying to update, you have to retool your site's navigation. And although change can be painful, it often provides the opportunity to rethink, streamline, and improve an initial design.

Experiment with different characters, like this:

Asterisks: Home * News * About * Contact Us

Two colons in a row: Home :: News:: About :: Contact Us

Square brackets: [Home] [News] [About] [Contact Us]

Curly brackets: {Home} {News} {About} {Contact Us}

Plain ol' parentheses: (Home) (News) (About) (Contact Us)

Vertical line (Shift + \): Home | News | About | Contact Us

Play around with initial caps, all lowercase, and small caps to give your navigation bar a different feel, as in these examples:

home * news * about * contact us

home :: news :: about :: contact us

[home] [news] [about] [contact us]

Increase the character spacing within each hyperlink word for a looser, relaxed style:

h o m e | n e w s | a b o u t | c o n t a c t u s

If you want a very loose look, simply type a space between each letter, as in the preceding example. For more precision, use the controls in the Font dialog box, on the Character Spacing tab. (We talk about adjusting character spacing in Chapter 3.)

At the bottom of your page, add a small, supplemental navigation bar that duplicates the main navigation, as shown in Figure 4-6 (from the Expression Web template Event 1). Especially useful with long pages, this supplemental navigation bar gives visitors access to your site's links without having to return to the top of the page.

Text hyperlinks in a vertical unordered list <ul>

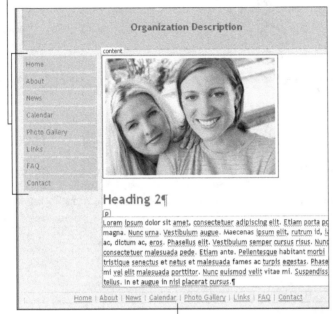

Figure 4-6:
This
navigation
bar uses the
vertical line
character to
separate
hyperlinks.

Text hyperlinks in a paragraph <p>

Use your imagination and play around until you get something you like. To use your navigation on all pages in your Web site, create a page template or include your navigation bar (or bars) in a Dynamic Web Template. (We talk about Dynamic Web Templates in Chapter 11.)

Here's what the code for the simple navigation bar shown at the bottom of Figure 4-6 looks like:

```
<p><a href="default.htm">Home</a> |
<a href="about/about.htm">About</a> |
<a href="news/news.htm">News</a> |
<a href="calendar/calendar.htm">Calendar</a> |
<a href="photo_gallery/photo_gallery.htm">Photo Gallery</a> |
<a href="maps/maps.htm">Maps</a> |
<a href="information_links/information_links.htm">Links</a> |
<a href="faq/faq.htm">FAQs</a> |
<a href="contact/contact.htm">Contact</a></p>
```

Notice that each hyperlink contains the relative URL for the Web page file as the hyperlink destination, the hyperlink source text, and a vertical line character. (We define the term *relative* earlier in this chapter.) In this case, the entire navigation bar is enclosed by HTML paragraph tags (<p> and </p>).

Using lists to create a navigation bar

A favorite trick among Web designers for creating a navigation bar is to use an unordered list of text hyperlinks. You can stack your hyperlink list vertically (refer to Figure 4-6), or line them up horizontally, as shown in Figure 4-7 (from the Expression Web template Organization 4). All the navigation bars in Expression Web templates are nothing more than gussied-up, unordered lists with a few formatting and positioning CSS styles applied. Each hyperlink in the navigation bar is a separate list item. (We talk more about styles for navigation bars in Chapter 8.)

Text hyperlinks in a horizontal unordered list <ul>

Figure 4-7:
The main navigation bar on this page uses an unordered list with styles applied for formatting and positioning.

Here are some techniques for making a hyperlink list look more like a navigation bar and less like your grocery list:

✔ **Banish the bullets.** The best way to do this is to set a style for the list. We show you how to create styles in Chapter 7.

✔ **Lose link underlining.** Click the links to select them, and on the Common or Formatting toolbar, click the Underline button to remove this formatting. Better yet, set a style for the whole list that turns off underlining. (We tell you how to create new styles in Chapter 7.)

✔ **Coordinate hyperlink colors.** Change default colors for hyperlinks to match your site's color scheme. We tell you how earlier in this chapter, in the section "Changing hyperlink color."

✔ **Decorate with graphical icons.** Create an icon that coordinates with the graphical elements in your site and place it next to each text hyperlink. (To do this, place the graphic next to your hyperlink or specify the graphic as the bullet style. We talk more about graphics in Chapter 5; see Chapter 3 for how to customize bullets in lists.)

✔ **Build in borders and backgrounds.** The best way to do this is to use CSS styles to format and position the navigation bar as a whole. We talk about creating styles in Chapter 7; we cover positioning with CSS in Chapter 8.

You may be tempted to copy a navigation bar from one of the Expression Web templates into your Web page and simply change the text and hyperlinks. It's not that simple. Expression Web templates use several layers of style sheets to format and position the different page elements. Not only that, the navigation bars are located on each template's Dynamic Web Template. Trying to figure out what controls what can quickly send the novice user into a conniption fit of frustration. We recommend sticking with simple text formatting for your navigation bars until you bone up a bit on Cascading Style Sheets (see Chapters 7 and 8) and Dynamic Web Templates (see Chapter 11). After you get the hang of how it all works together, it's much easier to tweak the different controls to get your navigation bars to look the way you want.

Here's what the code looks like for a simple list of hyperlinks:

```
<ul>
        <li><a href="default.htm">Home</a></li>
        <li><a href="news.htm">News</a></li>
        <li><a
         href="testimonials.htm">Testimonials</a></li>
        <li><a href="about.htm">About</a></li>
        <li><a href="contact.htm">Contact Us</a></li>
</ul>
```

Notice that each hyperlink is enclosed by the `<li></li>` tags.

We revisit creating navigation bars in Chapter 8, after we go over the ins and outs of using Cascading Styles Sheets for formatting and positioning.

Inserting an Interactive Button

If plain-text hyperlinks don't excite you, interactive buttons might. An *interactive* button is an animated button that, when clicked, activates a hyperlink, as shown in Figure 4-8. This type of button is a good way to add oomph to your links. When the visitor moves the cursor over the button before clicking it, the button changes color or shape. You can arrange interactive buttons on a horizontal line or stack them vertically to create an interactive button-navigation bar.

Figure 4-8:
An interactive button.

Home

By default, interactive buttons look like stylized rectangular boxes. If rectangles aren't your style, Expression Web gives you a bevy of button shapes to choose from, including capsules and tabs in several styles and colors.

Interactive buttons are produced by using JavaScript and therefore require that your visitors use JavaScript-capable browsers.

Adding an interactive button to your page

To create an interactive button, follow these steps:

1. **Choose Insert➪Interactive Button.**

   The Interactive Buttons dialog box appears with the Button tab visible, as shown in Figure 4-9.

2. **In the Buttons list box, click the type of button you want to create.**

   Chances are that the cryptic list items don't necessarily make sense to you, so scroll down the list box and click an option that looks promising. A preview of the interactive button appears in the dialog box's Preview area.

3. **In the Text text box, type the word or words that you want to appear on the button.**

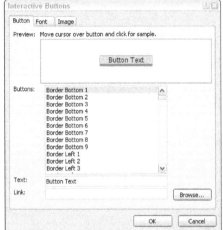

Figure 4-9:
The Button
tab in the
Interactive
Buttons
dialog box.

4. **In the Link text box, type the filename or URL of the page you want to appear when the interactive button is clicked.**

   Or click the Browse button to choose a link destination from the Edit Hyperlink dialog box. We describe how this dialog box works earlier in this chapter, in the section "Editing Hyperlinks."

5. **If you're happy with what you see, click OK to close the dialog box and insert the interactive button in your Web page.**

   If you want to further tinker with the interactive button's text formatting and image style, don't click OK — read the next section of this chapter for more directions.

Changing an interactive button's text formatting

You're not stuck with the text formatting that Expression Web provides when you create an interactive button. You can change text size, color, and more. Here's how:

1. **Insert an interactive button into your page. (Follow the steps in the preceding section.) Or, to change the text formatting on an existing button, in the page, double-click the interactive button to display the Interactive Buttons dialog box.**

2. **In the dialog box, click the Font tab to make those options visible, as shown in Figure 4-10.**

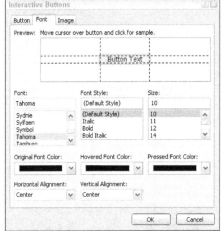

Figure 4-10:
The Font
tab in the
Interactive
Buttons
dialog box.

3. **Choose a font, font style, and text size from the appropriate list boxes.**

   For detailed information about each font effect, see Chapter 3.

4. **Choose text colors from the Original Font Color, Hovered Font Color, and Pressed Font Color list boxes:**

   • *Original Font Color:* When nothing is happening to the interactive button (the visitor isn't clicking it or moving the mouse over it), text appears in this color.

   • *Hovered Font Color:* When a visitor moves the cursor over the button without clicking it, text appears in this color.

   • *Pressed Font Color:* When a visitor clicks the interactive button, text appears in this color *while the button is being clicked.* When the click is finished (about a half-second later), text returns to its hovered color.

5. **To change how the text is aligned on the button, choose different options from the Horizontal Alignment and Vertical Alignment list boxes.**

   We don't waste your time describing each effect here. Just pick the effect that looks like what you want. After you finish creating the button, you can preview the page to see how the effect looks. If you don't like the effect, you can change this setting.

6. **When you're happy with what you see in the Preview area, click OK to close the dialog box and insert the interactive button in your Web page.**

   If you want to keep fiddling, don't click OK — read the next section of this chapter for more directions.

Altering an interactive button's image

You have a little wiggle room with the interactive button images that Expression Web gives you. You can change the image dimensions, as well as how they behave when clicked, by following these steps:

1. **Insert an interactive button into your page. (Follow the steps in the earlier section "Adding an interactive button to your page.") Or, to change how an existing button looks, in the page, double-click the interactive button to display the Interactive Buttons dialog box.**

2. **In the dialog box, click the Image tab to make those options visible, as shown in Figure 4-11.**

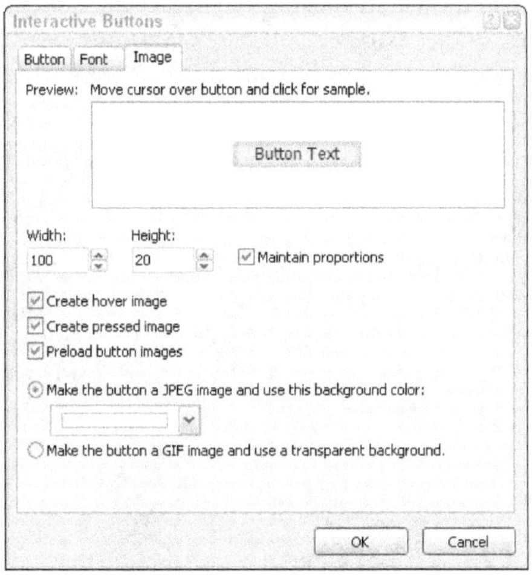

Figure 4-11: The Image tab in the Interactive Buttons dialog box.

3. **To change the button's dimensions, enter new pixel values in the Width and Height text boxes.**

   Be sure that the Maintain Proportions check box is selected so that the button image doesn't stretch in a funny way when you change its width or height.

4. **If you want the button to look the same whether or not the visitor hovers the cursor over it, deselect the Create Hover Image check box.**

5. **If you want the button to look the same while the visitor clicks the button, deselect the Create Pressed Image check box.**

6. **Make sure that the Preload Button Images check box is selected.**

When this check box is selected, Expression Web inserts JavaScript into the page's HTML code that tells the visitor's browser to load the button's images in the background while the rest of the page text loads. (The regular, hover, and pressed images are three separate picture files.) This way, when a visitor hovers the cursor over or clicks the interactive button, the images that create these effects are immediately available. Incidentally, browsers that don't understand JavaScript simply ignore the script and display only the original button image.

7. **If necessary, choose the interactive button's background color.**

By default, the interactive button's background color is white. You can see the interactive button's background color only if you chose a rounded button — a capsule or a rounded tab — *and* if the page's background color is something other than white. If this is the case, you can either set the interactive button's background color to be the same as the page's (choose a color from the Make the Button a JPEG Image list box), or you can give the button a transparent background color (select the Make the Button a GIF Image option).

8. **Click OK to close the dialog box and insert the interactive button in your Web page.**

If your site needs more than a handful of interactive buttons, consider using a third-party software option that can create multilevel navigation. Before you decide on one, make sure it plays by the rules, by complying with Web standards for code and accessibility. A good one is Ultimate Drop Down Menu, by Brothercake (`www.brothercake.com/site/products/menu`).

Swapping Images to Make Interactive Buttons

Designers often use a behavior called Swap Image to create dynamic graphical buttons, similar to the buttons Expression Web generates for interactive buttons (described earlier in this chapter). To do so, you need to have access to two image files. For the effect to look its best, the images should look similar, such as two button-shaped graphics that differ only in color or shading.

The Swap Images behavior use Dynamic HTML to make it work. (See the sidebar "What's Dynamic HTML?" in this section for more information.)

The first image sits in the page, and looks to all the world like a regular ol' button graphic. With the help of DHTML, the second image replaces the first based on the event you choose (most often, `onmouseover`).

The following steps describe how to create your own interactive button:

1. **Add the two graphical files into your Web site.**

   If you're not sure how to add files, refer to Chapter 1.

2. **Insert the first image into the page.**

3. **Click the image, and then choose Format➪Behaviors.**

   The Behaviors task pane appears.

4. **In the task pane, click the Insert box, and from the menu that appears, choose Swap Image.**

   The Swap Images dialog box appears. The main portion of the dialog box already contains the location of the selected graphic. You now must tell Expression Web which graphic you want to swap.

   If a warning about ActiveX content pops up, click Yes to continue adding the behavior and read the sidebar "What's Dynamic HTML?" later in this chapter.

5. **In the Swap Image URL text box, type the URL or location of the second image.**

   Or click the Browse button to select the image from a list of files.

6. **Be sure the Preload Images and Restore On Mouseout Event check boxes are selected.**

   Preloading images for this effect ensures that they're immediately visible when the page loads — a key element of this illusion's success.

   By selecting the Restore On Mouseout Event check box, you tell Expression Web to insert DHTML that causes the original image to reappear when the visitor moves the cursor off the image, thereby completing the swap.

7. **Click OK to close the Swap Images dialog box.**

   The dialog box closes, and the Swap Images behavior appears in the Behaviors task pane. (If you don't see Swap Images, be sure the image in the page is still selected.)

 8. **To turn your button into a hyperlink, in Design view, select the image and click the Insert Hyperlink button to hook it to the desired hyperlink destination, as described in the first part of this chapter.**

Save and preview the page to watch the Swap Image and Swap Image Restore effects do their things correctly. (Be sure to preview by using several browsers to see how the effect looks.) To change either effect, double-click their listings in the Behaviors task pane.

What's Dynamic HTML?

Dynamic HTML (or *DHTML*) isn't a "flavor" of HTML per se. It's a combination of different technologies, including HTML, JavaScript, Cascading Style Sheets, and other techie goodies that work together to create interesting effects. Expression Web calls these effects *behaviors*.

As you can imagine, coding DHTML takes some geeky mojo. But Expression Web comes with tools that do all the work for you. You find the Expression Web DHTML tools in the Behaviors task pane. (If you don't see this pane, choose Task Panes➪Behaviors.)

Really getting to know DHTML (and, by extension, understanding the Expression Web DHTML features) requires knowing HTML, CSS, and JavaScript. If this description fits you and you want to find out more, visit an excellent

DHTML tutorial at www.webmonkey.com/webmonkey/authoring/dynamic_html/tutorials/tutorial1.html.

Be aware that if you add DHTML elements to your Web page, Expression Web inserts scripts in your Web page's code. Many Web visitors have their browsers set to block or at least issue a warning if a page contains scripts. In fact your own computer's security settings may prompt a warning even when you add behaviors to your Web page. We recommend you preview your pages in browsers with script blocking turned on so that you can see your pages as your visitors will see them. We also suggest that you use DHTML as embellishments to your already useable page rather than as, say, the only way to navigate to a particular page.

In this section, we show you how to use the Swap Image behavior to create an interactive hyperlink button, but you can, of course, use the behavior however you like. For example, you can create a clickable before-and-after picture display in your Web site by using two photos that illustrate "before" and "after" and then attaching the Swap Image behavior to the onclick event. The possibilities are endless!

Embedding More than One Hyperlink in a Picture

An *image map* is simply a picture that contains more than one hyperlink. Visitors activate the different hyperlinks in the image map by clicking different places inside the picture (see Figure 4-12).

The clickable areas of the picture are *hotspots*. Hotspots work just like regular hyperlinks: They can link to e-mail addresses, downloadable files, or other locations in the Web site or on the Internet. Most often, however, image maps contain links to other places inside the Web site.

Figure 4-12:
The
"buttons"
show
visitors
where to
click to
activate a
hyperlink.

Expression Web contains tools you use to "draw" hotspots on the picture of your choice. Hotspots are visible to you as you work with the image map in Expression Web, but when visitors look at your page with a Web browser, hotspots are invisible. (Visitors see only the image map graphic.)

You don't want to turn just any old picture into an image map. Because hotspots are invisible to the visitor, the picture you choose should clearly indicate where to click, either with the help of a visual metaphor (the example shown in Figure 4-12 uses buttons) or with text labels. The ideal image map picture doesn't require explanation; the clickable areas should be obvious.

Don't worry if you can't get your hands on the ideal image map graphic. Even though image map hotspots are invisible when visitors view your page with a Web browser, the cursor changes shape and the hotspot's destination address appears on the browser's status bar when a visitor hovers the cursor over a hotspot. These clues are enough to prompt most visitors to click.

After you choose your picture, open the page in which you want the image map to appear and then insert the picture into the page. (Flip to Chapter 5 if you're not sure how to insert a picture.)

If you use an image map in your Web site, consider including a corresponding list of text hyperlinks somewhere else in the page. Visitors who surf the Web with their browsers' image-loading function turned off (or who use text-only browsers) cannot see regular pictures or image maps and, therefore, must rely on the text hyperlinks in order to move around.

Adding hotspots to a picture

After you find the right picture and insert it in your page, you're ready to draw the hotspots.

You use tools available on the Pictures toolbar to draw hotspots. You can draw rectangles, circles, and multisided shapes (polygons) around the areas you want to make clickable.

To draw hotspots on a picture, follow these steps:

1. **Open the page containing the image map graphic, and then click the picture.**

2. **Choose View⇨Toolbars⇨Pictures.**

   The Pictures toolbar appears.

3. **In the page, click the image map graphic to select it, and then, on the Pictures toolbar, click the Rectangular Hotspot, Circular Hotspot, or Polygonal Hotspot button.**

   Pick the shape that resembles the shape of the area you want to turn into a hotspot. You can always move or reshape the hotspot later or delete the hotspot and start over.

4. **Move the cursor over the picture.**

   The cursor turns into a little pencil.

5. **Click the hotspot area and drag the cursor until the resulting hotspot surrounds the area.**

   Where to click depends on the shape you chose. Here's what to do for the different hotspot shapes:

   - *Rectangle:* Click the corner of the hotspot area and drag the rectangle until the shape surrounds the area.

   - *Circle:* Click the center of the hotspot area and drag. (The circle expands from its center point.)

   - *Polygon:* Creating a polygonal hotspot is like playing connect-the-dots, except that you decide where the dots are: Click the first point, release the mouse button, and then move the cursor. (This action produces a line.) Stretch the line to the second point — click, stretch, click, stretch — until you enclose your hotspot area. After you finish defining the hotspot, click the hotspot's starting point, and Expression Web closes the hotspot for you.

You can overlap hotspots. If you do so, the most recent hotspot is on top, which means that this hotspot takes priority if a visitor clicks the overlapped area.

After you draw the hotspot, the hotspot border appears on top of your picture, and the Insert Hyperlink dialog box appears, enabling you to associate a hyperlink with the hotspot.

6. **Create a link for the hotspot, just as you would for a regular hyperlink.**

   Give your hotspot link a ScreenTip so that your visitors know where they'll go when they click the hotspot. (Click the ScreenTip button in the Insert Hyperlink dialog box; we explain ScreenTips earlier in this chapter.)

7. **Keep creating hotspots until you define all the clickable areas inside the picture.**

   Areas not covered by a hotspot don't do anything if clicked unless you specify a *default hyperlink*. (I show you how to do this in the following section.)

8. **When you're finished, click anywhere outside the picture to hide the hotspot borders.**

Here are some other handy tricks to know as you fine-tune your hotspots:

✔ **For a quick look at all the hotspots inside the picture,** click the Highlight Hotspots button on the Pictures toolbar. The picture becomes blank, and only the hotspot borders are visible. To return to the regular display, click the Highlight Hotspots button again.

✔ **To move a hotspot,** click the hotspot and then drag it to a new position.

✔ **To reshape a hotspot,** click the hotspot to make its size handles visible (those little square dots along the hotspot border), and then click a handle and drag it until the hotspot looks the way you want. Size handles act differently, depending on the shape of the hotspot. Working with handles isn't a precise science. Just keep clicking, dragging, and stretching until you're happy with the results.

✔ **To change a hotspot's hyperlink,** click the picture to make the hotspots visible, and then double-click the hotspot to open the Edit Hyperlink dialog box. Make any changes you want and then click OK to close the dialog box.

✔ **To delete a hotspot,** click the hotspot and then press the Backspace or Delete key.

Setting the default hyperlink

The final (and optional) step in creating an image map is setting the image map's *default hyperlink*. Visitors jump to the destination of the default hyperlink if they click anywhere on the image map not covered by a hotspot. If you forgo the default hyperlink, clicking an undefined area does nothing.

In general, we recommend skipping this step. Visitors expecting to click hotspots can get confused when they click outside a hotspot (which, intuitively, should accomplish nothing) and are still sent to a different location. However, if you find that it makes sense for your image map to have a default hyperlink, feel free to add one.

To set an image map's default hyperlink, follow these steps:

1. **Right-click the image map and then choose Picture Properties from the pop-up menu that appears.**

    The Picture Properties dialog box appears with the General tab visible.

2. **In the Hyperlink area of the tab, type the default hyperlink's URL in the Location text box.**

    If you can't remember the URL, click the Browse button to display the Edit Hyperlink dialog box. We explain how to use this dialog box in the "Editing Hyperlinks" section, earlier in this chapter.

    After you specify the URL, click OK to close the Edit Hyperlink dialog box. The Picture Properties dialog box becomes visible again, with the default hyperlink's URL visible in the Location text box.

     If you want the hyperlink destination to open in a new browser window, click the Change Target Frame button next to the Target Frame text box, and in the Target Frame dialog box that appears, choose New Window. Click OK to close the Target Frame dialog box. In the Picture Properties dialog box, in the Target Frame text box, New Window appears.

3. **Click OK to close the dialog box.**

    Expression Web applies the default hyperlink to the image map.

To test-drive the image map, preview your page and click away. (Refer to Chapter 2 if you're not sure how.)

Chapter 5

Graphically Speaking

*I*f the World Wide Web were made up of just text and hyperlinks, we would probably spend less time surfing and more time working. Pictures — photos, art, graphics, and logos — are what make most Web sites both enticing and useful. Pictures can even make or break your visitors' interest in what you have to say: How many times have you skipped over an eBay listing because it lacked a photo of the item? Nowadays, Web visitors demand pictures, and it's your job to deliver.

You have to walk a fine line, though. Overusing pictures can clutter your site and slow its load time to a crawl, and cheesy clip art (especially the blinking, winking, and jumping variety) can cheapen the look of your site. In this chapter, we show you what you need in order to work with pictures in your Web pages — the pitfalls and tricks and, of course, how to use the Expression Web graphic tools.

Note: We adopted the Expression Web term *pictures* to refer to all Web graphics, including photos, graphics, clip art, screen snapshots, and logos.

Understanding the Quirks of Web Pictures

Your goal, when using pictures in your Web site, is to get the highest-quality pictures with the shortest load times. The process is relatively straightforward because most graphics software programs have special features for preparing pictures for the Web.

Choosing Web-friendly picture formats

In the morass of graphical file formats and unpronounceable file extensions, you use only three formats to add pictures to your Web pages.

- **JPEG** (pronounced "jay-peg") is the most common format for Web-ready photographs. If you use a point-and-shoot digital camera, chances are it saves your photos as JPEGs. JPEGs are *bitmapped* images: They're made up of a bunch of *bits,* or colored dots. The JPEG format can stuff a wide range of colors with subtle variations into a small file size, which is exactly what makes it good for photos. The problem with JPEGs is that they're notoriously hard to resize. Resized JPEGs end up looking ragged and fuzzy.

- **GIF,** pronounced "giff" (or "jiff," depending on whom you talk to), stands for Graphic Interchange Format (which is why we say "giff"; it's a hard *g* sound, for crying out loud). GIFs are the heavy lifters of simple Web graphics: They're ideal for images that contain a limited color palette, like logos, buttons, text bits with fancy fonts, cartoons, and any other simple line drawings. The GIF format can also pack multiple pictures in a single file to create simple animation, called *animated GIFs.* A GIF is typically small in file size and can be resized and stretched without affecting the image quality. A GIF can also handle interlacing and transparency. (We talk about these features later in this chapter.) Because a GIF can display only up to 256 colors, it isn't a good choice for photos or complex art with many color variations.

- **PNG,** pronounced "ping," stands for Portable Network Graphics. The PNG format, which is the new kid on the block, was developed specifically for the Web. It displays subtle color variations well, like a JPEG does, but scales well, like a GIF. It also handles transparency better than GIF (although some browsers don't always display transparent PNGs properly). Browser support for PNG is continually improving, allowing the PNG format to take its rightful place at the Web graphics table. Look for the forthcoming Internet Explorer 7 to fully support the PNG format.

Which graphical format should you use? Your goal is to create the best-looking picture for the smallest file size. For simple line art and logos, choose GIF. You get a scaleable image with a small file size. If you have a more complex graphic with lots of colors, give PNG a try. You can preview your page in different browsers to see what it looks like. (We tell you how in Chapter 2.) For photos, JPEG is your best option.

Many graphics programs know how to create pictures specifically for the Web and let you compare the file size and image quality of different formats. In Adobe Photoshop Elements, which is a lighter-weight (and much cheaper) version of its big brother Adobe Photoshop, look for the Save for Web command.

If you want to delve deeper into Web graphics, here are some sites to get you started: The official PNG site, www.libpng.org/pub/png, tells you everything you would ever want to know about this format. Read the World Wide Web Consortium's analysis at www.w3.org/graphics. A particularly good comparison of image formats and when to use which one appears on www.r1ch.net/img-formats.

A word or two about colors

If you happen to hang around with Web designers, you may have heard about the *browser-safe* or *Web-safe palette*. This set of colors looks good on all browsers and monitors. The Web-safe palette was developed back in the days when computer monitors weren't as color savvy as they are now. Technology has improved, and now monitors can display millions of colors.

What does this mean for you? The colors that show up on your Web pages in a visitor's browser depend on what colors their monitor is capable of displaying. If your picture contains a color that isn't present in your visitor's system palette, your visitor's Web browser attempts to display the color by *dithering* — that is, mixing two other colors in a checkerboard pattern to approximate the color in the image. Dithered images, although better than nothing, lack clarity and definition.

You have to decide whether to stick to the "safe" colors or venture into the world of color possibilities. If you're unsure what to do, most Web hosting providers gather statistics about their visitors' monitor types. If an acceptable majority of visitors use 24- or 32-bit monitors, use color with abandon. If the few that are still using 8-bit monitors matter deeply to you, stick with the browser-safe palette.

Revving up your graphics in a graphics program

In general, you should prepare pictures for your Web pages — including file conversions, color editing, and sizing — in a program specifically designed for graphics work and then save the file in the Web-friendly format of your choice. A good choice if you're just preparing pictures for the screen is Adobe Photoshop Elements, the little brother of the full-blown (and expensive) Adobe Photoshop. Another good program is Corel Paint Shop Pro. Watch for the forthcoming release of the Expression Web companion product, Microsoft Expression Design. Expression Design is designed to work closely with Expression Web as part of a suite of Web-development programs.

Many graphics programs are available as free trial versions for a limited time so that you can test-drive a few and decide which one you like best. See `www.corel.com/paintshop` for more information about the Paint Shop suite of products. See `www.adobe.com/products/photoshopelwin/index.html` for information on downloading a trial version of Photoshop Elements. Before the full version of Microsoft Expression Design is available for sale, you can download a pre-release version to play around with by visiting `www.microsoft.com/products/expression/en/expression-design/free-trial.mspx`. (Microsoft Corporation wisely cautions against using beta software for final, production use.)

A good place to go for current statistics about browsers, operating systems, and monitors in use is `www.w3schools.com/browsers/browsers_stats.asp`. You can also read `www.w3schools.com/html/html_colors.asp` to find out more about color on a monitor. If you're looking for a more general discussion of color on the Web, check out *Web Design For Dummies,* 2nd Edition, by Lisa Lopuck (Wiley).

Creating quick-loading pictures

If your visitors must wait more than a few seconds for your site to appear in their browsers, your site risks falling victim to *clickitis,* a chronic condition that causes surfers to click elsewhere whenever they must wait a moment for something to download. Keeping load times brief prevents clickitis. Here are some ways to ensure that your graphics don't drag:

- ✔ **Reduce image dimensions.** Wherever possible, keep the picture file's dimensions small.

- ✔ **Limit colors.** You can shave precious seconds off the download time while maintaining your picture's quality if you use a graphics program to reduce the number of colors in your pictures.

✔ **Keep resolution low.** Save your picture files at a resolution of 72 ppi (pixels per inch). This resolution, although too low for high-quality print images, is ideal for images that are displayed on a computer monitor. Use anything higher and you're adding unnecessary bulk to your picture's file size.

✔ **Repeat pictures.** As much as possible, use the same pictures throughout your site. Web browsers *cache* picture files, which means that the browser saves a copy of the picture on the visitor's hard drive. The first time someone visits your site, the browser downloads the picture files from the host server. After the initial download, the browser displays the cached files instead — which load almost instantly. This strategy works especially well for background images. Many Web sites offer downloadable background images that, when repeated, look like a solid pattern. (See the section "Adding a Tiled Background Picture," later in this chapter, for more info about how to do this.)

Practicing graphical restraint

After you get the hang of adding pictures to Web pages, you can easily fall into the "more is better" trap. Exercise some graphical restraint. Each additional picture increases the overall load time of the page and should be added only if seeing the picture is worth the wait. Use only those pictures that communicate your site's purpose and make getting around the site easier or more pleasant for your audience.

Finally, make sure your visitors can understand your site without the pictures. Some surfers turn off their browser's image-loading option to speed up browsing sessions, especially on small-screen mobile devices. (We show you how to deal with this situation later in this chapter by specifying alternative text.)

Adding a Picture to Your Page

When you insert a picture in a Web page, Expression Web adds a reference inside the page's HTML tags that points to the location of the graphics file. (We help you take a peek at the HTML for graphics later in this chapter.) The reference tells the visitor's browser to fetch the picture and display it on the page at the location of the reference. In other words, when you look at a Web page that contains pictures, you're looking at more than one file simultaneously: the Web page (the file that contains the text and the references to the pictures) and each individual picture file.

Inserting a picture is similar to creating a hyperlink because you simply link two different files: the Web page and the picture file. So, like a hyperlink, a picture reference can point to a picture file stored inside the Web site or on a remote Web server.

If you don't have any pictures of your own or don't want to create any, plenty of excellent Web galleries encourage you to grab their pictures for your own, personal use. Search the Free Graphics collection at www.freegraphics.com to start looking for graphics of all types and styles. Chapter 16 includes other sources for finding pictures, available for free or for a minimal fee. Keep in mind that not every image you can download from the Web is free for the taking, however. Before using a picture on your site, check the terms of use on the Web site to make sure that you comply with copyright laws.

Importing pictures into your Web site

Before you add any pictures to your Web pages, we recommend that you first import them into your Web site. Expression Web can then keep tabs on where pictures are stored inside your Web site. If you move them around within the Web site, Expression Web makes note of it and updates all the internal links so that they continue to display properly.

To import pictures into your Web site, follow these steps:

1. **Launch Expression Web and open the Web site into which you want to import pictures.**

2. **In the Folder List task pane, select the folder where you want to store the picture files.**

   (See the later sidebar "Organizing picture files" for tips on where to store pictures inside your Web site.)

   If you don't want the pictures in any particular folder, select the name of the Web site folder itself (at the top of the Folder List task pane).

3. **Choose File⇨Import⇨File.**

   The Import dialog box appears.

4. **To import individual picture files, click the Add File button.**

   The Add File to Import List dialog box appears.

5. **Using the options in the dialog box, navigate to the folder containing the picture or pictures you want to import.**

6. Click to select the picture.

In the upper-right corner of the Add File to Import List dialog box, click the Views button and, from the drop-down menu that appears, click Preview. When you click a picture file, a preview of it appears in the dialog box so that you know you chose the right one.

If you want to select multiple pictures, hold down the Ctrl key and click each picture.

7. Click the Open button.

The Import dialog box appears again, listing the picture or pictures you selected, as shown in Figure 5-1.

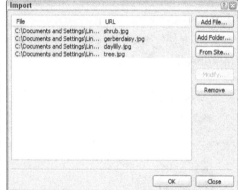

Figure 5-1:
The Import dialog box with pictures ready to be imported.

8. If you want to import more picture files, continue adding pictures to the Import dialog box by repeating Steps 4 through 7.

To add an entire folder containing pictures, click the Add Folder button and, in the File Open dialog box, navigate to the folder, click to select it, and click the Open button. All files located in the folder appear in the Import dialog box.

To remove a picture or folder from the Import dialog box File list, click to select it (hold down the Ctrl key to select multiple pictures) and click the Remove button.

9. After you add all the pictures you want to import to the Import dialog box, click OK.

Inserting a picture

After you import your pictures into your Web site, plugging the pictures into a page is easy. Follow these steps:

1. **Open the page into which you want to insert the picture, and then, in Design view, place the cursor where you want the picture to appear.**

   Expression Web knows how to place the cursor only inside a line of text or in a new, blank paragraph. If the cursor location doesn't exactly correspond to where you want the picture to sit inside your page, just do the best you can. We talk about other ways to position pictures later in this chapter.

2. **On the Common, Standard, or Pictures toolbar, click the Insert Picture from File button.**

   Pop open the Pictures toolbar by choosing View➪Toolbars➪Pictures.

   The Picture dialog box appears, as shown in Figure 5-2.

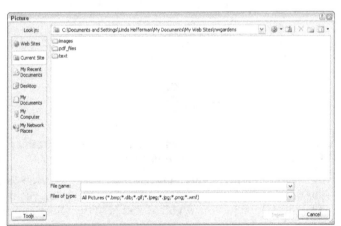

Figure 5-2:
The Picture
dialog box.

If you haven't done so already, click the Views button in the upper-right corner of the Picture dialog box, and, from the drop-down menu that appears, click Preview. When you click a picture file, a preview of it appears in the dialog box so that you know you chose the right one.

3. **In the dialog box's file list, navigate to the location of the picture you want to insert, and then double-click the file's icon.**

   The Accessibility Properties dialog box appears.

4. **In the Alternate Text text box, type the text you want to appear on the screen as an alternative to the picture.**

   Alternative text appears in these cases (see the nearby sidebar "Alternative text is mandatory" in this chapter):

   - If the visitor's browser is set to not display pictures

   - While the picture is loading

   - In some browsers, as hover text when the visitor's cursor passes over the picture

5. **Click OK.**

   The dialog box closes, and the picture appears inside the page.

Here's a quick way to insert a picture that you already imported into your Web site. From the Folder List task pane, drag the icon for the picture file into your Web page. Then add alternative text for the picture when the Accessibility Properties dialog box pops up (as just explained in Step 3) and click OK.

Take a look at the code for a picture:

```
<img alt="sunflower" src="images/sunflower.gif"
        width="193" height="174" />
```

Alternative text is mandatory

Some Web surfers, desperate to save seconds, turn off their browsers' capability to display pictures, as do many browsers on portable devices. Nowadays, Web pages need to be viewable in a lot of different "viewpoints" (as browsers are called by the World Wide Web Consortium, the folks who set the rules for Web standards and accessibility). To make your Web pages accessible to all, your pictures must contain alternative text, or *alt text,* as it's called in Web design circles. That's why Expression Web prompts you to enter alternative text in the Accessibility Properties dialog box as soon as you add a picture to your page. Of course, you can turn off the prompt by deselecting the

Show This Prompt When Inserting Images check box, but you just have to go back and add it later if you want your pages to pass their accessibility tests. (We talk about how to test your pages in Chapter 12.) Good alt text should briefly describe the picture so that Web surfers at least know what they're missing and screen readers can interpret images for vision-impaired visitors. You can read up on the guidelines for alt text at `www.w3.org/TR/html4/struct/objects.html#h-13.8`. See also `www.w3.org/WAI/References/Browsing` for a discussion of alternative browsing methods.

Notice that there's no separate closing tag for a picture tag. The tag opens and closes within one set of angle brackets, and `img` tells the browser to display an image in this location. Next comes the alt text; in this example, the word *sunflower* appears on the page (`alt="sunflower"`) if images are turned off.

The next part of the tag tells the browser the name of the picture file and its location in relation to the page, called a *relative* link: `src="images/sunflower.gif"`. In this case, the GIF file `sunflower.gif` is located in a subfolder named `images`. The next bit of information, `width="193" height="174"`, tells the browser how many pixels wide and high to reserve for this picture. (We talk more about picture dimensions later in this chapter.) Finally, the tag closes with `/>`.

Adding a picture from another application or location

You can also add pictures to your pages from other locations. Here's a brief rundown of your options:

- ✔ **Paste a picture from the Clipboard:** Copy the picture to the Clipboard from another application or from another Web page (either in the current site or in another Web site) and paste it into your page at the cursor location (choose Edit⇨Paste or press Ctrl+V).

- ✔ **Insert a picture from a scanner or a digital camera:** Hook up your scanner or camera to your computer, and then choose Insert⇨Picture⇨ From Scanner or Camera. In the Insert Picture from Scanner or Camera dialog box, choose your device, click the Web Quality option, and then click the Insert button. (Check the instructions for your device and Microsoft Expression Web Help for more information.)

- ✔ **Drag and drop a picture file into your Web page from Windows Explorer:** Find the picture file's icon and drag it into your Web page.

Regardless of how you add a picture to a Web page, Expression Web pops open the Accessibility Properties dialog box and prompts you to enter alternative text.

If you add a picture whose original file lives outside the current page's Web site, Expression Web needs to save a copy of the file inside your Web site. (Remember that a picture on a page is nothing more than a reference to the *file,* not to the picture itself.) This concept becomes especially important when you publish your Web site on the Internet so that the picture files don't get left behind.

To save a picture file inside your Web site, follow these steps:

1. **Save the Web page to which you added a picture or pictures. (We tell you how in Chapter 2.)**

   The Save Embedded Files dialog box appears when you save your page, as shown in Figure 5-3.

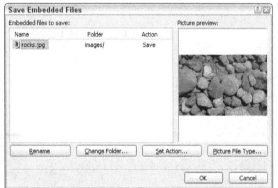

Figure 5-3:
The Save
Embedded
Files dialog
box.

2. **To rename the picture file, click the picture file to select it, click the Rename button, and type a new name.**

   Remember that your Web site's files should contain only lowercase letters; use the underscore character (_) rather than spaces.

3. **To specify where to save the picture file, click the Change Folder button, and, in the Change Folder dialog box, navigate to the desired folder (or create a new folder by clicking the Create New Folder button) and click OK.**

   Unless you tell it otherwise, Expression Web saves the file in the folder shown in the Embedded Files to Save list, in the Folder column.

4. **(Optional) If you want to change the picture format or set other options for the picture, click the Picture File Type button.**

   We talk about how to edit a picture later in this chapter.

5. **Click OK.**

Editing a Picture on a Page

Just because your picture is sitting there on your page doesn't mean that you can't change it. In fact, as you fiddle with your pages to get them looking the way you want, you most likely need to tinker with your pictures, too. Use the tools on the Picture toolbar to make minor adjustments to the picture or to change how it looks on the page. For more complex work, however, do your picture editing in a full-blown graphics program. You can set up Expression Web to open pictures in the graphics editor of your choice.

If you have Microsoft Office installed on your computer, you can make minor changes in the Microsoft Office Picture Manager. This miniprogram gives you all the image editing options on the Pictures toolbar plus a few more, such as red-eye removal and autocorrect.

Organizing picture files

Every Web designer has her preferred way to organize picture files in a Web site. Some prefer to create one folder (often named `images`) and place all pictures used in the whole Web site there. Others create separate image folders inside subfolders and store images specific to that area there. (You can see an example of this type of organization in the template Web sites provided with Expression Web.) How you decide to organize your picture files is up to you, but it helps to spend a little time upfront thinking about what makes the most sense, depending on the size of your Web site. For small sites with a manageable number of pictures, one centrally located image folder is probably sufficient. But if your Web site contains hundreds of pictures, you probably want to group their files into subfolders or create an image folder inside each subfolder of your Web site.

Regardless of which way you organize your picture files, here are a few tips to keep in mind:

✔ If the same picture is used on multiple pages, always link to the same picture file and store it in a central location; if your site is very large, you could create a folder named `shared_images` for these files. If you create duplicate versions of the same pictures, you unnecessarily bloat your Web site size, which affects how fast your pages are downloaded and displayed.

✔ Give picture files meaningful names that organize them alphabetically and help identify them at a glance. A Web designer we know (who's also a librarian) names her picture files with a combination of their function and their description. For example, she names all pictures used for page backgrounds `backgrnd_nameofpicture` or all pictures for buttons `button_nameofbutton`. This naming convention groups similar picture files and helps her more easily identify them at a glance and find the one she needs quickly.

Editing a picture in a graphics program

You can launch any number of graphics programs from within Expression Web and set your favorite as the default editor for images. To add a graphics editor to Expression Web, follow these steps:

1. **Choose Tools➪Application Options.**

   The Application Options dialog box opens.

2. **Click the Configure Editors tab.**

3. **In the Extensions list box, scroll until you see the entry for image files (jpg jpeg gif png), and then select it, as shown in Figure 5-4.**

Figure 5-4:
The
Configure
Editors tab
in the
Application
Options
dialog box.

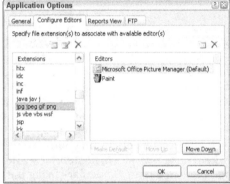

4. **If the program you want isn't listed, click the New Editor icon above the Editors list box.**

   The Open With dialog box opens, listing all applications that Expression Web could find installed on your hard drive. If you don't see the program you want to use (it might be on a network drive), click the Browse button and navigate to the application by using the options in the Browse dialog box.

5. **In the Open With dialog box (or the Browse dialog box), click the desired application and click OK (click Open in the Browse dialog box).**

   The selected application appears in the Editors list box.

6. **To make an application the default editor, click the application name and then click the Make Default button.**

7. **When you're finished, click OK to close the Application Options dialog box.**

You can add as many graphics editors to this list as you want.

To pick which graphics program you want to use to open the picture, follow these steps:

1. **In the page's Design view, right-click the picture.**

   Or, in the Folder List task pane, right-click the picture file icon.

2. **From the pop-up menu that appears, click Open With and then click the program.**

   The graphics program opens and loads your picture file.

To open a picture in the default graphics editor, in the Folder List task pane, double-click the picture file icon.

Setting a picture's display dimensions

Expression Web enables you to specify the width and height of a picture as it appears when viewed with a Web browser. By doing so, you don't affect the size of the graphics file itself; you affect only the dimensions of the picture as it appears inside a Web page. (Remember that the picture that appears in the Web browser and in Design view is a *reference* to the original picture file that's still sitting safely in a folder somewhere — on your hard drive, a network drive, or the server where your Web site is hosted.) It's kind of like looking at a small object through binoculars; the binoculars make the object look bigger, but the size of the object doesn't change.

You can use Expression Web to adjust the dimensions of your Web pictures, either in pixels or as a percentage of the browser window size.

To resize a picture quickly, in the page, click the picture and then drag the size handles that appear around the picture. If you want to maintain the picture's proportions (always recommended for JPEG photographs because of their resizing issues), hold down the Shift key while dragging the handles.

For more precise control over dimensions, follow these steps:

1. **In the page, double-click the picture.**

   The Picture Properties dialog box appears.

2. **Click the Appearance tab.**

   The Width and Height text boxes already contain the picture's dimensions.

3. **To change the picture's dimensions, select the Specify Size check box, and then type new numbers in the Width and Height text boxes.**

   You can specify a number of pixels, or you can choose a percentage of the browser window. To maintain the correct proportion, select the Keep Aspect Ratio check box. (Always select this option when working with JPEG photographs.)

4. **Click OK to close the dialog box and adjust the picture's dimensions.**

Unless you're just making minor size adjustments, you should resize your photos in a graphics program and then resave them in Expression Web. If you must change the photo slightly, always remember to maintain the same width and height proportions by holding down the Shift key when dragging or, in the Picture Properties dialog box's Appearance tab, make sure that the Keep Aspect Ratio check box is selected.

Resampling a picture

In the "Setting a picture's display dimensions" section, earlier in this chapter, we explain how to set a picture's display dimensions, and we mention that by changing dimension settings, you don't affect the dimensions of the graphics file itself — only the size as it appears inside a Web page. That is true. However, we're about to go back on our word.

If you decide that you prefer the new size of the picture, you can tell Expression Web to *resample* (or *optimize*) the picture to match its new size. Resampling doesn't perform magic, but it can smooth out the rough edges that sometimes appear when you resize a photograph. Resampling can also reduce the file size a bit. To resample a picture, follow these steps:

1. **Change the dimensions of the picture by dragging, as described in the previous section, and then click the Resample button on the Pictures toolbar.**

   If the Pictures toolbar isn't visible, choose View➪Toolbars➪Pictures.

   You can also click the little Picture Actions menu icon in the lower-right corner of the picture (click the picture to select it if you don't see this icon) and then choose Resample Picture to Match Size.

2. **Click Save to save the page and, in the Save Embedded Files dialog box, save the picture with a *different* name.**

   If you save the picture file with the *same* name, you overwrite the original picture file. Save it with a different name to keep the original file unchanged.

Creating a transparent GIF

The concept of a transparent GIF is more easily demonstrated than explained. In Figure 5-5, the image on the top is a regular GIF. See how the image's background color wrestles with the background color of the page? This problem disappears if you make the GIF's background color transparent, like the background of the image on the bottom. The transparent GIF blends nicely with the rest of the page.

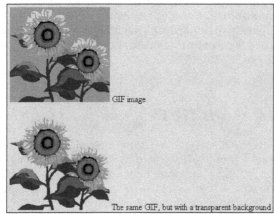

GIF image

The same GIF, but with a transparent background

Figure 5-5:
A regular
and a
transparent
GIF.

A transparent GIF has one of its colors erased (generally the background color) so that the color of the page shows through. The Pictures toolbar contains a "magic eraser" that can make regular GIFs transparent with a couple of clicks.

A GIF can have only one transparent color. Whichever color you slate for erasure disappears throughout the graphic. Unless the color you choose is unique, your GIF resembles Swiss cheese, because see-through spots appear throughout the picture. To avoid this problem, make sure that the GIF's background color doesn't appear anywhere else in the graphic. If you're working with ready-made graphics, you may need to alter them in a graphics program first.

To transform a regular GIF into a transparent GIF, follow these steps:

1. **Insert the GIF of your choice into your page.**

   See the section "Adding a Picture to Your Page," earlier in this chapter.

2. **In the page, click the picture.**

3. **On the Pictures toolbar, click the Set Transparent Color button and then, in the picture, move the cursor over the color you want to erase.**

   As you move the cursor over the picture, it turns into a little pencil eraser with an arrow sticking out the top.

4. **Click the mouse button.**

   The color disappears!

To change a picture's transparent color, click the Set Transparent Color button and then click a different color inside the picture. The original color reappears, and the newly chosen color becomes transparent.

To turn a transparent GIF back into a regular GIF, click the Set Transparent Color button and then click the transparent area. The old color comes back.

If you try this trick on a JPEG image, Expression Web prompts you to convert the picture to GIF format. (GIF and PNG are the only Web graphics formats that can be made transparent.) Proceed with care, however, because the GIF format can't accommodate as many colors as JPEG can, and your picture's quality and file size may suffer as a result. Again, turn to your graphics program for this kind of picture editing.

Cropping a picture

Cropping a picture involves trimming away parts of the picture and leaving only the stuff you like. To crop a picture, do this:

1. **In the page, click the picture you want to crop.**

2. **On the Pictures toolbar, click the Crop button.**

   A set of handles and a cropping border, shown in Figure 5-6, appear inside the selected picture. The handles, which are shaped like little squares, allow you to change the shape of the cropping border (the dotted lines).

Figure 5-6:
Cropping a
picture.

3. **Click and drag one of the handles, and keep reshaping the cropping border until it surrounds the part of the picture you want to keep intact.**

   You can also click inside the cropping border and drag the border around without reshaping it. After you crop the picture, the stuff inside the cropping border stays, and the stuff outside the border goes.

4. **After you get the cropping border right where you want it, click the Crop button again.**

   Snip! The unwanted portion of the picture goes away.

 If you decide that you don't like the newly cropped picture, click the Undo button on the Common or Standard toolbar to start over.

 Cropping a picture changes the actual image file. If you want to keep the original picture file unchanged, save the page and, when the Save Embedded Files dialog box pops up, save the cropped picture file with a different name.

Applying a special effect to a picture

The Pictures toolbar contains a few tools that apply special visual effects to your pictures. Table 5-1 shows the buttons on the Pictures toolbar and explains what effects the buttons apply. To use any of these effects, click the picture you want to change and then click the corresponding button.

Table 5-1	Visual Effects Options on the Pictures Toolbar	
Button	**Button Name**	**What It Does**
	Bring Forward and Send Backward	Increases and decreases the picture's z-index value; used when positioning pictures on a page in relation to other elements. (We talk about positioning in Chapter 8.)
	Rotate Left and Rotate Right	Rotates the picture 90 degrees to the left or right.
	Flip Horizontal and Flip Vertical	Flips the picture horizontally and vertically.

Button	Button Name	What It Does
	Increase Contrast and Decrease Contrast	Increases or decreases the picture's contrast.
	Increase Brightness and Decrease Brightness	Increases or decreases the picture's brightness.
	Color	Shows two pop-up options: Grayscale and Washout (useful when you want inactive graphical hyperlink buttons to look inactive in your page).
	Bevel	Transforms a regular, flat picture into a raised button of sorts; works best with square and rectangular graphics.
	Select	"Turns off" a button effect and returns the cursor to its usual cursor function.
	Rectangular Hotspot	Creates a rectangular hotspot. (See Chapter 4 for details about hotspots.)
	Circular Hotspot	Creates a circular hotspot. (See Chapter 4 for details about hotspots.)
	Polygonal Hotspot	Creates a polygonal hotspot. (See Chapter 4 for details about hotspots.)
	Highlight Hotspot	Highlights the hotspots inside an image map. (See Chapter 4 for details about hotspots and image maps.)
	Restore	Returns the picture to its original state if you're not happy with any of the effects. (Just be sure *not* to save the changes first; otherwise, the Restore button doesn't work.)

Deleting a picture

Erasing a picture from your page hardly takes a thought. Just click the picture and press the Backspace or Delete key. That's it. (Remember that this action deletes only the reference to the picture file on this page. The picture file itself remains in your Web site folder.)

Using Thumbnails to Speed Up Your Page

Adding pictures to a Web page increases the page's load time. Because Web surfers' annoyance levels rise with every second they must wait for a page to appear on-screen, you're wise to limit the number of pictures to keep the site loading fast.

What if your site relies on pictures? Suppose that you're building an online catalog or a Web-based art gallery. For these sites, the pictures are the main attraction. Are you (and your visitors) doomed to a slow-moving site?

Thankfully, no. Your salvation is a *thumbnail,* a tiny version of the picture that you want to display in your page. Because a small picture loads faster than a big picture, a thumbnail takes only moments to appear on-screen. The thumbnail is hyperlinked to the full-size picture, so if visitors want to see more detail, they can click the thumbnail. (Presumably, they're willing to wait a few moments for the full-size version to appear.)

Thumbnails are ideal for graphics-heavy sites because visitors wait only for the pictures they really want to see. Furthermore, you can insert several thumbnails into a page and still keep the load time minimal.

Keep in mind that a page with bunches of pictures, no matter what their size, slows down the page's loading time. If necessary, break hefty pages into several more sparsely filled pages.

In Expression Web, thumbnails take only moments to create by following these steps:

1. **In the page, insert the picture that you want to turn into a thumbnail.**

2. **Click the picture, and then, on the Pictures toolbar, click the Auto Thumbnail button.**

Note: If the Auto Thumbnail button appears dimmed, you cannot use the selected picture as a thumbnail. Expression Web gives you the thumbs down on the Thumbnail option in the following cases:

- The picture is already hyperlinked.
- The picture's original dimensions are smaller than the thumbnail.
- The picture is an image map. (We introduce you to image maps in Chapter 4.)

After you click the Auto Thumbnail button, the picture shrinks, and a colorful border appears around the picture, indicating that it is now a graphical hyperlink.

3. **To see the thumbnail in action, save your changes, preview the page in a browser (we tell you how in Chapter 2), and click the thumbnail.**

 When you save the page, the Save Embedded Files dialog box appears, suggesting a name for the thumbnail picture file, like this: barn_small. jpg. Click OK to save the files. We explain how to use this dialog box earlier in this chapter, in the section "Adding a picture from another application or location."

You can control the dimensions, the border thickness, and the bevel setting that Expression Web uses to create thumbnails. To access the Expression Web thumbnail settings, choose Tools➪Page Editor Options to display the Page Editor Options dialog box. In the dialog box, click the Auto Thumbnail tab.

If you don't like the thumbnail pictures that Expression Web creates, turn to your graphics program. Many graphics programs have built-in features for creating and saving thumbnails for Web pages.

Here's what the code for a thumbnail picture looks like:

```
<a href="images/barn.jpg">
<img alt="old barn" src="images/barn_small.jpg"
        width="100" height="66" class="stylex" /><!--
        MSComment="autothumbnail" xthumbnail-orig-
        image="file:///C:/Documents and Settings/My
        Name/My Documents/My Web
        Sites/travelsite/images/barn.jpg" --></a>
```

Remember that a picture on a Web page is nothing more than a reference to the picture file. So, when Expression Web creates a thumbnail, it replaces the original img link to the picture file with a hyperlink to it: <a href="images/ barn.jpg">. (We show you the code for hyperlinks in Chapter 4.)

Photo gallery savvy

You can turn any ordinary Web page into an online photo gallery by using the Expression Web Auto Thumbnail feature to create miniatures from your masterpieces that link to the real photo. Also, many graphics programs have features for creating Web photo gallery pages.

If you don't want to do it yourself, check out some of the great photo-archiving sites and software available on the Web. Here are a few favorites among Web designers: JAlbum (`http://jalbum.net`), Flickr (`http://`

`flickr.com`), and Picasa (`http://picasa.google.com/features/features-share.html`).

If you have a site you built in FrontPage with a photo gallery created by the FrontPage Photo Gallery Web Component, don't worry. It still works in Expression Web. You just can't create any new photo galleries for it in Expression Web. (The code for the FrontPage Photo Gallery didn't measure up to the strict Expression Web code standards.)

The next line contains a new `img` tag pointing to the new, smaller picture file, complete with width and height dimensions (`<img alt="old barn" src="images/barn_small.jpg" width="100" height="66"`). Notice that `class="stylex"` means that Expression Web has written a style rule for the thumbnail that sets the border style (solid or dotted, for example) and the border width properties. If you scroll to the top of the page, you see this style rule:

```
.stylex {
        border-style: solid;
        border-width: 2px;
}
```

We show you how to rename automatically generated styles and change their properties in Chapter 7.

The next bit of information is enclosed in HTML comment tags: `<!-- comment -->`. If we were to translate this comment into English, it would go something like this: "I created an Auto Thumbnail version of this picture file, found at this location." Notice that the `</a>` closing tag comes at the end of all this information, completing the hyperlink code. Whew! Aren't you glad you didn't have to type all that into your code?

Controlling a Picture's Position on the Page

After you insert a picture into your page, you can change how the picture is displayed on the page. For example, you can control how it aligns with surrounding text, how much space surrounds the picture, and whether it has a border. Because Expression Web uses CSS styles to control all these characteristics, you get to be precise and nitpicky about how your pictures look. In this section, we introduce you to a few positioning options as they relate specifically to pictures. Check out Chapter 8 for more information about using CSS styles to position pictures and other elements on your Web pages.

Aligning a picture with surrounding text

Generally, aligning pictures with text is best accomplished after you get into the finer points of laying out your pages, either with CSS positioning or in table layouts. (We cover positioning with CSS in Chapter 8 and table layouts in Chapter 10.)

However, when you insert a picture at the start of a paragraph of text and you simply want to control how the text flows around it, these steps do the trick:

1. **In the page, double-click the picture.**

   The Picture Properties dialog box appears with the General tab visible.

2. **Click the Appearance tab.**

   Figure 5-7 shows the contents of the Appearance tab.

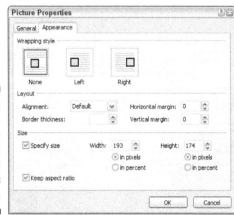

Figure 5-7: The Appearance tab in the Picture Properties dialog box.

3. **To align the picture against the left or right margin and have the text wrap around it, select either Left or Right in the Wrapping Style area.**

Figure 5-8 shows the results of the Left and Right wrapping style options.

Figure 5-8:
The results
of the Left
and Right
alignment
options.

You use the options in the Alignment drop-down list box to fine-tune how the picture aligns vertically with the text by specifying which part of the text to use as a reference point. Play around with the choices and see whether you get the results you want. Here are your choices:

- **Baseline:** Aligns the picture with the text baseline. The *baseline* is the invisible line that the page's text sits on, something like the lines on a piece of notebook paper.

- **Sub:** Moves the picture slightly downward in relation to the text.

- **Super:** Moves the picture slightly upward in relation to the text.

- **Top:** Aligns the top of the picture with the text.

- **Text-top:** Aligns the top of the picture with the top of the tallest text in the line.

- **Middle:** Aligns the middle of the picture with the text.

- **Bottom:** Aligns the bottom of the picture with the text.

- **Text-bottom:** Aligns the picture with the bottom of the text in the line.

4. **Click OK.**

The dialog box closes, and the picture alignment changes accordingly.

Take a look at the code for the wrapping-style alignment we describe in Step 3 of the preceding instructions. In this example, we aligned a picture to the left of a block of text:

```
<img alt="old barn" src="images/barn.jpg" width="320"
        height="207" style="float: left" />
```

Notice the style information that Expression Web has inserted in the `img` tag: `style="float: left"`. This is an *inline style* because it appears inside an HTML tag. We talk in Chapter 7 about the different places where Expression Web writes style information and why it matters. For now, we want you to notice the style information: `"float: left"`. This *style declaration* (as a style property and value pair are called in CSS) indicates that the picture should move on over to the left edge of the page and let other elements (in this case, a paragraph of text) flow around it. If we had clicked Right (on the Appearance tab, in the Wrapping Style area of the Picture Properties), the style would read `style="float: right"`, and the picture would align on the right side of the page with the text wrapping around it on the left. Figure 5-8 shows the result of applying these two options.

When it comes to flowing text around a picture, `float` is your new best friend. You can use it for page elements other than pictures, too. You find out how in Chapter 8.

Controlling the amount of space surrounding a picture

When you insert a picture in a text block or among other elements on your page, it can get a bit crowded. To give your pictures some elbowroom, you can increase the margins around the left and right sides and the top and bottom of the picture. To adjust margins around a picture, follow these steps:

1. **In the page, double-click the picture.**

   The Picture Properties dialog box appears.

2. **Click the Appearance tab (refer to Figure 5-7).**

3. **In the Horizontal Margin text box, type the number of pixels of blank space that you want to insert to the left and right of the picture.**

   The specified margin width is inserted on both the left and right sides. For example, if you type 6 pixels, 6 pixels of blank space appear to the left and to the right of the picture.

4. **In the Vertical Margin text box, type the number of pixels of blank space that you want to insert above and below the picture.**

   The specified margin width is inserted on both the top and the bottom. For example, if you type 6 pixels, 6 pixels of blank space appear above and below the picture.

5. **Click OK to close the dialog box and adjust the spacing.**

When you adjust the margins around a picture by using the options on the Appearance tab, Expression Web writes a CSS style for the picture with the margin widths you enter. You can get much more precise margins by editing the style rule. You can even set different margin widths for the left, right, top, and bottom. We show you how to edit automatically generated style rules and describe your options in Chapter 7.

Adding or removing a picture border

You can place borders around pictures in several ways. The method we describe here simply places a black box around the selected picture. But because the border is controlled by styles, you have many more options for line style, line width, and line color. You can even set different border types for each side individually. (We tell you how in Chapter 7.)

With all these choices, you can easily get carried away and apply borders with wild abandon. But keep basic design principles in mind and preview your pages often to make sure that borders don't unnecessarily create visual clutter on your pages. (We describe how to preview your Web pages in different browsers in Chapter 2.)

To give your picture a simple border, or to remove an existing border, follow these steps:

1. **In the page, double-click the picture.**

   The Picture Properties dialog box appears.

2. **Click the Appearance tab (refer to Figure 5-7).**

3. **In the dialog box's Border Thickness box, type the thickness, in pixels, of the picture border.**

   We recommend nothing thicker than 2 pixels. Anything much thicker tends to look gaudy, but experiment to see what you prefer.

   To *remove* borders, specify a border thickness of 0 pixels.

4. **Click OK to close the dialog box and apply the border setting.**

Take a peek at the code for border styles. In this example, we specified a border thickness of 2 pixels on the Picture Properties Appearances tab. Here's the code for the picture that is the lucky recipient of the border (it also has the `float: left` style applied to it; we explain `float` earlier in this chapter):

```
<img "sunflower" src="images/sunflower.gif" width="100"
        height="100" style="float: left: class="stylex"
```

Notice that, rather than add the style rule for the border in the `img` tag, Expression Web added `class="stylex"` and wrote the style rule at the top of the page (your style rule may contain other or different style definitions, depending on what you've done to your picture):

```
.stylex {
        border-style: solid;
        border-width: 2px;
}
```

By default, Expression Web writes different types of style information either inline (inside the HTML tag) or at the top of the Web page (called *internal* or *embedded* style rules). We explain more in Chapter 7 about different types of styles and why it matters where they appear.

Adding a Tiled Background Picture

You can use a picture to create a tiled background for your Web page, with your text or other content sitting on top of it. The Web browser *tiles* the picture, by repeating it over and over until it fills the browser window, much like you would tile your bathroom floor. Figure 5-9 shows a Web page using a leaf pattern picture that creates a seamless background texture.

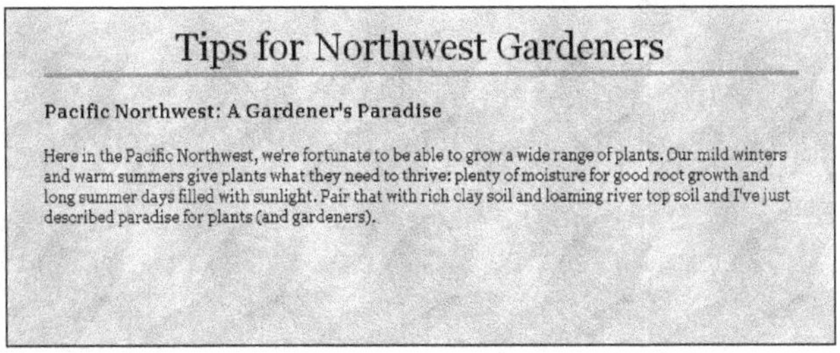

Figure 5-9:
A Web page
with a tiled
background
image.

Tips for Northwest Gardeners

Pacific Northwest: A Gardener's Paradise

Here in the Pacific Northwest, we're fortunate to be able to grow a wide range of plants. Our mild winters and warm summers give plants what they need to thrive: plenty of moisture for good root growth and long summer days filled with sunlight. Pair that with rich clay soil and loaming river top soil and I've just described paradise for plants (and gardeners).

If you decide to use a background image, choose one that harmonizes with the colors in your site. If the picture is too busy, the background may obscure the text and make the page difficult to read. Additionally, background images, like regular pictures, add time to your page's total download speed. The smaller and simpler your background image is, the faster the page loads.

To insert a background image, follow these steps:

1. **With a page open in Design view, choose Format⇨Background.**

   The Page Properties dialog box appears, with the Formatting tab visible.

2. **In the dialog box, select the Background Picture check box.**

3. **In the corresponding text box, type the graphic file's path.**

   Alternatively, click Browse to select the file from another location.

4. **If you want the background to appear fixed, select the Make It a Watermark check box.**

   Watermarks are the same as regular backgrounds, except that watermarks appear fixed in place if viewed with a Web browser — when a visitor scrolls around the screen, the text appears to float above the fixed background. (With regular background images, the background and text move together when a visitor scrolls around the page.)

5. **Click OK to close the dialog box.**

   The background image appears in your page.

If the background image is stored in a location other than in the open Web site, the Save Embedded Files dialog box offers to import the graphics file to your Web site the next time you save the page. Click OK to import the file. (We tell you how to use this dialog box earlier in this chapter, in the section "Adding a picture from another application or location.")

Here are some tips to keep in mind when creating a background for your page:

- ✔ **You can choose a solid color rather than a picture as your page background.** Solid background colors load instantly and are often easier to coordinate with the color scheme of the page. To specify a background color, choose Format⇨Background to display the Page Properties dialog box. Choose a color from the Background list box (or choose More Colors to pick a color from the More Colors dialog box), and then click OK.

- ✔ **Expression Web stores page background instructions in the page's style rules.** By customizing the style for a page's background, you get more options than the ones described here. For example, you can specify that the background picture not repeat or repeat only horizontally or only vertically. We show you in Chapter 7 how to customize the styles that Expression Web writes.

✔ **Many of the Web site templates that come with Expression Web use tiled pictures as page backgrounds.** If you see one you like, you can save the Web template and import the background picture file into your Web site to use on your pages. (We tell you how to import picture files earlier in this chapter.) You can also search for background textures and pictures on the Web. The Microsoft Office Online site contains a large collection of picture files for download, at http://office.microsoft.com/clipart/default.aspx?!c=en-us. (If this link doesn't work — Microsoft moves things around frequently — search for **Microsoft Office clip art and media** in your Web browser). You can also create your own background pictures in a graphics program.

✔ **Using CSS styles, you can create a "container" for your page's content so that the content appears to sit on top of your page background, much like a place mat sits on top of a tablecloth.** This method is an attractive way to use page backgrounds and keeps them from interfering with a visitor's ability to read your content. Take a look at the Web site templates that are available with Expression Web for some examples of using background images this way (the templates Personal 5, 6, and 7 all use tiled background images). We talk more in Chapter 8 about laying out pages by using CSS, and we tell you how to create a Web site from a template in Chapter 1.

Look at the code for a background image:

```
<body style="background-image: url('leaftexture.gif')">
```

The <body> HTML tag identifies the start of all the page content that is displayed in the Web browser. Everything related to the page — pictures, headings, paragraphs, lists, links — goes between the opening <body> and closing </body> tags. (Scroll to the bottom of your page; you see the closing tag, right before the "back cover" of all HTML pages, </html>.)

To specify the background picture for the entire page, Expression Web inserts an inline style in the body tag: style="background-image: url('leaftexture.gif')".

If you make the page background picture into a watermark (select the Make It a Watermark check box on the Page Properties Formatting tab), Expression Web adds the background-attachment style property to the body tag, like this:

```
<body style="background-image: url('leaftexture.gif');
            background-attachment: fixed">
```

Using styles, you have a lot of other options for customizing your page background. We talk in Chapter 7 about how to customize the styles that Expression Web automatically generates.

Chapter 6

Forms for Any Purpose

*W*hat's the first thing that pops into your mind when we mention forms? Bureaucracy-perpetuating pieces of paper? Multipage monstrosities in triplicate? Well, put those thoughts aside for a moment, because in this chapter, we introduce you to the wonders of the *interactive form.* Interactive forms allow you to survey your visitors and ask for their opinions. And you don't even need to hire an accountant.

Looking at How Forms Work

Before you build a form, understanding the basics of how forms work can help. If this stuff seems a little tricky, don't worry. Expression Web takes care of the hard part. All you need to do is decide how you want to use forms in your Web site.

Like paper forms, interactive forms collect different types of information. Web site visitors fill in *fields,* either by typing information or selecting an item from a list. After visitors complete the form, they click a button to submit the information. The form shown in Figure 6-1 illustrates how this process works.

Figure 6-1:
A typical
Web page
form.

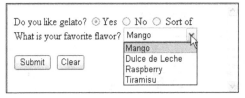

The information submitted from forms is organized into a list of field names (also known as variable names) and field values. The *field name* is a unique identifying descriptor assigned to each field in your form. The field name is invisible to your visitors; it exists inside the form's HTML and is visible only to the person (or computer) receiving the information submitted from the form. The pieces of text you see in Figure 6-1 — Do you like gelato? and What is your favorite flavor?, for example — aren't field names; they're bits of regular text sitting inside the page and prompting the visitor to fill in the accompanying field.

The *field value* is the information that the visitor submits. Depending on the type of field, the value is either the stuff the visitor types or an item that the visitor chooses from a list you define. (In Figure 6-1, for example, the value of the favorite flavor field is Mango.)

What happens to that information after a visitor submits the completed form depends on the type of form handler assigned to the form. A *form handler* is a program that resides on the host Web server (the computer on which your Web site will eventually be published). This program receives the form data and then does something with it. Depending on the type of form handler, the program might, for example, save the data (also known as the *form results*) in a text file, format the results as a Web page, or send the information back to the site administrator in an e-mail message.

Depending on the type of form handler you use, spammers may eventually find a way to fill your survey fields with junk that gets sent on to your inbox because the form handler can't differentiate between legitimate survey answers and ads for Rolex knockoffs. If your form falls prey to spammers, you can do a couple of things about it. Ask someone at your Web host whether it has spam-protected form handlers. If not, some Web-based services and third-party software products offer form security for a small fee. (Take a look at www.formbreeze.com and www.hform.com.)

If something beyond the simple user-input form is what you're after (such as a form that interacts with a database or a survey that requires authentication), consider taking a look at the more advanced ASP.NET site-building features that Expression Web offers. (ASP.NET sites are beyond the scope of this book, but you can find ASP.NET resources for beginners at www.dummies.com.)

Forms, FrontPage Server Extensions, and Expression Web

Suppose that you already have a form-enhanced Web site that you built in FrontPage. The forms work just fine, but they require that the host server have FrontPage Server Extensions installed in order to work. Expression Web no longer uses FrontPage Server Extensions, so what do you do? Not to worry — you can open your FrontPage-created site in Expression Web, publish it to your Web server with FrontPage Server Extensions enabled, and continue to use your forms as you set them up in FrontPage. The built-in form handler continues to validate and process your form results as before. But here's what you *can't* do in Expression Web:

✔ The Form Wizard and FrontPage form templates have gone bye-bye. You have to build any new forms for your site by hand. (It's not difficult; we show you how later in this chapter.)

✔ Built-in form field validation has also gone by the wayside. If any of your form fields has data-entry requirements, you cannot modify its data rules from within any Expression Web form-related dialog box. (If the data rules are stored in a script in your Web page, they're written in either VBScript or JavaScript, whichever you specified when you set up form validation. With some scripting-language know-how, you *can* modify the data rules in the Expression Web Code view.)

Even though your existing forms that rely on FrontPage Server Extensions continue to work (as long as you publish your site to a Web server with FrontPage Server Extensions available *and* as long as your Web host continues to offer FrontPage Server Extensions), you eventually have to find another solution. Check with your Web host to see whether its form handlers offer field validation. If not, you can build form validation into your form by using JavaScript. Check out *JavaScript For Dummies,* 4th Edition, by Emily A. Vander Veer (Wiley) to find out more.

If you're feeling ambitious, the ASP.NET controls in Expression Web offer all sorts of form options. The catch is that you have to build an ASP.NET Web site rather than an HTML Web site. The topic of building an ASP.NET site is beyond the scope of this book. Check out *ASP.NET 2 For Dummies,* by Bill Hatfield (Wiley) and *ASP.NET 2.0 Everyday Apps For Dummies,* by Doug Lowe (Wiley).

Creating Forms and Form Fields

A *form* is nothing more than a particular type of HTML that sits inside a page. You can, therefore, add a form to any Web page. Or, you can create a form on a blank page.

Form fields are the collection plates into which visitors drop bits of information. The kinds of fields you include in your form depend on the kinds of information you want to gather. Do you want visitors to select from a predefined list of choices? Would you rather let them fill in whatever information they like? The answers to these questions determine the types of fields you should use in your form.

To create your form, you first add a *form area* to a Web page (which tells Expression Web, "This part of the page is a form"). You then fill the form area with the fields you want your form to contain. Finally, you customize the fields so that they look and act the way you want. By *customize,* we mean that you assign each field a *name* — in some cases, a *value* — and you adjust how the field looks. (We explain what field names and values are in the preceding section.)

You can add as many fields as you like to your form. You can cut, copy, and paste fields and then drag and drop them in different locations within the form area. Add any explanatory text you want, and use the text formatting options we talk about in Chapter 3 or apply styles that match your site's formatting and layout (we talk about styles in Chapter 7).

Each of the following sections ends with a look at the code for the form element. Why should you be familiar with the HTML code for forms? When you look at the form results compiled by your form handler, they're written in a format that looks more like Code view for your form than the form your Web visitors see in their browsers. When you look at your form results, it doesn't seem like a foreign language. We show you a sample form result at the end of this chapter, in Figure 6-10.

Beginning with a form area

To add a form area to a Web page, follow these steps:

1. **In the Toolbox task pane, scroll down the list until you see Form Controls, as shown in Figure 6-2.**

   If you don't see the Toolbox task pane, choose Task Panes⇨Toolbox.

Figure 6-2:
The Toolbox task pane, with Form selected.

2. **From the Toolbox, drag the Form control in the Expression Web Design view to the page where you want the form to appear.**

   The cursor changes to a rectangular box with a plus sign.

   You can also drag the Form control into Code view.

3. **When you arrive on the page where you want the form to appear, release the mouse button.**

   The form appears on your page as a dotted rectangular box with a tab in the upper-left corner that says form.

In Code view, the following HTML tags appear:

```
<form method="post" action="">
</form>
```

The HTML tags `<form></form>` define the start and end of the form. All form controls go between these tags. When it's time to hook up the form to the form handler, the `method` and `action` attributes tell the form handler what to do with the form results after the visitor submits the form. We talk about how to add instructions for the form handler later in this chapter.

Here are a couple of tips to keep in mind as you work with forms:

✔ **When you add fields to a form, you must insert the fields *inside* the form area.** If you insert a form field outside the form area, Expression Web thinks that you want to create a second form and creates a new form area. These two forms then work independently of each other. Although, technically, one Web page can contain multiple forms, we assume that your intention is to create a single form.

✔ **As you create your form, be sure to preview the page to get a more accurate picture of how the page will look after it's published.** If you're not sure how to preview a page, refer to Chapter 2.

Text boxes

Text boxes are plain-vanilla fields into which visitors type a single line of text. Use a text box when you want to collect small bits of information, such as a name or an e-mail address. Figure 6-3 shows a filled-in text box as it appears in a Web browser.

Figure 6-3: A text box field.

E-mail address: me@mydomain.com

To add a text box to your page, follow these steps:

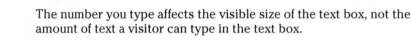 **1. From the Toolbox task pane, drag the Input (Text) form control inside the form area.**

   A text box appears on your page with a tab in the upper-left corner that says input.

2. In the page, double-click the text box.

   The Text Box Properties dialog box appears.

   In the dialog box's Name text box, Expression Web suggests the field name Text*x*.

3. In the Name text box, type your own field name.

   Choose a one-word, generic name that describes the *information* that the text box collects. If, for example, you're creating a text box to collect a visitor's e-mail address, type **Email** or **Email_address**.

   Always keep your field names restricted to one word. (You can use the underscore character to cheat a bit, as we did in the preceding example.) Some Web servers cannot process forms with longer field names. The name you choose doesn't need to match the text descriptor that you insert in the page to identify the field to visitors. Rather, the name should tell you what type of information that field gathered from your visitors.

4. If you want the text box field to appear with default text inside (rather than be empty), type the text in the Initial Value text box.

5. In the Width in Characters text box, type the visible width of the text box field.

   The number you type affects the visible size of the text box, not the amount of text a visitor can type in the text box.

   If you prefer to adjust the width of a text box by hand, skip this step. Instead, after you finish defining the text box's properties, click the text box in the page and then drag the field's size handles until you're satisfied with its new width.

6. Optionally, type a number in the Tab Order text box.

   The *tab order* is the order in which the cursor advances to the next field when a visitor presses the Tab key. By default, the tab order is sequential; the visitor fills out the first form field and then presses Tab to advance to the next field in the form. By entering a number in the Tab Order text box, you can control the sequence in which the cursor moves. For example, type **1** in the Tab Order text box if you want the current field to be the first field in which the cursor appears, even if that field isn't the first field on the page.

Form design tips

Here are a few tricks to make your homegrown forms easy for visitors to fill out:

Place helpful text next to each field. If, for example, you include a field in your form for the visitor's e-mail address, add `E-mail address (username@domain.com)` to make absolutely clear what information you want.

Help visitors provide you with the correct information. If your form contains mandatory fields or fields that require information to be entered in a certain way, include a note next to the field that demonstrates the correct format or at least that reads *This field is required.*

Pay attention to the order of the fields. Most Web browsers enable visitors to press the Tab key to advance to the next field. You, therefore, should arrange fields in sequential order on the page. If you place fields sequentially, pressing

the Tab key advances from one field to the next in a left-to-right, top-to-bottom order. Always test the form in various browsers with the Tab key before you send it out to your visitors.

Use grid marks to help line up fields. Turn on gridlines in Design view by choosing View⇨ Ruler and Grid⇨Show Grid.

Use default text in text box fields (also known as the field's initial value) to save visitors time and effort. For example, if your form asks the visitor's country of origin and most of your visitors are American, use *USA* as the field's default text.

Consider rewarding your visitors for taking the time to fill out the form. Enter them in a drawing (with their permission) or give them access to free downloadable goodies.

---

7. **Specify whether the text box is a password field.**

   Password fields are no different from regular text boxes except that, when viewed with a browser, text that someone types into a password field appears on-screen as dots or asterisks. These characters prevent nosy passersby from seeing the characters you type.

   Including a password field in your form *does not* automatically add password protection to your Web site.

8. **Click OK.**

   The dialog box closes, and any default text you specified appears inside the text box. If you changed the width of the text box, it stretches or shrinks accordingly.

Here's what the code for a text box form field for entering an e-mail address looks like:

```
<input name="email" type="text">
```

The field name for this text box, `email type="text"`, indicates that it's a text input field. Notice that there is no matching closing tag for `<input>`. All information about the form field appears inside the angle brackets. If you specify a character size in the Text Box Properties dialog box, the tag contains the size as well, like this:

```
<input name="email" type="text" size="25">
```

If, rather than enter a character width, you make the text box wider by dragging its right edge in Design view, the size is specified in pixels, like this:

```
<input name="email" type="text" style="width: 185px">
```

Text areas

Text areas are just like text boxes, except that this type of field holds more than one line of text. Text areas are ideal for verbose visitors who want to send lots of comments.

To create a text area, follow these steps:

1. **From the Toolbox task pane, drag the Text Area form control inside the form area.**

   A text area field appears on the page with a tab in the upper-left corner that says textarea.

2. **In the page, double-click the field.**

   The TextArea Box Properties dialog box appears.

   In the dialog box's Name text box, Expression Web suggests the field name TextArea*x*.

3. **In the Name text box, type your own field name.**

   The name you choose doesn't need to match the text descriptor that you insert in the page to identify the field to visitors. Use a one-word name that tells you what kind of information the field collects.

4. **If you want the text area to appear with default text inside, type that text in the Initial Value text box.**

5. **In the Width in Characters text box, type the visible width of the text area.**

6. **In the Number of Lines text box, type the number of lines of text that the text area can hold.**

   Effectively, this option controls the field's height. You can also adjust the height and width by hand (after you finish defining the field's properties) by clicking the text area and dragging the size handles until the field is the size you want.

7. **(Optional) Type a number in the Tab Order text box.**

   You can find out more about the tab order in Step 6 in the section, "Text boxes," earlier in this chapter.

8. **Click OK.**

   The dialog box closes, and any default text you specified appears inside the text area. If you changed the size of the text area, it stretches or shrinks accordingly.

Here's what the code for a text area form field for entering free-form comments on a form looks like:

```
<textarea name="comments" cols="50" rows="2">Use this
         space to tell us what you think...</textarea>
```

The field name for this text area is `comments`; the character width is expressed as columns, like this: `cols="50"`; `rows="2"` indicates that this text area is two text lines high. In this example, you want the text area to contain this text (in the Initial Value field in the TextArea Box Properties dialog box): "Use this space to tell us what you think." Notice that this HTML field tag has a matching closing tag, `</textarea>`, and the initial text value appears between the opening and closing tags.

Check boxes

Check boxes are like teenagers: They're independent but still prefer to hang around in groups. (Figure 6-4 shows an example of what a group of check boxes looks like in a Web browser.) Use check boxes if you want visitors to select as many items as they want from a predefined list. You can include one check box or many in your form.

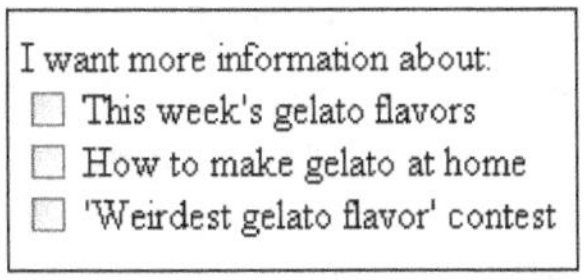

Figure 6-4:
A gang
of check
boxes.

I want more information about:
☐ This week's gelato flavors
☐ How to make gelato at home
☐ 'Weirdest gelato flavor' contest

To insert a check box, follow these steps:

1. **From the Toolbox task pane, drag the Input (Checkbox) form control inside the form area.**

   A check box appears on your page with a tab that says `input`.

2. **In the page, double-click the check box.**

The Check Box Properties dialog box appears.

In the dialog box's Name text box, Expression Web suggests the field name `Checkboxx`.

3. **In the Name text box, type your own field name.**

The name you choose doesn't need to match the text descriptor that you insert in the page to identify the field to visitors. You should, however, stick to one word for the field name.

4. **In the Value text box, type a word or two that describes what the selected check box means.**

Suppose that you're using a check box to enable visitors to request more information about a particular product. Using the first check box in Figure 6-4 as an example, `flavors` is a good name choice, and `more info` is a good value choice, because if visitors select that check box, their choice means "I want more information about gelato flavors."

5. **If you want the check box to appear selected initially, select the Checked option.**

6. **If you want to specify a tab order, type a number in the Tab Order text box.**

You can find out more about the tab order in Step 6 in the section "Text boxes," earlier in this chapter.

7. **Click OK to close the Check Box Properties dialog box.**

To add more check boxes, repeat these steps until you have all the check boxes you want.

Here's what the code for a check box looks like:

```
<input name="send_info" type="checkbox" value="Yes"
        checked="checked">
```

In this example, Web visitors select this box if they want information sent to them, so we named the check box field `send_info`. In the Check Box Properties Value field, we entered Yes (`value="Yes"`) and set the Initial state option to Checked (`checked="checked"`). Notice that, like the text box form field, this HTML code has no closing tag; `type="checkbox"` indicates what type of input field it is.

Group boxes make your forms friendlier

You build a long form. It contains many fields. Your users have visions of final exams, tax day, and associated unpleasantness.

Don't like where this image is heading? Take it from us, neither do your visitors. When you include a form in your site, you must give your visitors every reason to fill it out. A surefire way to scare away your respondents is to load your form with lots of time-consuming fields.

Group boxes can ease the sting of a long form by creating visual groupings of related form fields. Group boxes are empty, captioned rectangles into which you can insert form fields. Group boxes don't *do* anything per se, but, if your form must contain lots of fields, group boxes visually divide your form into palatable chunks of information. Suppose that users must fill in a lengthy survey form. Rather than bombard your visitors with 30 empty fields, you can group related questions inside group boxes to break the form into more manageable pieces.

See whether your form can benefit from the addition of a group box or two. Adding group boxes is easy; just follow these steps:

1. **From the Toolbox task pane, drag the Group Box form control inside the form area.**

A group box appears inside your form.

2. **Insert the fields of your choice inside the group box, or drag existing fields into the group box.**

You can do anything inside the group box that you can do inside the form area — add descriptive text, format text, and more.

3. **To change the group box caption, select the caption and type new text.**

4. **To change the caption alignment, right-click inside the group box and choose Group Box Properties from the pop-up menu that appears.**

The Group Box Properties dialog box appears.

5. **Choose an option from the Align list box and then click OK to close the dialog box.**

You can nest group boxes (place group boxes within group boxes) and you can format the caption text with styles (see Chapter 7 for more information about styles). Note that group boxes can look different in different browsers.

Option buttons

If check boxes are independent teens, *option buttons* (or *radio buttons*) are a giddy high-school clique. Option buttons are never seen alone and base their identity solely on the others in the group.

Use a group of option buttons to present visitors with a list of choices from which only one option can be selected. Figure 6-5 shows an example of what a group of option buttons looks like in a Web browser.

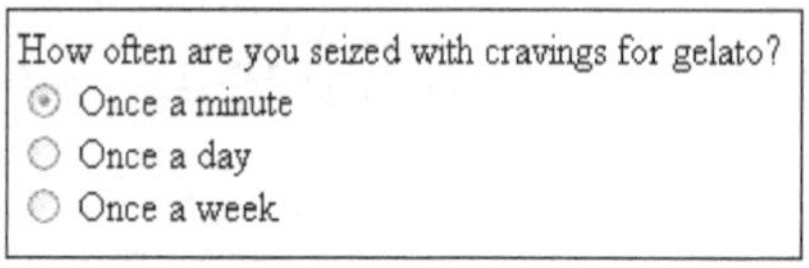

Figure 6-5:
A gathering
of option
buttons.

How often are you seized with cravings for gelato?
⊙ Once a minute
○ Once a day
○ Once a week

To create an option button group, follow these steps:

1. **From the Toolbox task pane, drag the Input (Radio) form control inside the form area.**

   A single option button appears on your page with a tab that says `input`.

2. **In the page, double-click the option button.**

   The Option Button Properties dialog box appears.

3. **In the Group Name text box, type a name that applies to the entire group (even though you created only one option button).**

   In the example shown in Figure 6-5, the group name is `gelato_craving`.

   The group name you choose doesn't need to match the text descriptor that you insert in the page to identify the list of option buttons to visitors.

4. **In the Value text box, type the value for the individual option button.**

   In the example shown in Figure 6-5, the value for the first option button is `minute`.

5. **If you want the option button to appear deselected initially, click the Not Selected option button.**

   By default, the first option button in a group appears selected.

6. **If you want to specify a tab order, type a number in the Tab Order text box.**

   You can find out more about the tab order in Step 6 in the section "Text boxes," earlier in this chapter.

7. **Click OK to close the Option Button Properties dialog box.**

Now you must create at least one more option button to complete the group. To do so, follow these steps:

1. **From the Toolbox task pane, drag the Input (Radio) form control inside the form area (ideally, near the first option button field).**

   A second option button appears on the page.

2. **In the page, double-click the second option button.**

   The Option Button Properties dialog box appears. The group name is the same as for the first option button. (We *told* you that they stick together.) All you need to do is give the second option button a unique value. In the example shown in Figure 6-5, the value for the second option button is day.

3. **Choose the option button's initial state.**

If you want the second option button to appear initially selected, click the Selected option. (By default, the first option button in a group appears selected. If you choose this option, the first option button in the group appears initially empty.) If you want the second option button to appear empty, click the Not Selected option.

4. **If you want to specify a tab order, type a number in the Tab Order text box.**

5. **Click OK to close the Option Button Properties dialog box.**

Here's what the code for the options buttons in Figure 6-5 looks like:

```
<input name="gelato_craving" type="radio" value="minute"
        checked="checked"> Once a minute<br>
        <input name="gelato_craving" type="radio"
        value="day"> Once a day<br>
        <input name="gelato_craving" type="radio"
        value="week"> Once a week<br>
```

In this example, the group name for the whole gaggle of option buttons (or radio buttons, as they're called in the code) is called gelato_craving (name="gelato_craving"); type="radio" identifies this input field as a radio button. Notice that the value for each radio button (value="minute", value ="day", and value="week") tells you which radio button is which. We specified that we want the first radio button selected: checked= "checked". After each radio button's closing angle bracket (>), its accompanying text appears, followed by a
 (line break) tag. This tag tells the Web browser to display the next bit of HTML on a new line.

Drop-down boxes

Drop-down boxes are so named because, after you click the field, a list of choices "drops down." Figure 6-6 shows how a drop-down box works when viewed with a Web browser.

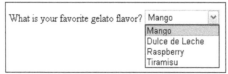

Figure 6-6:
A drop-down box.

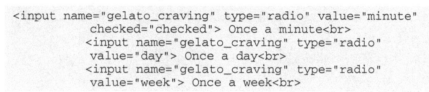

Like option button groups, drop-down boxes let visitors choose from a predefined group of options. In some cases, drop-down boxes have some advantages over option button groups, such as these two:

✔ Drop-down boxes save space on your page by popping open only after a visitor clicks the down arrow next to the option.

✔ You can set up a drop-down box to accept more than one choice at a time.

To create a drop-down box, follow these steps:

1. **From the Toolbox task pane, drag the Drop-Down Box form control inside the form area.**

   A drop-down box field appears on your page with a tab that says select.

2. **In the page, double-click the drop-down box.**

   The Drop-Down Box Properties dialog box appears, as shown in Figure 6-7.

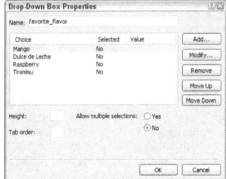

Figure 6-7: The Drop-Down Box Properties dialog box.

3. **In the Name text box, type the field name.**

   In the example in Figure 6-7, the name is favorite_flavor.

   The name you choose doesn't need to match the text descriptor you insert in the page to identify the field to visitors.

4. **To add menu choices, click the Add button.**

   The Add Choice dialog box appears, as shown in Figure 6-8.

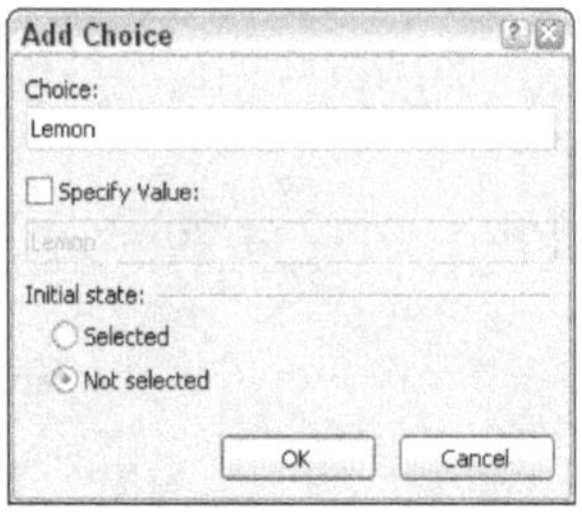

Figure 6-8:
The Add
Choice
dialog box.

5. **In the Choice text box, type the text that you want to appear in the drop-down box.**

   In the example shown in Figure 6-7, the choices are Mango, Dulce de Leche, Raspberry, and Tiramisu.

6. **If you want the choice's value to be something other than the information you type in the Choice text box, select the Specify Value check box and then type the value in the accompanying text box.**

   For example, you might add a choice of Chocolate/Fudge to the drop-down box, but when you transfer the form results into a database, the database program cannot process the slash / character. By selecting the Specify Value check box in the Add Choice dialog box, you can instead specify a value of Chocolate_Fudge. That way, visitors select from the drop-down box an item that reads Chocolate/Fudge, but the database receives the value Chocolate_Fudge.

7. **If you want the choice to appear initially selected, click the Selected option.**

8. **Click OK to close the Add Choice dialog box.**

9. **Repeat Steps 4 through 8 to add more menu choices until the drop-down box is complete.**

   You can rearrange, modify, or remove menu items by selecting the item in the list and then clicking the Move Up, Move Down, Modify, or Remove button (in the Drop-Down Box Properties dialog box).

10. **In the Height text box (refer to Figure 6-7), type the number of menu choices that are visible before a visitor clicks the drop-down box and causes it to drop down.**

    You can manually adjust the width of a drop-down box (after you finish defining the field's properties) by clicking the drop-down box in your page and dragging its size handles. You can change the height with the handles only if you specified two or more menu choices in Step 10.

11. **To enable visitors to select more than one item from the list, select the Yes option in the Allow Multiple Selections area of the dialog box.**

When visitors view the form with a Web browser, they select more than one option by pressing and holding the Ctrl key or the Apple Command key (⌘) as they click their selections.

12. **If you want to specify a tab order, type a number in the Tab Order text box.**

    You can find out more about the tab order in Step 6 in the section "Text boxes," earlier in this chapter.

13. **Click OK to close the Drop-Down Box Properties dialog box.**

    The first menu choice becomes visible in the drop-down list in your page. (If you specified that more than one menu choice is initially visible, the drop-down list expands to display the specified number of choices.)

Here's the code for the drop-down option box shown in Figure 6-6:

```
<select name="favorite_flavor">
        <option>Mango</option>
        <option>Dulce de Leche</option>
        <option>Raspberry</option>
        <option>Tiramisu</option>
        </select>
```

Notice the opening and closing `<select></select>` tags. All options are nested between these tags, which define the beginning and end of the drop-down box options. The field name (`name="favorite_flavor"`) indicates what this drop-down box is about. Notice that each option appears between a pair of opening and closing `<option></option>` tags, much like list items (`<li></li>`). In this list of options, the value is the same as the choice. If we add another option and define a different value for it (as in the example in Step 6), the code looks like this:

```
<option value="Chocolate_Fudge">Chocolate/Fudge</option>
```

If we want the Mango option selected initially, the code looks like this:

```
<option selected="selected">Mango</option>
```

Submit and Reset buttons

After you create your form and add the controls you want, you need to give your visitors a way to send their results to you. The *Submit button* is the linchpin of the entire operation. After visitors click this powerful button, their browsers activate the form handler program, which takes over from there and processes the form results.

Inserting a Submit button

You add a Submit button to your form just like you add all the other form controls, by dragging it from the Toolbox task pane into your form and plopping it in place.

If a standard gray Submit button is too boring for your taste, you can replace it with a *picture field.* Rather than insert a staid button, you can insert a snazzy picture. Clicking the picture submits the form results, just as a Submit button does.

To insert a Submit button, follow these steps:

1. **From the Toolbox task pane, drag the Input (Submit) form control inside the form area.**

   A push button field (with the label submit) appears on your page. A tab appears above the push button form control that says input.

2. **In the page, double-click the push button field.**

   The Push Button Properties dialog box appears.

   In the dialog box's Name text box, Expression Web suggests the field name Submit*x.*

3. **In the Name text box, accept the name or type a new one.**

4. **In the Value/Label text box, type the label you want to appear on the button.**

   How about something vivid? A Submit button could read Come to Mama!

5. **In the Button Type area, select the Submit option.**

6. **If you want to specify a tab order, type a number in the Tab Order text box.**

   You can find out more about the tab order in Step 6 in the section "Text boxes," earlier in this chapter.

7. **Click OK to close the Push Button Properties dialog box.**

Here's what the code for a Submit button looks like:

```
<input name="submit" type="submit" value="Submit">
```

We changed the field name to Submit (name="submit") rather than Submit1, which Expression Web suggested. (Our form has only one Submit button.) We also changed the label to an initial capital letter: value="Submit".

Inserting a picture field

To use a picture field in place of a Submit button, follow these steps:

1. **From the Toolbox task pane, drag the Input (Image) form control inside the form area.**

   A box with an X inside appears on the page. A tab that says `input` appears above the form control.

2. **In the page, double-click the image form control.**

   The Picture Properties dialog box appears, with the Form Field tab open.

   `Imagex` appears in the Name text box.

3. **In the Name text box, type a name for the image button.**

   Give the image a name that describes the information the button collects. *Submit* is a perfect name because it describes what the button does.

4. **In the Picture Properties dialog box, click the General tab to display its options.**

5. **In the Picture text box, type the name of the image file or click Browse to locate the image file.**

   If you click Browse, the Picture dialog box opens. Use the dialog box's options to navigate to the picture file. Click the picture file and then click Open. You return to the Picture Properties dialog box, and the Picture text box contains the full path of the picture file.

   If the picture file is outside the current Web site, Expression Web pops open the Save Embedded Files dialog box when you save your Web page. (We tell you how to use this dialog box in Chapter 2.)

6. **On the General tab, in the Alternate Text text box, type the text that a Web visitor should see in case images are set to not show (such as Submit).**

   We talk about the importance of using alternative text in Chapter 5.

   If you want to change the size or layout of the image, click the Appearance tab and set options there. (We talk about sizing images in Chapter 5).

7. **Click OK to save the image as a Submit button.**

Take a peek at the code for a Submit button that uses an image rather than the plain-Jane gray button:

```
<input name="submit" type="image"
       src="/images/submit_button.gif" alt="Submit"
       width="25" height="23">
```

The code `name="submit" type="image"` indicates that this is indeed a Submit button, but of the image variety. The rest of the code defines the image file's location relative to the form page (`src="/images/submit_button.gif"`) and provides alternative text (`alt="Submit"`) that tells the visitor what the button does in case images aren't displayed. The width and height measurements for the image are also indicated (`width="25"` `height="23"`; pixels, that is). We talk more about images in Chapter 5.

Inserting a Reset button

The Reset button is another handy form tool. After visitors click the Reset button, their browsers clear all the information they entered into the form so that they can start over. Alas, Reset buttons cannot be replaced by picture fields and are fated to look like plain gray rectangles.

To add a Reset button, follow the same steps we describe for adding a Submit button, but drag the Input (Reset) form control into your form instead.

Your Reset button could read something like `I changed my mind.`

The code for a Reset button looks a lot like the code for a Submit button:

```
<input name="reset" type="reset" value="Oops, changed my
        mind!">
```

We used the text `Oops, changed my mind!` for the Reset button rather than the boring old `Reset`.

Another push button field type sits quietly inside the Push Button Properties dialog box: the Normal push button. You can program this type of button to do just about anything. You can, for example, include a button in your Web page that plays a sound clip or opens a new Web page when a visitor clicks the button.

For such a feature to work, however, you need to write an *associated* script (a miniprogram that gets embedded into the page's HTML code) using a client-side scripting language, such as JavaScript. If you're intrigued, check out *JavaScript For Dummies,* 4th Edition, by Emily A. Vander Veer (Wiley) to find out more. Or, take a look at what ASP.NET has to offer.

Specifying What Happens to Form Results

All the real action occurs *after* a visitor submits the form. What happens to the form results is up to you. You specify where and in what manner to send the form results. For this task, you need a form handler script. Chances are good that your Web host has a form-handling script or two already in place on your Web server. Speak to your Web host technical service or administrator to discover the script's capabilities and find out where the script (that is, the script's URL) is located on the server. If form results are sent to you via e-mail, you need to tell your Web host which e-mail address you want to use to receive form results.

Many form handlers provide additional options, such as customizing the form results e-mail message with a Subject line and specifying a confirmation page that appears when the visitor clicks the Submit button. (We talk about creating a confirmation page in the next section.) Other scripts offer more advanced options, such as *input field validation*. What does that term mean? If you've ever typed your e-mail address incorrectly into a Web site and received the message E-mail address not valid, you've been on the receiving end of a script for input field validation.

If you need special data-processing capabilities beyond what your Web host's form handler can provide, you can write your own custom script and embed it into your Web page (for which you need programming experience or a programmer friend who owes you a big favor.) Prebuilt form-handling scripts for specific purposes are also widely available on the Internet, some even for free, depending on their features and capabilities.

Regardless of the form handler script you choose, hitching your form to a form handler in Expression Web is easy. In this section, we use a simple e-mail form handler as an example (such as your Web host would typically provide), to show you what dialog boxes you need to visit to introduce your form and your form handler to each other. Our sample form handler offers two additional options:

- ✔ A subject line for the form results e-mail
- ✔ The ability to specify a confirmation page

Depending on the form handler script you pick, you need to enter slightly different information, but the basic steps to get the form and the form handler to communicate nicely with each other are the same.

To hook up your form to this type of form handler, follow these steps:

1. **Right-click inside the form area and, from the pop-up menu that appears, choose Form Properties.**

   The Form Properties dialog box appears.

2. **Select the Send to Other option.**

The corresponding list box comes into view, with the Custom ISAPI, NSAPI, CGI, or ASP Script option visible.

If you must know, ISAPI stands for Internet Server Application Programming Interface, NSAPI stands for Netscape Server Application Programming Interface, CGI stands for Common Gateway Interface, and ASP stands for Active Server Pages.

3. **In the dialog box, click the Options button.**

   The Options for Custom Form Handler dialog box appears.

4. **In the Action text box, type the URL of the form handler.**

   If you don't know the URL, ask your Web host or system administrator.

   In our example, our form handler is named gdform.asp, and it lives in the same place as our Web site, so we would enter http://www. domain.com/gdform.asp.

5. **If post isn't already visible, choose it from the Method list box.**

6. **Leave the Encoding Type text box alone.**

7. **Click OK to close the Options for Custom Form Handler dialog box.**

   You just hooked up your form to the form handler.

8. **To set up additional options, click the Advanced button.**

   The Advanced Form Properties dialog box appears.

   We first set up the option to specify the Subject line for the form results e-mail.

9. **In the Advanced Form Properties dialog box, click the Add button.**

   The Name/Value Pair dialog box appears.

   The instructions for our form handler specify to use the field name subject.

10. **In the Name text field, type** subject.

11. **In the Value field, enter the text for the Subject line that you want to appear in the form results e-mail.**

    You can enter anything you want. (We entered Gelato Survey Results.)

12. **Click OK to close the Name/Value Pair dialog box.**

    In the Hidden Fields list in Advanced Form Properties dialog box, subject appears in the Name column and the Subject line text appears in the Value column (see Figure 6-9).

These fields are *hidden* because the visitor never sees them on your form. The fields sit backstage in the HTML code and direct the form handler to do specific things after the visitor clicks the Submit button.

Repeat Steps 9 through 12 to add options.

In Figure 6-9, we added the field name `redirect` (from the form handler instructions) and the value `survey_confirm.htm`, the confirmation page we want the visitor to see after clicking the Submit button.

Figure 6-9:
Options
for e-mail
subject
line and
confirmation
page.

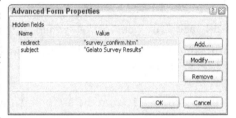

13. **When you are done adding options, click OK to close the Form Properties dialog box.**

Now that we've introduced our form to its handler, take a peek at the form code:

```
<form method="post"
        action="http://www.mydomain.com/gdform.asp">
```

The code `action="http://www.mydomain.com/gdform.asp"` tells the Web browser where to find the form-handling script.

We give you a sample URL here; contact your Web host to find out the URL of the form handler you use for your site.

Here's the code for specifying the Subject line for the form results email:

```
<input type="hidden" name="subject" value="Gelato Survey
        Results">
```

This code fetches and displays the confirmation page after the visitor clicks the Submit button:

```
<input type="hidden" name="redirect"
        value="survey_confirm.htm">
```

TIP

Figure 6-10 shows an example of an e-mail message sent by a form handler.

```
From: formmailer@secureserver.net [mailto:formmailer@secureserver.net]
Sent: Wednesday, October 04, 2006 6:33 PM
To: me@gelatonut.com
Subject: Gelato Survey Results

emailaddress: joe@crazyaboutgelato.com
favorite_flavor: Mango
firstname: Joe
gelato_craving: Minute
lastname: Gelato
submit: Submit

-----------------------------------------------------------------
This e-mail was generated from a form submission on your website: gelatonut.com
```

Figure 6-10:
E-mail
results from
a form.

Creating a Confirmation Page

If your form handler allows it, you can create a simple confirmation page for your form. A *confirmation page* is a Web page that appears after visitors submit a form. This page lets visitors know that the form submission was successful and (depending on the capabilities of your form handler and how you set up the page) confirms the information that visitors entered in the form. A confirmation page is a nice way to reassure visitors that the information they just sent didn't float off into the ether after they clicked the Submit button.

Create a confirmation page just as you create any other Web page. We suggest that you use design elements from other Web pages so that it blends in nicely with the rest of your site's design. (If you submit your form to a custom script, the script's programming determines whether it can work in conjunction with a confirmation page. Your Web host technical support team or system administrator can fill you in on the script's capabilities.)

The confirmation page can be as simple as a polite acknowledgment and a hyperlink back to the Web site's home page ("Thank you for filling out our survey. Return to the Acme home page."). Some scripts allow you to include some of the information the visitor entered in the form on the confirmation page. Check the capabilities of the script you're using to find out how to create and use this type of confirmation page.

TIP

If you use a Dynamic Web Template to unify the design of your site (covered in Chapter 11), consider hooking it to your confirmation page.

Making Sure Your Form Works

After you finish your form, you may as well check to see whether the darn thing works. Unfortunately, testing your form isn't as simple as previewing the page and filling out the fields.

Because forms require a form handler to be able to work, you must go a step further: You must call on the services of a Web server. To do so, you must publish your Web site and then preview and test the live version of the form. (For directions on how to publish your site, see Chapter 12.)

Part III

Great Design Doesn't Have to Be Difficult

The 5th Wave   By Rich Tennant

"Okay, I think I forgot to mention this, but we now have a Web management function that automatically alerts us when there's a broken link on The Aquarium's Web site."

In this part . . .

Some styles are as changeable as the weather during the Pacific Northwest springtime — but not the kind that take your Web page content beyond the ordinary.

In this part, we go in depth into Cascading Style Sheets and how to use styles to get your pages looking their best. Chapter 7 covers what makes styles special and how to create them, and we introduce you to some basic CSS concepts. Chapter 8 shows you some ways to use CSS to make stuff on your pages sit and stay. Chapter 9 covers how to style other pages by using external style sheets. In Chapter 10, we show you how to put tables to work lining up stuff on your pages. And in Chapter 11, we let you in on the timesaving technique of using Dynamic Web Templates to speed up designing and updating pages within a Web site.

Chapter 7

Using Styles to Gussy Up Your Content

In This Chapter

▶ Understanding the advantages of using styles for formatting

▶ Getting comfortable with CSS terminology and the Expression Web style tools

▶ Understanding classes, IDs, and other selectors

▶ Working with automatically generated styles

▶ Creating, modifying, applying, and deleting style rules

*I*n earlier chapters in this book, we introduce you to some of the ways Expression Web uses styles to format elements on your page. In this chapter, we cover styles in depth — how to work with the styles that Expression Web writes into your site's code and how to build your own styles. We also guide you through the basics of using Cascading Style Sheets and introduce you to the Expression Web style tools. Understanding how CSS works requires grappling with a bit of code, but after you get comfortable with the CSS big picture, you find out just how powerful and handy the Expression Web CSS tools really are.

The first several sections of this chapter cover the fundamentals of CSS: style sheets and how they cascade and style rules and how they work. If you're already CSS savvy and want to get right to using styles in Expression Web, you may want to skim the first part of this chapter and read the parts that aren't familiar. If you're a CSS newbie, however, we suggest that you read the entire chapter. And, if you're new to HTML, be sure to read through the first section in Chapter 14, in which we cover the basic HTML concepts you need to know to combine CSS with HTML.

Don't be surprised if you don't "get" CSS right away. This intermediate-level stuff takes time and practice to master. CSS is central to good Web design, which is why we encourage you, when you're ready, to take a deep breath and dive right in.

Miles of styles

Last time we checked our local technical bookstore, no fewer than five bookshelves were devoted to Cascading Styles Sheets. And Web sites abound that explain particular techniques for elegantly styling page elements with CSS — not to mention entire conferences dedicated to the meeting and brain melding of CSS masterminds. In this chapter, we introduce you to the basic concepts of CSS and show you how to work with styles in Expression Web, but we can't begin to do justice to this huge topic. Fortunately, you can find oodles of resources for getting the most from CSS, ranging from beginning-level tutorials to the nitpicky details of positioning page elements by using some of the more baffling CSS properties. Here are a few suggestions to get you started:

- *CSS Web Design For Dummies,* by Richard Mansfield (Wiley): Covers the basics and not-so-basics with Dummies-style wit and illumination.

- *HTML 4 For Dummies*, 5th Edition, by Ed Tittel and Mary Burmeister (Wiley): Explains HTML, XHTML, and CSS and how they work together.

- Several CSS reference books explain every single CSS property, such as *CSS Pocket*

Reference, 2nd Edition (O'Reilly Media, Inc.). Do some browsing and pick the one you like the most. Be sure to choose a book with a recent publication date, to ensure that it includes the latest changes to CSS.

If you prefer to let your computer do the walking, check out these online CSS tutorials:

- W3 Schools at `www.w3schools.com/css` offers basic CSS tutorials with online tests that introduce CSS concepts little by little.

- An excellent in-depth CSS tutorial that goes beyond the basics is at `www.westciv.com/style_master/house/tutorials/index.html`.

- Max Design at `http://css.max design.com.au/` offers tutorials on particular topics, such as Selectutorial, Floatutorial, and Listamatic. Their site contains a plethora of useful and informative articles by leading CSS experts.

- The Web Design Group's quick tutorials cover a wide range of CSS topics in short, accessible chunks at `www.htmlhelp.com/reference/css`.

What's So Great about Styles?

In Web design-ese, all things style related fall under the umbrella term *Cascading Style Sheets,* or *CSS.* The biggest contribution CSS makes to Web design is the ability to separate your site's *content* (the text and pictures that the site contains) from its *design* (how the site looks).

Whereas HTML puts the *content* on the Web page — the paragraphs, headings, lists, and hyperlinks, for example — CSS describes how they look. HTML says, "This is a first-level heading, and here's what it says." CSS says, "You know that first-level heading? Here's what it looks like: bold, small caps, red."

Here's another way to think about the relationship between CSS and HTML: Imagine that your favorite romance novel author (bear with us here) describes the physical appearance of the hero and heroine *every time* they're mentioned in the book. "Kate, who's slender, 5-foot-5-inches tall with unruly red head, cornflower blue eyes, and a heart-shaped face, gazed longingly at Kevin, that dark-haired, muscular, 6-foot-2-inch tall man with swarthy good looks and a brooding countenance hinting at dark secrets in his past." By the end of the first chapter (if you ever get that far), Kevin's swarthy good looks and Kate's unruly red hair make you want to run screaming from the room.

The code behind a Web site built without the benefit of CSS works like the novel we just described: Every paragraph, heading, bulleted list, and hyperlink has to announce to the Web browser how it's supposed to look every time it appears on the page. Before CSS, that's how Web designers had to write Web page code if they wanted their sites to look anything different from the boring ol' defaults.

Enter CSS, the romantic lead of Web design, flexing its rock-hard muscles. CSS says to HTML (in a deep and booming hero's voice), "Leave the heavy lifting of formatting to me, little HTML. You just focus on getting the content right." And CSS (who, despite the gleaming teeth, is also an efficiency geek) thinks, "Hmm, we shouldn't have to tell the browser more than once how a heading looks" — just like you, dear novel reader, shouldn't have to suffer through more than one description of Kevin and Kate.

Sound like a lot less coding work? It is. And because the powerful combination of CSS and HTML generates a lot less code, you get leaner, faster-loading pages. Not only that, if you want to change the formatting for a particular HTML element (return to our novel analogy for a moment to change Kate's hair color, for example, from red to blonde), you need to change the formatting in only one place (rather than in every appearance Kate makes on the page).

Want to see the heroic powers of CSS in action? Take a stroll through CSS Zen Garden at `www.csszengarden.com`. This site illustrates how a single CSS style sheet transforms a plain-and-simple Suzy HTML page into sultry Svetlana. Figure 7-1 shows the plain, nonstyled page that forms the basis for all the different styles showcased on the CSS Zen Garden site.

Figure 7-2 shows what happens when a CSS style sheet gets attached to this content page. Figure 7-3 shows how the whole page changes just by attaching a different style sheet.

Understanding How Styles Cascade

The *C* in CSS stands for *cascading* because of the multiple levels of styles that *cascade,* or fall onto each other, on the road to styling something (like text) on a Web page.

Figure 7-1:
The CSS
Zen Garden
HTML
content
page with
no style
sheet
attached.

Figure 7-2:
The same
HTML
content
page styled
with CSS.

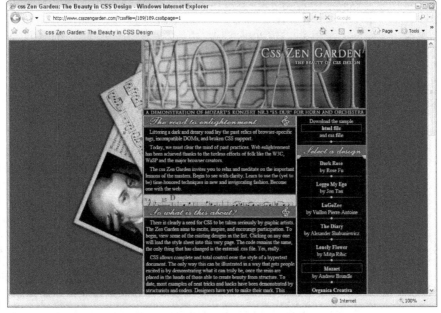

Figure 7-3:
The same
HTML
content
page styled
with the
Mozart style
sheet.

Consider the following:

- In Joe Web Surfer's Web browser, the default font for all text is set to Times New Roman. The software company that makes the browser set the font for that browser. It's called a *browser style sheet* because styles are set by the browser (or browser manufacturer).

- Joe Web Surfer hates Times New Roman, so he changes the default font in his browser to Helvetica. By changing his font, Joe Web Surfer has set a *user* style sheet that overrides the font set by the browser style sheet.

- You, the Web page designer, decide that you want the default font for your Web site to be Georgia. You write this style rule in a style sheet and attach it to all pages in your Web site, which changes all your text to Georgia. Your style sheet is an *author* style sheet because you're the author of your Web site and thereby the author of the style sheet attached to the Web site.

If Joe Web Surfer has the Georgia font installed on his computer, your page's text uses Georgia in his Web browser because the *author* style sheet (which uses Georgia) has higher authority than Joe's *user* style sheet (Helvetica), which in turn overrides his *browser* style sheet (Times New Roman). If Joe Web Surfer also hates Georgia, the only way he can override your *author* style sheet is to uninstall Georgia from his computer.

If, instead, you did *not* specify the font for your page's text, your page would be displayed in Helvetica in Joe Web Surfer's browser because his *user* style sheet overrides the font set by the *browser* style sheet. Which font would be displayed in Joe Web Surfer's roommate's browser (who never bothers to change defaults)? Text would be displayed in Times New Roman, the font specified by the *browser* style sheet.

You, as the Web page designer, also have control over your own cascading styles when you build your Web pages. Here's how they work:

1. You set the font for your Web site to Georgia by writing a style rule and saving it in an *external* style sheet attached to all the Web pages in your site. (We introduce external style sheets later in this chapter and describe them in detail in Chapter 9.)

2. You then decide that on *one particular page*, you want the font for all first-level headings to be Matisse. You write a style rule for first-level headings and, rather than move the style rule to the external style sheet — where it would affect *every* first-level heading throughout your entire site — you leave the style rule on this single page, in the page's <head> section (known as an *internal,* or *embedded,* style).

3. You then decide that on that same page you want *one particular first-level heading* to be Verdana. So you insert a style rule inside its <h1> HTML tag (called an *inline* style).

What font does that *one particular first-level heading* on that *one particular page* end up using when Joe Web Surfer looks at it in his browser? As long as he has Verdana on his computer, the heading uses Verdana because the inline style takes precedence over all other styles. (If Joe Web Surfer's computer doesn't have Verdana, the internal, or embedded, style rule written in the <head> section of the Web page takes precedence, and the heading appears in Matisse. If Joe doesn't have Matisse, the heading appears in Georgia, the font specified by the style sheet attached to the Web page.)

We show you what these style rules — external, internal or embedded, and inline — look like in Expression Web later in this chapter.

Introducing Classy Classes and Other Selectors

In this section, you take a closer look at how style rules are put together and how each style rule knows which element on your page to style. If this information seems like a lot to take in, bear with us. We show you a little later in this chapter how to put your new knowledge to use, to work with the style rules that Expression Web writes for you and to write your own style rules from scratch.

A style rule isn't much use if it doesn't know what to style. To figure out which thingy gets which styling, CSS uses selectors. A *selector* is the part of the style rule that tells it *what* to format, just like we tell our paintbrush-brandishing kids what they *can* paint on.

Element-based style rules

Style rules can apply to HTML elements, like the examples we show in this section. These are *element-based* style rules. In each case, the selector (the item being formatted, or *targeted,* by the style rule) is an HTML element:

Here's a style rule that applies the Georgia font to all *first-level headings:*

```
h1 {
        font-family: Georgia;
}
```

In this style rule, h1 is the selector, referring to the HTML element <h1>, and affects all the content between the <h1> and </h1> tags.

The following style rule applies the Georgia font to all *paragraphs:*

```
p {
        font-family: Georgia;
}
```

In this style rule, p is the selector, referring to all content between the HTML tags <p> and </p>.

In Expression Web, element-based style rules appear in the Apply Styles task pane list under the heading Contextual Selectors. If you know that you want a specific HTML element to look a certain way, you would create in Expression Web a style rule that targets that type of element (for example, a first-level heading or paragraph). Expression Web doesn't create an element-based style automatically. See the section "Creating a style rule from scratch," later in this chapter, for the details about how to create your own style rules.

For a chart of the most common HTML elements and their tags, take a look at Chapter 14.

Anatomy of a style rule

Here's an X-ray view of a style rule, with its various parts on display.

```
   selector        declaration              declaration
   h1 {text-align:  center;  color:  #008000;}
                    property   value   property   value
                           declaration block
```

Expression Web writes style rules on separate lines, like this:

```
selector {
property: value;
property: value;
}
```

The advantage of this format is that each style declaration appears on a separate line, making the declarative block easy to read and modify. You can just as easily write a style rule on one line, like in the diagram.

You can change the way Expression Web writes style rules by choosing Tools⇨Page Editor Options and then clicking the Code Formatting tab and changing the options in the CSS area.

Class-based style rules

Now we get more specific. The following style rule colors in red *any* HTML element that contains the attribute/value pair class="warning" in its HTML tag (#FF0000 is the hexadecimal code for red; see the sidebar "Hexa-what? How CSS understands color," later in this chapter):

```
.warning {
        color: #FF0000;
}
```

This is a *class-based* style rule. The period in .warning indicates that the style rule applies to an HTML tag containing the attribute class, and warning matches the attribute's value (class="warning"). Here are some HTML elements with class="warning" in them:

A paragraph:

```
<p class="warning">Never cross the street without looking
        both ways!</p>
```

A second-level heading:

```
<h2 class="warning">Watch for snakes!</h2>
```

An unordered list:

```
<ul class="warning">
        <li>Always look both ways</li>
        <li>Never cross when the light is red</li>
        <li>Do not assume cars can see you</li>
</ul>
```

Notice that it doesn't matter what the HTML element is. As long as it has `class="warning"` in its tag, it's colored red.

If you want to change the color of every element with `class="warning"` (for example, from red to blue), you simply change the color property value in the style rule (from #FF0000 to #0000FF, the hexadecimal number for blue).

When you format elements on your Web page, Expression Web automatically writes most formatting information as class-based styles with generic class values, such as `style1`, `style2`, and so on. Expression Web makes it easy to change automatic class-based styles and write your own style rules. We show you how to tweak automatic style rules and write your own, in the section "Performing Common Style-Rule Maneuvers," later in this chapter.

Hexa-*what?* How CSS understands color

When you look at color values in CSS, you notice that some CSS books and Web sites refer to colors by name: red, green, blue. Some even get more specific: CornflowerBlue and Khaki. But when you look at the color properties that Expression Web writes in style rules, you see six-digit letter-number combinations, like this: #FF0000 (red), #0000FF (blue), #008000 (green), #6495AD (CornflowerBlue), and #F0E68C (Khaki). These letter-number combinations are hexadecimal numbers. *Hexadecimal* numbers describe every one of the 16,777,216 colors that a modern computer monitor can display with a unique combination of letters and numbers. Wow!

Hexadecimal color numbers are sometimes abbreviated to three digits, like this: #FFF (white) or #000 (black). You can abbreviate a hexadecimal color number *only* if the two digits representing *each* color value are the same (the full color value for white is #FFFFFF; black is #000000).

Although all browsers understand the same set of basic color names (the Standard Colors set shown in many color areas of Expression Web and other Microsoft programs), *all* browsers understand hexadecimal numbers, so you should specify color values by hexadecimal number. A great color gizmo for picking Web colors is at `www.febooti.com/products/iezoom/online-help/online-color-chart-picker.html`. If you use Photoshop Elements as your graphics program, the Color Picker feature tells you a color's hexadecimal number, too. (See *Photoshop Elements For Dummies*, by Barbara Obermeier and Ted Padova (Wiley), for a detailed look at this program.) And, if you feel like geeking out over the finer points of color for the Web, check out the Wikipedia explanation at `http://en.wikipedia.org/wiki/Web_colors` or *Web Design For Dummies*, by Lisa Lopuck (Wiley).

ID-based style rules

ID-based style rules come in handy when you're using CSS to position HTML elements on your page, which we get to in Chapter 8. Whereas `class` is used to identify a *group* of elements, `id` identifies a *unique* element on a page.

Here's an example of an ID-based style rule that sets the font size for the element on the page that has `id="copyright"` in its HTML tag. ID-based style rules always have the symbol # preceding their name:

```
#copyright {
        font-size: xx-small;
}
```

Here's the style rule applied to a paragraph on the Web page with the attribute/value pair `id="copyright"`:

```
<p id="copyright"> Copyright 2006. All rights
        reserved.</p>
```

Pseudo classes and other selectors

In addition to elements, classes, and IDs, all sorts of other selectors — and ways to combine selectors — let you target content precisely with your style rules. For example, `a:active`, `a:hover`, `a:link`, `a:visited` are *pseudo classes;* they allow you to set different properties for each of the four hyperlink states. (We talk about hyperlinks in Chapter 4.) The selector `p.warning` shows you how you can combine selectors to target only those paragraphs (p) that have `class="warning"` in their tags.

Check out your favorite CSS reference book for more information about selectors. (We list some of our favorite CSS resources in the sidebar "Miles of styles," earlier in this chapter.)

Recognizing Style Rule Geography

In the section "Understanding How Styles Cascade," earlier in this chapter, we explain how different types of style rules — internal (or embedded), external, and inline — take precedence over each other to apply a font to a heading. In this section, you take a look at what inline, internal, and external style rules look like in the Expression Web Design view and Code view. We show you a bit of code, and we also introduce you to the visual cues and workspace areas you use when working with styles in Expression Web.

TIP

If you're completely new to CSS, this section makes you comfortable with what different types of style rules look like and how they appear in Expression Web. If you're already familiar with style rules and want to get right down to creating and modifying style rules, you may want to skip ahead to the section "Performing Common Style-Rule Maneuvers," later in this chapter.

Internal (embedded) styles

An *internal* (or *embedded*) style appears in the <head> section of its Web page's HTML code, and thus internal style rules control formatting for only the elements on that page. You can't apply an internal style rule that's embedded in one page to an element on another Web page.

Most of the style rules that Expression Web writes automatically are *internal class-based* styles. (We explain class-based styles earlier in this chapter.) If you already fiddled around with formatting, you probably have a smattering of style rules sitting inside your page named style1, style2, and style3, for example.

Figure 7-4 shows a paragraph with an internal style applied to it. This example shows a typical style rule that Expression Web writes when you choose a font family for a paragraph.

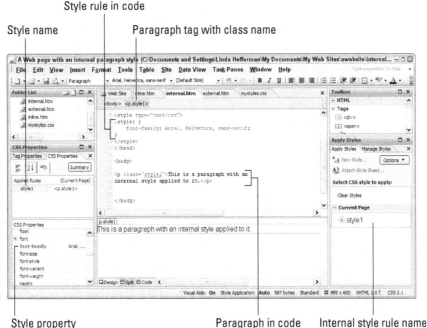

Figure 7-4:
A paragraph with an internal style rule applied.

Expression Web gives you information about the page's internal styles in a number of ways:

- ✔ **In Design view:** Displays a little tab on the paragraph that says p.style1, indicating that this paragraph has a class attribute whose value is style1.
- ✔ **The Quick Tag Selector bar:** Shows the paragraph tag with the class attribute <p.style1>.
- ✔ **The CSS Properties task pane:** Shows the name of the style rule in the Applied Rules column and, under (Current Page), shows the paragraph tag <p.style1> exactly as it appears on the Quick Tag Selector bar.
- ✔ **In the CSS Properties list:** Displays font-family in bold and blue and displays the font family name in the Value column.
- ✔ **In the Apply Styles task pane:** Shows the style rule .style1 as well, decorated like the text it applies to. A box around the style rule indicates that this style rule applies to the element that's selected on the page — in this case, the paragraph. The green dot identifies the style rule as class based. The circle around the dot means that the style rule is in use on this page.

Hovering your cursor over the style rule in the Apply Styles, Manage Styles, or CSS Properties task pane displays the style rule, exactly as it is written in your Web page's code. (We talk more about these task panes later in this chapter.)

Here's the style rule for our example (the rule's selector is in bold type), which appears in the <head> section of the Web page:

```
.style1 {
         font-family: Arial, Helvetica, sans-serif;
}
```

Here's what this style rule says in English: "Find the thing with style1 in it, and make its font family Arial, Helvetica, sans-serif." The period preceding the style rule name tells the style rule that it's looking for something with a class selector (class="style1").

Here's a closer look at the code for the paragraph itself (the class attribute that the style rule selects is in bold type):

```
<p class="style1">This is a paragraph with an internal
         style applied to it.</p>
```

Because this style is an internal one, you can add class="style1" to any HTML element on the page, and the CSS code in the <head> section tells the browser to apply the class-based .style1 rule to it. An easy way to do this in one step is to select the element, such as another paragraph, and, in the

Apply Styles task pane, click .style1. (We talk more about applying style rules to elements in the section "Applying style rules to page elements," later in this chapter.) If you decide that the chosen fonts in .style1 don't look quite right, all you need to do is change the style properties of .style1 in the internal CSS style rule to change all elements formatted with that style at one time. We show you how to edit style rules in the section "Modifying an existing style rule," later in this chapter.

Expression Web is pretty smart about working with style rules. As much as possible, when creating internal style rules, it adds additional properties to the same style rule instead of creating a whole new style rule. In the code example below, we selected the paragraph that had a font style applied to it and then clicked the Center Align button on the Common toolbar. Expression Web adds the new style declaration to the existing style rule, like this:

```
.style1 {
        font-family: Arial, Helvetica, sans-serif;
        text-align: center;
}
```

We say "pretty smart" because occasionally Expression Web does seem to write separate style rules when one would suffice, and these instances have left us scratching our heads. You will undoubtedly experience a few of these situations, too! No harm done, though. You may end up with an extra style rule or two, but we show you how to edit and delete style rules later in this chapter.

To quickly and accurately select an element on your Web page, click its tag on the Quick Tag Selector bar, as shown in Figure 7-5.

Figure 7-5:
Quick Tag
Selector
bar.

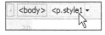

External styles

Internal style rules can easily be moved to an *external style sheet,* which is simply a separate file that contains a bunch of style rules. Moving style rules to an external style sheet makes them available for use on any page you attach the style sheet to — pages you haven't yet created and any plain-Jane content pages waiting around to get dressed up. Ah, here's the true power of style sheets: instant sitewide formatting with a few clicks!

TIP

Move internal styles to a separate style sheet after you fiddle with the formatting on a page and get everything looking the way you like it, *and* after you rename any Expression Web-generated styles. (We explain the virtues of renaming styles, such as `.style1`, to something more descriptive in the section "Renaming a class-based style," later in this chapter. We show you how to move styles to an external style sheet in Chapter 9.)

To show you what an external style rule looks like, we moved the internal style rule from Figure 7-4 for the formatted paragraph to an external style sheet without changing its name (something you wouldn't normally do because `.style1` doesn't convey any useful information about what the style is used for). Figure 7-6 shows the style rule after it packed its bags and moved to the external style sheet named `mystyles.css`.

Style rule location

Link to style sheet

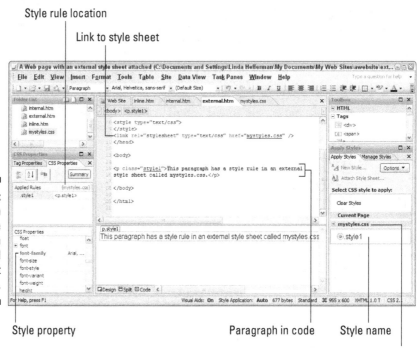

Figure 7-6:
A paragraph with a style rule from an external style sheet applied to it.

Style property   Paragraph in code   Style name

Style location is now external style sheet

Notice that the information in the CSS Properties task pane looks exactly like it did in the example with the internal style, as does the Quick Tag Selector bar. The paragraph also looks the same. But in the Apply Styles task pane, the style rule appears under the external style sheet filename `mystyles.css` rather than under (Current Page). The Manage Styles task pane shows the same information, indicating that the style rule now lives in the `mystyles.css` style sheet. (We talk more about the Apply Styles, Manage Styles, and CSS Properties task panes in the next section of this chapter.)

Peek at the code in the `<head>` section of the Web page:

```
<link rel="stylesheet" type="text/css" href="mystyles.css" />
```

Expression Web replaced the style rule with a *link* to the external style sheet named `mystyles.css`.

After you move a style rule to an external style sheet, you have to *modify* the style rule if you want to apply additional formatting to the elements it's applied to. For example, if we were to select our sample paragraph and click the Center Align button on the Common toolbar or change the text color, Expression Web wouldn't automatically add the new style property to the style rule located in the external style sheet. Instead, a *new* internal class-based style rule gets created in the `<head>` section of the page. Although this behavior seems quirky, Expression Web makes it easy to modify a style rule regardless of where it lives (in your page or in an external style sheet). Simply right-click the style rule in either the Apply Styles or Manage Styles task pane and, from the pop-up menu that appears, select Modify Style. (We show you in more detail how to do this in the section "Modifying an existing style rule," later in this chapter.)

If you find this behavior annoying, just refrain from moving your internal style rules to an external style sheet until you finish most of the formatting on your page. This way, you let Expression Web take care of writing internal style rules while you focus on clicking toolbar buttons and selecting dialog box options.

Inline styles

We would be remiss if we ended this style geography tour without a glance at inline styles and a description of what they look like in Expression Web. An inline style rule lives inside the HTML element's tag that it affects. In Figure 7-7, we manually modified the code to show you what our sample paragraph would look like if it were controlled by an inline style. (Expression Web would not write this kind of style rule by default.)

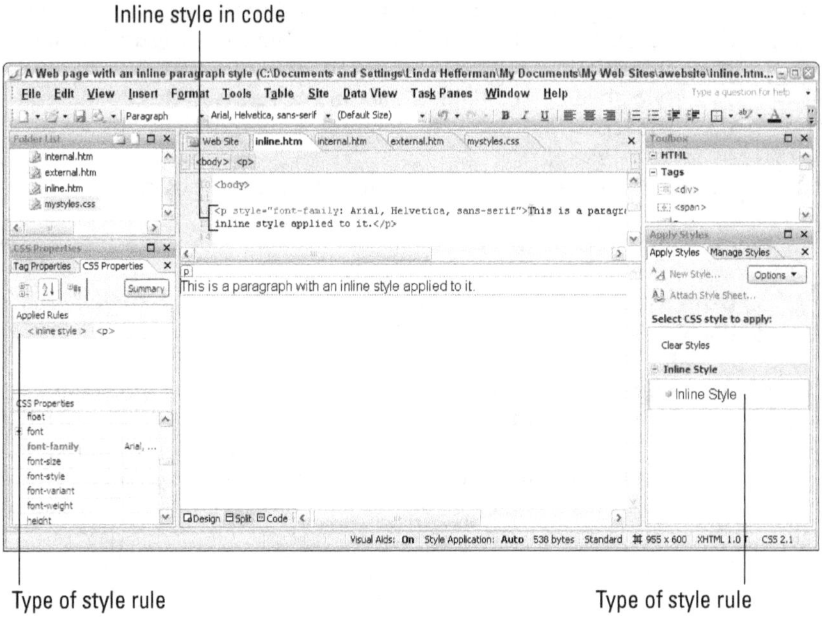

Inline style in code

Figure 7-7:
The sample
paragraph
with an
inline style
rule applied.

Type of style rule

Type of style rule

In Figure 7-7, notice where Expression Web gives you information about the selected paragraph and the style that formats it:

- ✔ **The CSS Properties task pane** tells you that an *inline* style is applied to the selected HTML element, <p>. This task pane also shows you exactly which style property is being used, by bolding the font-family property, coloring it blue, and showing its value: Arial, Helvetica, sans-serif.

- ✔ **The Apply Styles task pane** tells you that an inline style is applied to the selected paragraph and displays the name of the style (Inline Style) formatted exactly like the element being styled (the paragraph).

We talk more about the CSS Properties and Apply Styles task panes later in this chapter.

Here's the code for the paragraph being styled, with the inline style in bold:

```
<p style="font-family: Arial, Helvetica, sans-serif">This
        is a paragraph.</p>
```

By default, Expression Web writes inline CSS style codes for only two types of properties (we talk more about these properties and why you may want to change the Expression Web defaults in Chapter 8):

✔ Web page properties applied to the <body> tag (such as background, page margins, and page text color)

✔ Sizing, positioning, and floating properties that specify where elements appear on the Web page

Checking Out Your Style Tools

The Microsoft development team managed to make the Expression Web style tools relatively easy for beginners to use, yet flexible enough for more advanced users. Because Web designers like to work with styles differently, many of the style tools in Expression Web do the same thing by using slightly different techniques. As you get comfortable with using styles to format your page elements, you will most likely find your own favorite ways to do things with the Expression Web style tools.

In this section, we give you a brief overview of the different style tools and functions that we think are most useful. Some of them you were introduced to elsewhere. Others are tucked away, out of sight and ready to be called into service with a few clicks of the mouse.

If you need quick information about these style tools as you're working in Expression Web and don't have this book handy, remember that you can access the help system by choosing Help➪Microsoft Expression Web Designer Help or pressing the F1 key.

Apply Styles task pane

The Apply Styles task pane (shown in Figure 7-8; choose Task Panes➪ Apply Styles) shows you all the style rules that are working in the open Web page, including inline styles, internal style rules embedded in the page, and style rules that live in any external style sheets attached to the page.

Figure 7-8:
The Apply Styles task pane.

Because the styles appear in the list dressed in their formatting, the Apply Styles task pane is most useful for working closely with particular styles: creating new styles, modifying existing styles, and applying styles to page elements. Table 7-1 describes what the colored dots next to the style rules mean.

Table 7-1	Spotting the Dots in the Apply Styles Task Pane
Dot	**What It Indicates**
Green	A class-based style rule
Blue	An element-based style rule
Red	An ID-based style rule
Yellow	An inline style rule
Circled dot	A style rule applied to at least one element in the open page

Here are some tips for using the Apply Styles task pane:

- ✔ Hover your cursor over a style rule to view the complete style rule as it's written in your code so that you can glance at all the style properties it includes.

- ✔ Click the drop-down arrow to the right of the style to display a menu of commands. These commands let you do such tasks as modify the style and copy style properties to a new style, in addition to many other style-related functions explained later in this chapter.

- ✔ Click New Style to pop open the New Style dialog box and create a new style rule from scratch.

- ✔ Click Attach Style Sheet to attach an existing external style sheet to the page.

- ✔ Click the Options button to change the way styles are categorized in the list and to select which style rules to show. These choices let you customize the order and level of detail displayed in the Apply Styles task pane.

- ✔ Select an element on your Web page, and then click a style rule to apply it to the selected element.

Manage Styles task pane

Like the Apply Styles task pane, the Manage Styles task pane reveals the styles operating in the page. You display this task pane, shown in Figure 7-9, by clicking the Manage Styles tab or by choosing Task Panes➪Manage Styles.

The styles appear only by name (although a preview of the selected style appears at the bottom of the task pane). Using this pane, you can apply styles in the CSS Styles list, create new styles, and modify existing ones. You can also attach an external style sheet.

Figure 7-9:
The
Manage
Styles task
pane.

Here are some tips for using the Manage Styles task pane:

- ✔ Hover your cursor over a style rule to view the complete style rule as it's written in your code.

- ✔ Right-click a style rule to display a pop-up menu of style-related commands that let you modify the style rule, copy its style information to a new style, or delete the style, to name a few.

- ✔ Click New Style to pop open the New Style dialog box and create a new style rule from scratch.

- ✔ Click Attach Style Sheet to attach an existing external style sheet to the page.

- ✔ Click the Options button to change the way styles are categorized in the list, choose which style rules to show, and determine whether to display a preview area of the selected style.

- ✔ Select an element on your Web page, and then click a style rule to apply it to the selected element.

- ✔ Move a style rule somewhere else in the list by dragging it. The order in which styles appear in this list correspond to how they appear in either the external style sheet or the <head> section of the Web page. Changing the order here changes their order in the code, which is especially useful because some style rules must appear in a particular order (such as pseudo classes for hyperlink states, which must appear in this order: a:link, a:visited, a:hover, a:active).

- ✔ Move a style rule from the current page to an external style sheet by dragging it from one section to the other in the CSS styles list. (We talk more about external style sheets in Chapter 9.)

CSS Properties task pane

The CSS Properties task pane, shown in Figure 7-10, packs a lot of information into a small piece of screen real estate. By default, the CSS Properties task pane hangs out in the lower-left corner, behind the Tag Properties task pane. (If you don't see it, choose Task Panes⇨CSS Properties or Format⇨CSS Properties).

✔ **In the top half of the task pane,** under the heading Applied Rules, you see all the rules in use on the page, with the style rule applied to the selected element highlighted.

✔ **In the bottom half,** you find every single CSS property you can set in Expression Web under the heading CSS Properties. This list indicates which properties are set in the style rule highlighted in the Applied Rules section.

Figure 7-10:
The CSS
Properties
task pane.

The CSS Properties task pane can be a little intimidating at first, but after you get more comfortable working with styles, it's useful for viewing which style rules affect a particular element and how they interact with each other. If you're well versed in CSS, you may find that it's also a quick way to add or change style properties without having to use the Modify Style dialog box.

Here are some tips for using the CSS Properties task pane:

✔ Click an applied rule at the top, and then scroll through the properties list to see which properties the rule contains, along with their values.

 ✔ Click the Show Categorized List button to display properties in groups under a category header. These categories correspond to the categories in the New Style and Modify Style dialog boxes. (We explain how to use the New Style dialog box later in this chapter.)

✔ Click the Show Alphabetized List button to sort properties alphabetically, from A to Z.

✔ Click the Show Set Properties on Top button to group the properties used in a selected style rule at the top of the alphabetized list or the categorized list.

✔ Click any element in your Web page, and click the Summary button. The CSS Properties list shows just the properties applied to the selected element. (If no style rule is applied to the element, the Summary button is blank.) Click a property, and Expression Web shows you the style rule that contains it in the Applied Rules section. Cancel Summary view by clicking the Summary button again.

✔ If a property has a red line through it, another applied rule has the same property declaration. Hover your cursor over the red-lined property to see a pop-up tip.

✔ Change or enter a property's value by clicking it in the CSS Properties list and then typing a value or clicking the drop-down arrow that appears and selecting a value from the list.

✔ Click the small plus-sign button next to a style property to expand the list and show a more detailed breakdown of its values. For example, click the small plus-sign next to the `border-width` property to display `border-top-width`, `border-right-width`, `border-bottom-width`, and `border-left-width`, as shown in Figure 7-11.

✔ Right-click in the CSS Properties list to display a pop-up menu of style-related commands.

Figure 7-11:
Set individual properties for border width in the CSS Properties task pane.

Style toolbar

The Style toolbar, shown in Figure 7-12, performs some of the same tricks as the Apply Styles task pane, such as applying existing class or ID-based style rules to selected page elements, creating new styles, and attaching an external style sheet. To open the Style toolbar, choose View➪Toolbars➪Style.

Figure 7-12:
The Style
toolbar.

One useful function of the Style toolbar, however, is the ability to add a new `class` or `id` attribute to a selected page element. Adding a new `class` or `id` attribute from the Style toolbar doesn't create a matching style rule, so you have to create the style rule yourself.

Here are some tasks for which the Style toolbar comes in handy:

- **Add a *new class* to a page element:** In Design view, select the HTML element to which you want to add the new class and then, in the Style toolbar's Class text area, type the class value. Press the Enter key to add the class.

- **Add a *new ID* to a page element:** In Design view, select the HTML element to which you want to add the new ID and then, in the Style toolbar's ID text area, type the ID value. Press the Enter key to add the ID. You can also have Expression Web assign a unique ID to the selection by clicking the drop-down arrow and choosing Assign Unique ID. Expression Web creates a simple, sequentially numbered `id` value, however, such as p1. You're better off creating your own ID with a more meaningful name. IDs are most useful when you're using CSS to position page elements. We talk more about IDs in Chapter 8.

- **Apply an existing class-based or ID-based style rule to a page element:** Select the element to which you want to apply the style rule and then, from either the Class or ID drop-down list box, click the style name. Press the Enter key to apply the rule.

- **Remove a class or an ID from an element:** Select the element from which you want to remove the class or ID (it may or may not have a style rule that targets it) and then, in the Class or ID text area, delete the class or `id` value. Press the Enter key.

- **Open the New Style dialog box:** On the Style toolbar, click the New Style button.

- **Attach an existing style sheet to the open page:** On the Style toolbar, click the Attach Style Sheet button. (We cover external style sheets in Chapter 9.)

You can also assign, change, or delete an element's `class` or `id` value by selecting the element and typing the value in the Tag Properties task pane, next to the attribute (`class` or `id`). If necessary, choose Task Panes⇨ Tag Properties to display the Tag Properties task pane.

Style Application toolbar

The Style Application toolbar, shown in Figure 7-13, is most useful after you're experienced enough with CSS to decide for yourself how you want your style rules written each time you format something on your Web page. We assume that working with raw CSS isn't at the top of your list, so for this feature we pass the buck to the Expression Web Help system. (To access Help, choose Help⇨Expression Web Help or press F1.) To display the Style Application toolbar, choose View⇨Toolbars⇨Style Application or double-click Style Application: Auto in the lower-right portion of the status bar.

Figure 7-13:
The Style
Application
toolbar.

If you plan on using Expression Web in manual-style writing mode, dock the Style Application toolbar at the top of the workspace window so that its options are accessible but not in the way.

Performing Common Style-Rule Maneuvers

If you're a complete newcomer to CSS, the style rules that Expression Web generates can help you understand how CSS works. As you become more comfortable using styles, you can graduate to writing your own style rules. Eventually, you may even find it easier to do some of your work in Code view.

In this section, we cover the basics of dealing with automatically generated styles as well as how to write your own style rules from scratch. We also show you how to apply style rules to different elements on your page and how to modify and delete styles.

When we refer to a style rule's *name,* the name matches its *selector.* For example, the style rule named `.style1` is a class-based style rule that targets any element with `class="style1"` in its tag. The style rule named `h1` is an element-based style rule that targets all first-level headings (`<h1>`) in the page. The style rule named `#copyright` is an ID-based style rule that targets the single HTML element on a page that contains `id="copyright"` in its tag.

Renaming a class-based style

Because Expression Web writes class-based styles for almost all formatting you do, your Web page can quickly accumulate a bunch of sequentially numbered style rules. And `.style1`, `.style2`, and `.style3` don't exactly tell you anything useful about what they do. Fortunately, Expression Web makes it easy to rename class-based style rules.

When you rename a class-based style in Expression Web, you have the option of also renaming the `class` attribute in the HTML element so that the style rule still knows what it's supposed to format. (Why this is optional we don't know, because you must do it for the style rule to work). To rename the `class` attribute, follow these steps:

1. **In the Apply Styles task pane, click the drop-down arrow to the right of the style you want to rename.**

   Or, in the Manage Styles task pane, right-click the style name.

2. **From the pop-up menu that appears, choose Rename Class *Stylename*.**

   The Rename Class dialog box appears, as shown in Figure 7-14.

Figure 7-14: The Rename Class dialog box.

Rename Class	? ☒
Defined in: internal.htm	
Current name: style1	
New name:	
☑ Rename class references in this page.	
OK Cancel	

The style rule's location appears in the Defined In area. For an automatically generated style, this location is always the open Web page. The Current Name area displays the class name.

3. **In the New Name text box, type a new name for the style.**

When choosing names for class-based styles, keep these tips in mind:

- *Use words that describe the purpose of the style rather than its properties.* For example, a style that sets the text color to red should not be named `redtext` because you may change your mind and decide to make that text green later on. A better name is `alert` or `warning` if the purpose of the red text is to alert the Web visitor.

- *Use a single word for the style name.*

- *Use all lowercase letters.*

4. **Leave the Rename Class References in This Page check box selected.**

   If you deselect this check box, Expression Web changes only the name of the style rule selector (`.stylename` to `.newname`). The `class="stylename"` attributes in the HTML tags don't change to match the new selector, and the style rule doesn't know which page element (or elements) to style. If you inadvertently deselect this check box, the easiest way to fix it is to edit your page's code directly. In the code, find the element with the old class attribute value, and change it to match the style name. Chapter 14 covers how to work in your page's code.

5. **Click OK.**

Follow these instructions to rename *any* style rules and their associated class attributes, not just the ones that Expression Web automatically generates.

If you were to apply some other formatting to an element whose automatically generated style you renamed, Expression Web doesn't add the new style property to the renamed style. Instead, it creates a brand-*new* automatic style named `stylex` and gives the element the new `class` attribute `class="stylex"`. If you want to add the style property to your renamed style, follow the instructions for modifying existing styles later in this chapter.

Removing styles from page elements

When you're experimenting with formatting on your Web page, you will probably end up with a bunch of automatically generated class-based styles that you don't need. Not a problem. You can easily clear the class-based styles that Expression Web generates from an element on your page and delete the associated style rules in one fell swoop. To do so, select the element whose style (or styles) you want to clear and, in the Apply Styles task pane, click Clear Styles.

The Clear Styles command can also clear *inline* styles from a page element's HTML tag.

If you already renamed an automatically generated style, Clear Styles removes the `class` attribute from the page element but leaves the style rule in the `<head>` section of your Web page. If you want it gone from your page, you have to delete it separately. (We tell you how later in this chapter.)

The Quick Tag Selector bar can help you make sure that you're selecting the right HTML element. In Figure 7-15, suppose that you want to clear the style rule named `style1`, which makes the word *select* underlined. You know that the correct tag is selected because the Quick Tag Selector bar displays `<span. style1>` (a class-based style rule applied to a span tag with `class= "style1"`).

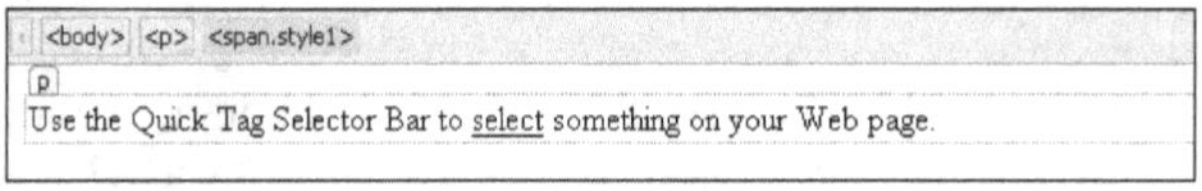

Figure 7-15:
The Quick Tag Selector bar shows you exactly which element is selected.

`<body>`	`<p>`	`<span.style1>`
p		

Use the Quick Tag Selector Bar to <u>select</u> something on your Web page.

Removing a class or an ID from an element

Deleting a class- or ID-based style doesn't remove any associated `class` or `id` attributes and their values in an element's HTML tag. You have to remove these attributes separately. Here are four quick ways to remove a `class` or `id` attribute from a selected page element:

- ✔ On the Quick Tag Selector bar, click the drop-down arrow next to the tag you want to edit, and then choose Edit Tag. In the Quick Tag Editor that appears, select the `class` or `id` attribute and value (for example, `class="stylex"`), and then press the Delete key.

- ✔ Pop open the Style toolbar (choose View➪Toolbars➪Style) and, in the Class or ID field, select the value and press the Delete key.

- ✔ In the Tag Properties task pane, select the `class` or `id` value and press the Delete key.

- ✔ In Code view (or the code portion of Split view), select the `class` or `id` attribute and its value and press the Delete key.

Creating a style rule from scratch

After you get the hang of how your HTML and CSS styles work together, you can write your own style rules by using the tools in Expression Web. Expression Web makes it easy to write any kind of style rule — element-based, class-based, or ID-based. You can specify whether the style rule is inline, internal, or saved to an existing external style sheet. When you write a new style from scratch, you have access to all the formatting properties that are scattered throughout the various Expression Web dialog boxes and tool-bar buttons in one place so that you can pick the exact ones you want your style rule to include.

When you create a new class- or ID-based style rule, you also have the option of telling Expression Web to create the style rule *and* add the class or id value to the element or item selected in Design view. Or, you can add class and id values separately (see the section "Style toolbar," earlier in this chapter, to find out how to add class and id values to your page elements, or refer to Chapter 14 for instructions on working in the Expression Web Code view).

When you create your own style rules, it's helpful to have a good Cascading Style Sheet reference manual handy so that you can look up the purpose of any properties you aren't sure about. We give you some book suggestions at the beginning of this chapter, in the sidebar "Miles of styles." Also, see the Cheat Sheet, inside the front cover, for a list of the most commonly used style properties.

To create a new *internal* or *inline* style rule, follow these steps:

1. **Do one of the following:**

   • Choose Format⇨New Style.

   ✔ In the Apply Styles or Manage Styles task pane, click New Style.

   • On the Style toolbar (choose View⇨Toolbars⇨Style); click the New Style button.

   The New Style dialog box appears, as shown in Figure 7-16.

2. **In the Selector text box, tell Expression Web what the style rule will target (the *selector*) by doing one of the following:**

   • To create an *element-based* style rule, select the HTML element that the style rule will apply to from the drop-down list. For example, to create a rule to set properties for all first-level headings on the page, select h1.

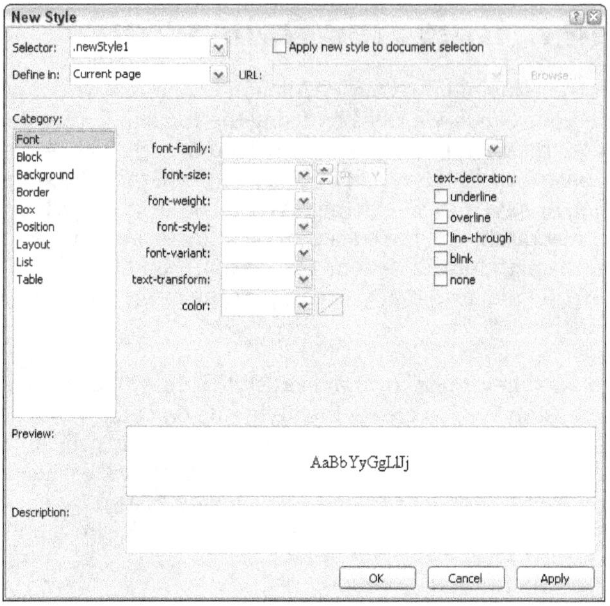

Figure 7-16:
The New
Style dialog
box.

- To create an *inline* style rule, select (`inline style`) from the drop-down list.

- To create a *class-based* style rule, type a period (.), and then type the class value. (Make sure that no space appears between the period and the class value.) For example, if you want to target *all* HTML elements that contain the class value `warning` in their tags, type **.warning**.

  If you want Expression Web to also add the `class` value to the selected HTML element, select the Apply New Style to Document Selection check box. In the preceding example, Expression Web would create the style rule `.warning` and add `class="warning"` to the selected element on your page.

- To create an *ID-based* style rule, type the # character (press Shift+3), and then type the `id` value. (Make sure that no space appears between the period and the `id` value.) For example, if you want to target an HTML element that contains the `id` value `copyright` in its tag, type **#copyright**.

  If you want Expression Web to also add the `id` value to the selected HTML element, select the Apply New Style to Document Selection check box. In the preceding example, Expression Web would create the ID-based style rule `#copyright` and add `id="copyright"` to the selected element on your page.

- If you know how to create complex selectors or if you want to target multiple HTML elements, type the selector in the Selector text box. For example, to create a style rule that targets *all* heading levels, type **h1, h2, h3, h4, h5, h6.**

3. **To save the style rule in the open page (an *internal* style rule), leave the Define In option set to Current Page.**

   This option isn't available if you're creating an *inline* style because an inline style is saved inside the HTML element's tag.

   If you choose to save the style to an *external* style sheet (either a new style sheet or an existing style sheet), see the additional steps a little later in this section.

4. **To choose the properties and their values, first click the type of property you want to set in the Category list, and then, from the displayed properties, set values for the ones you want your style rule to include.**

   The New Style dialog box contains all possible CSS properties, grouped by category. See Table 7-2, a little later in this section, for more information about which type of properties each category contains.

   The Preview area gives you a peek at what the selected element will look like as you select properties and set their values.

   The Description box shows you the style declarations as they will appear in the code.

5. **Continue setting properties and their values by clicking the type of property in the Category list and setting values for the properties you want to use.**

   If a category contains a defined property, the category name appears in bold type in the Category list. In Figure 7-17, properties are defined in the Font, Background, and Box categories.

6. **When you are finished setting properties, click OK to close the New Style dialog box and save the style rule.**

If you selected the Apply New Style to Document Selection check box, the selected element gets styled as defined in the style rule. Notice also that the new style rule appears in both the Apply Styles and Manage Styles task panes. The Apply Styles task pane shows the style rule with its formatting applied, whereas the Manage Styles task pane simply lists the style.

If you choose to save the new style rule to an *external* style sheet, you have a few additional steps to go through, depending on whether you chose a new style sheet or an existing style sheet in the Define In list box. (Refer to Step 3 in the preceding set of steps).

Figure 7-17:
Categories
with defined
properties
appear in
bold.

If you chose to save the style rule to a *new* style sheet (in the Define In list box), Expression Web pops open a dialog box asking whether you want to attach the new style sheet for the new style to your open page. Follow these steps:

1. **Click Yes to save the new style sheet.**

   Expression Web creates a new style sheet named `Untitled_1.css`, saves the new style in it, and attaches it to your page.

2. **Save your page. (We tell you how in Chapter 2.)**

   The Save As dialog box opens and prompts you to save the new style sheet file with a new name.

3. **In the File Name text box, type the new name *without* deleting the extension `.css`.**

   Try to use one-word, all-lowercase filenames for style sheets.

4. **Click OK to save the style sheet.**

If you chose to save the style rule to an *existing* style sheet (in the Define In list box), follow these steps:

1. **In the URL text box in the New Style dialog box, type the name and path of the style sheet.**

   Or, click the Browse button and, in the Select Style Sheet dialog box that appears, use the options to navigate to the style sheet you want to save the new style rule in. Click the style sheet name to select it and then click Open.

If you want to save the style rule to a style sheet that isn't located in your open Web site, you should import the style sheet into the Web site first, *before* saving new styles to it. We tell you how to import files into a Web site in Chapter 1.

The name and path of the style sheet file appear in the URL text box.

2. Click OK to save the new style rule.

Expression Web opens the style sheet in which you saved the style rule in the editing window, but doesn't make it the active window.

3. Click the style sheet tab to make it the active window, and click the Save button to save the style sheet.

We talk more about external style sheets in Chapter 9.

If you created an element-based style rule, (such as a style rule for all paragraphs), those elements receive their new formatting as soon as you click OK to save the style rule.

Table 7-2	Style Categories and Their Property Types
Category	*What the Property Type Controls*
Font	The way the characters (the letters, numbers, symbols, and special characters) look on the page. These properties correspond to the buttons and commands on the Font tab (choose Format⇨Font) in the Font dialog box and to the font-formatting buttons on the Common and Formatting toolbars.
Block	The spacing between lines of text within a block of text (a paragraph or heading), the spacing between letters in words and between words, and the alignment (indenting, centering, or right or left alignment) of a block of text on the page. These properties correspond to the commands in the Paragraph dialog box (choose Format⇨Paragraph), the Character Spacing tab (choose Format⇨Font) in the Font dialog box, and the paragraph alignment and indent buttons on the Common and Formatting toolbars.
Background	The way the background of the selected element looks and behaves: its color, the image it uses, whether it repeats and in which direction (horizontally, vertically, or both), and whether the background is fixed in one position or scrolls with the page. These properties correspond to the commands on the Shading tab in the Borders and Shading dialog box (choose Format⇨Borders and Shading) and on the Highlight button on the Common and Formatting toolbars.

(continued)

Table 7-2 *(continued)*

Category	What the Property Type Controls
Border	The border style (solid, dashed, dotted, or grooved), width, and color of the selected element. These properties correspond to the commands on the Borders tab in the Borders and Shading dialog box (choose Format⇨Borders and Shading) and on the Outside Borders button on the Common and Formatting toolbars.
Box	Margins and padding properties, the amount of space between the contents of an element and its border (padding) and the amount of space between the border and other surrounding elements (margins). To set padding and margin properties, you must understand the concept of the CSS box model. Chapter 8 gives you more information about margins and padding.
Position	The dimensions (width and height) of page elements — headings, paragraphs, and other items, such as navigation bars and footers, defined as block-level elements using <div> tags. These properties also control an element's position on the page. We talk more about these properties in Chapter 8.
Layout	The way that elements on the page act and interact with each other on the page. For example, you can control how elements wrap around each other by using the float property (we talk about using float for aligning a picture with surrounding text in Chapter 5) or whether an element should always appear below its preceding elements (clear). We talk about these properties in Chapter 8.
List	Ordered and unordered lists. These properties let you set the type of numbering or bullet style you use (or turn off bullets and numbers) and specify how a list is positioned on the page. These properties correspond to the commands in the Bullets and Numbering dialog box (choose Format⇨Bullets and Numbering).
Table	A table's position on a Web page, and the appearance of table cells, caption, and borders (although not the color and line style — those properties are set in the Borders category).

By the way, in Design view, if you click at the end of the text in the styled paragraph and press Enter, the paragraph style is carried over to the next paragraph. You may or may not want that to happen. If you don't want the style to carry over to the next paragraph, click in Design view below the selected paragraph rather than press the Enter key. (We show you how to apply and remove styles later in this chapter.)

Copying style properties to a new rule

Just as you can use a Web page as the basis for another Web page, you can use a style rule as the basis for another style rule. You can then save time if you want to create a new style rule that contains some of the same properties as another rule.

To copy style properties from an existing rule to a new rule, follow these steps:

1. **In the Apply Styles task pane, click the drop-down arrow to the right of the style rule you want to use as the basis for the new style rule and, from the menu that appears, choose New Style Copy.**

   The New Style dialog box appears; `stylenameCopy` appears in the Selector field. The original style rule's properties and values appear in each category.

2. **In the Selector field, type the style rule selector you want to use, or choose an HTML element from the drop-down list.**

3. **In the Define In list box, tell Expression Web where you want the new rule defined.**

   We cover how to use the Define In list box earlier in this chapter, in the section "Creating a style rule from scratch."

4. **If you want the new style rule to apply to an element selected in the Web page, select the Apply New Style to Document Selection check box.**

   If you just want to create the rule without applying it, leave this box deselected.

5. **Set new properties or change values for the properties already set by the original rule by clicking a property category in the Category list box and selecting the properties you want the rule to include.**

6. **When you finish defining the new rule, click OK to save it.**

There's no limit to how many style rules you can have and use. And, you can apply multiple styles to a single element. When you're first getting used to formatting your page elements with styles, you may find it easier to create many style rules with only a few properties apiece. As you gain style prowess, you may find that you prefer to create fewer style rules with more style properties.

Applying style rules to page elements

After you create a style rule you like, you can apply it to other elements on your page. You can apply the same rule to multiple elements, and you can apply multiple rules to a single element or to multiple elements.

To apply style rules to a single page element or multiple elements, follow these steps:

1. **In Design view or Code view, select the element to which you want to apply the style.**

   To select multiple elements, hold down the Ctrl key while clicking each element.

2. **In the Apply Styles task pane, click the style rule you want to apply to the element.**

3. **To apply another style rule to the selected elements, hold down the Ctrl key and, in the Apply Styles task pane, click the next style rule.**

Modifying an existing style rule

Did you change your mind about a style? Did you decide that you want green text rather than red? Expression Web makes it easy to modify your style rules.

To modify a style by using the Modify Style dialog box, follow these steps:

1. **In the Apply Styles task pane, click the drop-down arrow next to the style rule you want to modify.**

2. **From the pop-up menu that appears, choose Modify Style.**

   The Modify Style dialog box appears, as shown in Figure 7-18. The Modify Style dialog box displays all the properties and their values that are set by the rule.

3. **Make the changes you want to the style rule by selecting properties and setting their values.**

   If you want to delete a property from the style rule, clear its value by deleting any information that appears in its value field.

   If necessary, change the rule's selector in the Selector field.

Figure 7-18:
The Modify
Style dialog
box.

4. Click OK to save the changes.

5. Depending on where the style rule is located, do one of the following:

- If the style rule is an internal style rule embedded in the open page (or if it's an inline style), save the Web page. (We tell you how in Chapter 2.)

- If the style rule is defined in an external style sheet, save the page and, in the Save Embedded Files dialog box that appears, click OK to save changes to the style sheet file.

Deleting style rules

Delete any style rule that you no longer need. The process for deleting a style rule is almost the same, regardless of whether the style rule is embedded in the open Web page or located in an external style sheet.

To delete a style rule, follow these steps:

1. In the Apply Styles task pane, click the drop-down arrow next to the style rule you want to delete and, from the menu that appears, choose Delete.

In the Manage Styles task pane, right-click the style rule you want to delete and then choose Delete from the pop-up menu.

2. **In the message box that appears, asking you to confirm deleting the style, click Yes.**

   If the style you're deleting is located in an external style sheet, save the Web page that has the style sheet file attached to it. In the Save Embedded Files dialog box that appears, click OK to save changes to the style sheet.

Chapter 8

Putting Page Elements in Their Place

. . . .

. . . .

*I*f you've ever used a desktop publishing program, such as Adobe InDesign or Microsoft Publisher, you've experienced putting stuff on a page and having it sit and stay where you left it. Trying to do the same with a Web page is like trying to hold water in your hands: No matter how hard you grasp, things seem to slip around all over the place. For years, Web designers used tables to corral Web page parts into submission. (We talk about tables in Chapter 10.) But tables have fallen from grace in favor of CSS positioning. CSS has quite a few advantages over tables, not the least of which is that CSS banishes layout and formatting code from the page's content; you can use different style sheets to dress up a plain page for the Web, strip its fancy formatting to make it accessible for all visitors, straighten it out for printing, and simplify it for viewing on a pocket-size PDA.

One thing that makes positioning items on a Web page so tricky is that you have control over only a few size-related factors when you put together your page. Unlike designing for print, when you know the final size of your printed page, your Web visitors set size-related options themselves: monitor resolution, Web browser window size, and text size. Your challenge as a Web designer is to get the best-looking page that works well in a variety of different resolutions and browsers and that doesn't turn into a mishmash of text and pictures when a visitor increases the browser's text size or resizes the browser window.

In this chapter, we introduce you to some CSS positioning concepts and show you some of the Expression Web CSS positioning tools. CSS positioning falls into the realm of intermediate Web page building; this stuff takes time to figure out and even longer to master. It's worth the work, though, because it will soon form the foundation of every well-designed Web site. And, the excellent features in Expression Web help make the concepts you need to know a little easier to grasp. So, have patience, and don't worry if you're still scratching your head after tinkering with it for a while. You're not alone. Plenty of competent Web designers struggle with CSS positioning, partly because of inconsistent browser support and partly because it's just plain tricky stuff. Throughout this chapter, we point you to some excellent sources on the Web for more practice and help.

Many of the instructions in this chapter require you to work more closely with your Web page's code than you do in earlier chapters. If you're a newcomer to HTML, give the first part of Chapter 14 a read-through. If you're new to styles, be sure to read Chapter 7 before taking on CSS positioning. Keep in mind that there are many ways to position page elements by using CSS and there's often no single *right* way. Find the method that works best for your site and your content, and go from there.

See Chapter 7 for a list of good CSS books and online tutorials. Also, visit Chapter 16 for a list of Web design resources. One of our favorite tutorials on CSS and, specifically, CSS for positioning is at www.westciv.com/style_master/house/tutorials/index.html.

The Positioning Building Blocks

Underlying every CSS-positioned page are three basic concepts. Understand these, and you're well on your way to wrestling CSS positioning to the ground. We explain each of these concepts in more detail, but here they are, in their briefs (descriptions, that is):

- ✔ **The almighty `<div>` element:** HTML contains a special set of tags — `<div>` tags — for corralling disparate bits of content into meaningful Web page chunks, or *divisions* (hence the tag name `<div>`). On their own, `<div>` tags don't do much. They don't change the appearance of the content they surround, and they don't make anything happen in the browser. Combine `<div>` tags with CSS, though, and `<div>` tags obediently do the grunt work of making your layout work.

- ✔ **The CSS box model:** We've heard Web designers refer to the CSS box model as the "layout bread and butter." Here's the basic concept: Think of each heading, paragraph, and `<div>` element as a box. (We're talking *block-level* element here, the kind that always starts on a new line and forces a new line to start after it; see Chapter 14 for more information about block-level elements.) Each "box," or block-level element, has four parts:

- *Content area:* The amount of space that the actual text, picture, and other <div> element contents occupy on the screen

- *Padding:* The space between the content and the borders that gives the content breathing room

- *Borders:* The lines on each side of the content — top, right, bottom, and left; content can have borders on any combination of sides or no borders at all

- *Margins:* The space between the borders and other block-level elements

CSS gives you a slew of properties for controlling in minute detail how each side of each part of the box looks. Understand how these properties interact with each other, and you understand how to fine-tune the appearance of each box. Figure 8-1 shows the CSS box model with its parts labeled.

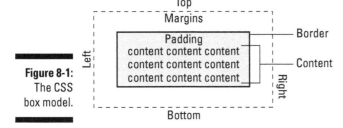

Figure 8-1:
The CSS
box model.

The CSS box model applies also to *inline* HTML elements, such as a chunk of text or a word surrounded by <span> tags or a hyperlink. For the purpose of this chapter, we focus on just block-level boxes.

✔ **Document flow:** No matter what a page looks like in a browser and despite any fancy CSS formatting and layout, the content sits in a document in a particular order. In the absence of any positioning or fancy formatting, the first item appears in the upper-left corner of the browser, followed vertically by the next item, and the next, and so on down the page. Wherever an element is in the document flow affects what it does and where it goes on the page when you start moving it around with CSS positioning properties.

Divide and Conquer with <div> Tags

To move content on a Web page into position, take a step back from the minutiae of the individual headings, paragraphs, and pictures and identify the big chunks of content that will become the different parts of the page. After you figure out what the different parts are, you surround each part with special HTML tags known as <div> tags. Using <div> tags to divide page content into sections is like putting a bunch of items into a clear plastic box. In fact, each <div> *element* (by which we mean the opening and closing <div> tags and the content between them) becomes its own "CSS box" for which you can define properties for the content area, padding, borders, and margins.

A simple example of a nonformatted page with its parts labeled appears in Figure 8-2. It has four sections:

✔ A header or title (a first-level heading)

✔ A list of hyperlinks for site navigation (an unordered list)

✔ The main page content (which consists of a second-level heading, a few third-level headings, and some paragraphs)

✔ A footer paragraph for the copyright information

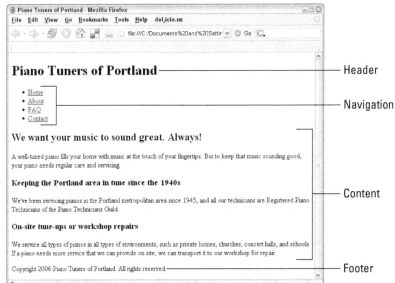

Figure 8-2:
A non-formatted Web page with four main parts.

Put plenty of time into structuring your page content so that it follows a logical flow and a hierarchical heading structure. You'll find it easier to build your page layout because you can easily identify the purpose of each part and where it should go on the page. See Chapter 14 for more information.

Wrapping <div> tags around existing page content

After you decide what the main parts of your page are, you need to enclose each page part with a set of <div> tags. This process is often called *wrapping a <div>* because that's essentially what you're doing — *wrapping* the opening and closing <div> tags around the chunk of content so that you can create styles for formatting and positioning it as a whole element. You can wrap a pair of <div> tags around a single element — such as a paragraph or heading — or a chunk of content, such as multiple headings, paragraphs, or pictures or a table or form (or any combination).

To wrap a <div> around a single element on a page, follow these steps:

1. **In Design view, place the cursor in the element around which you want to wrap the set of <div> tags.**

   For instance, place the cursor in a paragraph or heading.

2. **On the Quick Tag Selector bar, click the down arrow next to the selected item's tag and, from the drop-down list, select Wrap Tag, as shown in Figure 8-3.**

   To wrap a <div> around a *list*, click the <ul> or <ol> tag, not the <li> tag, which selects only that single item in the list.

Figure 8-3:
The Quick Tag Selector bar menu.

   The Quick Tag Editor appears, showing an opening and closing angle bracket in the text entry area. The cursor blinks patiently between them.

3. **Type div and then click the check mark to close the Quick Tag Editor and write the <div> tag into the page's code.**

Notice that the item you wrapped the <div> around doesn't look any different in Design view and you can't see the <div> tags. However, if you place the cursor in the element and click the <div> tag on the Quick Tag Selector bar, Expression Web selects the <div> in Design view and shows you the <div> element's default margins as pink, diagonal line shading, as shown in Figure 8-4. (The margins are one part of the CSS box, which we explain in more detail later in this chapter.)

Figure 8-4:
A selected
`<div>`
element in
Design
view.

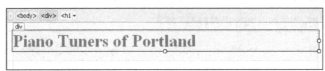

Take a peek at your page's code after you wrapped the `<div>` tag around a single element. Here's the first-level heading shown in Figure 8-2:

```
<div>
        <h1>Piano Tuners of Portland</h1>
</div>
```

If this happened to be the *only* content on our Web page, the content tags would be nested in this order:

```
<body>
<div>
        <h1>Piano Tuners of Portland</h1>
</div>
</body>
```

Wrapping a `<div>` around *more than one* element on your page — such as some headings and paragraphs — is a little more involved and requires that you roll up your sleeves and edit your page's code slightly. We walk you through the process step by step.

All content that belongs together as part of one `<div>` element must sit together on the page. In other words, you can't wrap a set of `<div>` tags around a heading at one end of the page and another set of `<div>` tags around a paragraph at the other (leaving everything between them out in the cold) and expect them to be treated as one `<div>` element. Think of it as calf roping: If two calves are standing next to each other, you can lasso both of them in one throw (well, maybe). If the two calves you want are on opposite ends of the corral with a bunch of other calves (and maybe the rodeo clown) between them, you're out of luck. (Our apologies if this concept seems obvious; we just want you to fully grasp how to wrap `<div>` tags because your success with CSS positioning depends on it!) Here's how to wrap a `<div>` around a chunk of content on the page:

1. **In either Code view or the code portion of Split view (at the bottom of the workspace window, click Code or Split), place the cursor directly to the left of where you want the `<div>` tag to begin.**

In the Web page shown in Figure 8-2, we want to wrap a set of <div> tags around the page's *main content* area, so we placed the cursor to the left of the first <h2> tag, as shown in Figure 8-5.

Figure 8-5:
Starting
position
for the
<div> tag.

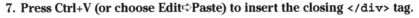

```
<h2>We want your music to sound great. Always!</h2>
<p>A well-tuned piano fills your home with music at the touch of your finge
But to keep that music sounding good, your piano needs regular care and se
<h3>Keeping the Portland area in tune since the 1940s </h3>
```

2. **To make your code easier to read, press the Enter key to insert a blank line and then move the cursor up to the blank line (you place the opening <div> tag on the blank line).**

3. **Type an opening angle bracket (<).**

   A drop-down list of HTML tags appears.

4. **On the drop-down list, double-click the div option (you have to scroll the list), and then close the tag by typing the closing angle bracket (>).**

   Notice that as soon as you type the closing bracket, the closing </div> tag appears, like this: <div></div>. The <div> tags aren't properly wrapped around the content. In the next step, you move the closing tag to its rightful home.

5. **Highlight the closing </div> tag and press Ctrl+X (or choose Edit⇨Cut).**

6. **Scroll down through your page's code until you find the last closing tag of the page content around which you're wrapping the <div> tags.**

   To make your code easier to read, insert a blank line to hold the closing </div> tag.

7. **Press Ctrl+V (or choose Edit⇨Paste) to insert the closing </div> tag.**

   Make sure the closing </div> tag comes after the last closing tag of the content around which you're wrapping the <div>.

   For example, in the Web page shown in Figure 8-2, the "content" <div> tag would end after the paragraph that ends with the word *repair;* therefore, the closing </div> tag comes after the last </p> tag, like this: repair.</p></div>.

You may notice that various tags in the code turn red and highlighted as you type and that squiggly lines appear under some tags. That's Expression Web's IntelliSense (the "code police") jumping into action, letting you know that something is amiss. In this case, you can ignore it; as soon as you finish adding your <div> tags, all will be well. (See Chapter 14 for more information about IntelliSense.)

Again, note that your content looks the same in Design view. Click the <div> tag on the Quick Tag Selector bar, however, and Expression Web shows you the <div> element with the content it contains and its default margins.

Adding <div> elements and then adding content

Rather than wrap <div> tags around *existing* page content, you can add a <div> element to a blank part of an existing Web page or to a blank new page. This process works best if you already thought out what content goes into which page part, but haven't yet added the content to the page, or if you plan to copy and paste content from somewhere else into a new <div> element.

To add a set of <div> tags to a page (to which you later add content), follow these steps:

1. **Open the page to which you want to add the <div> element.**

2. **In the Toolbox, drag the <div> icon to the page's Design view.**

   A light gray, dotted rectangle appears on the page, highlighted with a thin blue line and with div on its tab, as shown in Figure 8-6.

Figure 8-6:
A <div> element without content, in Design and Code views.

To add content to the empty <div> element, click inside the <div> element's dotted rectangle and type or add content just as you add content to a blank part of the page. Text added inside the <div> element doesn't automatically get formatted as a paragraph, like it does when you type directly on a blank part of a Web page. Be sure to select and format each piece of text by choosing from the drop-down list of text styles (such as Paragraph <p>, Heading 1 <h1>, or Heading 2 <h2>) on either the Common or Formatting toolbar.

Choose View⇨Formatting Marks⇨Show, and then make sure that Tag Marks is selected on the drop-down list of formatting marks. This action turns on visual markers for opening and closing tags so that they're displayed in Design view. You can see the start and end positions for the <div> tags in addition to the tags for other bits of content. Being able to see the tags helps you drag and drop content from somewhere else on the page into the <div> element or shift things around within the <div>. You probably want to turn off Show Tag Marks when you're done, though; tag marks are a bit clunky and distracting.

You can add pictures and other elements to the <div> element. When you're finished adding content, check to ensure that the <div> tags wrap around everything you want included in the <div> element.

Although it's tempting, keep yourself from dragging the sides of the <div> element's dotted rectangle in Design view to change its dimensions. Doing so gives it a fixed width and height. Instead, add the content and let the <div> element resize accordingly. Later in this chapter, we show you how to create style rules that target the <div> element so that you can control its location on the page and its size more precisely.

Here's what a chunk of content wrapped in <div> tags looks like in the code:

```
<div>
            <h2>A subheading</h2>
            <p>a paragraph</p>
            <h3>A sub subheading</h3>
            <p>another paragraph</p>
</div>
```

Giving a <div> element an identity all its own

To get the full benefit of using <div> elements for positioning, you need to name each <div> element with either a class or an ID. You can then use the class or ID name as the selector for a style rule that controls every aspect of how the <div> element looks and where it's placed on the page.

For the main content sections of a Web page, Web designers use IDs rather than classes because each <div> element identifies a *unique* part of the Web page, of which there's only one: the *one* page header, the *one* navigation area, the *one* main content area, and the *one* footer. Think of <div> elements with IDs as labeled, plastic storage boxes in a downstairs closet: You have *one* box labeled Old Photos ("I'll sort those one of these days"), *one* box labeled Unfinished Sewing Projects ("I'll finish these when I have more time"), and *one* box labeled Clothes for Johnny to Grow Into ("The reason that those photos aren't sorted and those sewing projects are unfinished!").

You have a number of ways to add an ID to a `<div>` tag. Here are a few of the easiest:

✔ **Use the Quick Tag Selector bar:** On the Quick Tag Selector bar, click the down arrow next to the `<div>` tag and, from the drop-down list, select Edit Tag. In the Quick Tag Editor text box, type the `id` name inside the `<div>` tag. Make sure that it's properly formatted, as shown in Figure 8-7.

✔ **Use the Tag Properties task pane:** Unless you moved or closed the Tag Properties task pane, it lives in the lower-left corner, with its buddy, the CSS Properties task pane. (If you don't see it, choose Task Panes➪Tag Properties to pop it open.) In the Tag Properties task pane's Attributes column, type the ID's value in the text box next to the `id` field, as shown in Figure 8-8.

✔ **Use Code view:** Inside the `<div>` element's opening tag, click to the right of the word `div`, press the spacebar, and enter `id="name"`. (Expression Web's code IntelliSense helps you enter it correctly by providing a menu of attributes and adding the quotation marks; see Chapter 14 for more information about IntelliSense.)

Figure 8-7:
The `id` value in the Quick Tag Editor.

Figure 8-8:
The Tag Properties task pane.

If you're ready to create a style for the `<div>` element, you can create an ID-based style rule and add the ID to the `<div>` in one fell swoop. We cover creating style rules in detail in Chapter 7, and we talk more about style rules for positioning later in this chapter. Here are the basic steps for creating an ID-based style rule:

1. **Select the `<div>` element by putting the cursor anywhere inside the `<div>` and then, on the Quick Tag Selector bar, clicking the `<div>` tag.**

2. **Choose Format⇨New Style; or, in the Apply Styles or Manage Styles task pane, click New Style.**

   The New Style dialog box appears.

3. **In the Selector text box, type the # character (press Shift+3), and then type the ID name.**

   The # character tells Expression Web (in CSS-ese) that the style rule targets an HTML element with an ID.

   No space should appear between # and the name, like this: `#idname`.

4. **Select the Apply New Style to Document Selection check box.**

5. **Define properties for the style rule and then click OK to save the style rule and apply the ID name to the selected `<div>` element.**

Returning to our sample Web page shown in Figure 8-2, here's the code for the page header's opening `<div>` element after we added the ID to it:

```
<div id="header">
        <h1>Piano Tuners of Portland</h1>
</div>
```

Here are all the IDs for our page, in order of each part:

```
<div id="header">
<div id="navigation">
<div id="content">
<div id="footer">
```

You can give your `<div>` elements any `id` value you want, as long as the name is unique. (You can't have two `<div id="content">` elements on the same page.) In general, keep names to one word or two words joined with an underscore (_), like this: `main_content`.

In this section, we describe using `<div>` elements to define *unique* content areas on a page that then get *unique* ID names. But you can wrap `<div>` tags around *any* chunk of content on a page that you want to identify as a `<div>` element and create styles for, regardless of whether it's unique. Here's an example of when you would want to assign a *class* rather than an ID to a series of `<div>` elements: You're creating a photo gallery page with a bunch of styled "boxes," each of which contains a different photo and caption but has the same borders, background, and font, for example. You would wrap each photo and caption in a `<div>` (thereby making each one a separate `<div>` element) and then create a *class*-based style (such as `.photo`) that controls the formatting of all `<div class="photo">` elements on the page. Figure 8-9, later in this chapter, shows a series of `<div>` elements controlled by a class-based style.

The CSS Box Is No Ordinary Box

Combine the almighty <div> element and the CSS box model, and you get an unbeatable duo, like peanut butter and jelly, snow and December, or mashed potatoes and gravy. After you wrap a bunch of content in <div> tags, you have a box with its requisite four parts — content, padding, borders, and margins — ready to accept orders from the CSS styles you create for it.

Understanding the CSS box

We borrow an analogy from Richard Mansfield's *CSS Web Design For Dummies* (Wiley) to help explain the box concept and how boxes interact with one another. Picture a series of matted and framed pictures hanging on a wall: Each item takes up a certain amount of space on the wall, determined by the four parts of its box. The box *content* is the space taken up by the piece of art itself, inside the mat window. The mat represents the box's *padding,* the visual space that separates the content from its frame. The frame represents the box's *borders,* and the space between each item on the wall comprises the box's *margins*. Figure 8-1, earlier in this chapter, shows a diagram of the CSS box model and its parts.

Figure 8-9 shows three items in the Expression Web Design view, with the item in the middle selected to show you how Expression Web displays a box's padding and margins. Each item shown in Figure 8-9 is a <div> element with the class attribute "box" (<div class="box">; we used a class rather than an ID because there are several boxes, each styled the same).

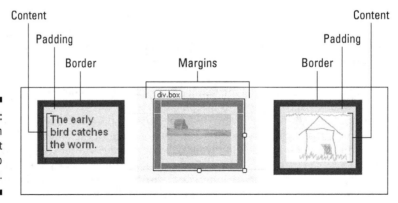

Figure 8-9: In Design view, select an item to see its box.

CSS layouts to go

If you want to order up a ready-to-use set of <div> elements that are already created and ID-ed, you can start a new page by using one of the CSS layouts that come with Expression Web. Here's how:

1. **Choose File⇨New⇨Page.**

2. **On the Page tab in the New dialog box, click to select CSS Layouts in the first column. Then select a page layout style in the second column.**

   The Preview area shows a sketch of the selected layout style, and the description area tells you a little about the layout.

3. **Click OK to create a page with the selected layout.**

   Expression Web creates a Web page containing <div> elements with a unique id already added for each part (Untitled_

x.htm), along with an attached CSS style sheet file (Untitled_x.css) complete with style rules ready to be filled with properties. (We talk more about external style sheets in Chapter 9.)

4. **Save the page file.**

   Expression Web prompts you to name the page file and then the CSS file. You can then add content to your heart's content (no pun intended) and style away.

   Depending on which layout you choose, some style properties may already be set to position columns and set widths. The Preview area shows you which columns get wider or narrower when the visitor changes the browser (indicated by a double arrow and dotted line) and which columns use fixed widths (indicated by a solid line).

Here's how the elements are set up:

- ✔ The <div> element's background is gray (the text color is black). This means that the background color for all content is gray.

- ✔ Ten pixels of *padding* have been added to all sides of the content.

- ✔ The *borders* are 10 pixels wide and black.

- ✔ The *margins* are set to 20 pixels on all sides.

- ✔ The *content* of the left box is the paragraph text "The early bird catches the worm." The *content* of the middle and right boxes are pictures (a photo JPEG and a GIF image). We specified a width of 100 pixels for the content area of all boxes; the pictures are each 100 pixels wide, so they take up the full content width. We did not set a height so that the box could adjust vertically to accommodate the height of the content. (To display the boxes side by side, we *floated* them; we talk about float later in this chapter.)

Notice that in the left box you can't distinguish the padding from the content background. That's because the *padding* background is always the same as the *content* background. In the middle and right boxes, the padding adds space between the content (the picture) and the borders so that the gray content background color shows up. Margins are always transparent, so the page background color surrounds each object. You can see the margins only if you select the <div> element in Design view, as we did in Figure 8-9.

When figuring out the *width* that a block-level element takes up on the page (such as the <div> boxes shown in Figure 8-9), you add together these individual width values: `margin-left`, `border-width-left`, `padding-left`, `width` (the *content* width), `padding-right`, `border-width-right`, and `margin-right`. In Figure 8-9 the width of each <div> is 180 pixels (`margin-left: 20px; border-width-left: 10px; padding-left: 10px; width: 100px; padding-right: 10px; border-width-right: 10px; margin-right: 20px;`). When laying out boxes side by side in your page — such as <div> elements displayed side by side (the boxes shown in Figure 8-9) — add the margins, borders, padding, and content of all the elements to figure out their combined width. We show you a fixed-width, two-column layout example later in this chapter. (See the later section "Creating and positioning a page content 'container'" for more details on fixed versus relative layouts, and see the later section "Using float to create a two-column layout" for the example.)

The box model has a couple of quirks. The first one has to do with the way the CSS box works. The second is a browser bug. (Grrrr.)

✔ If two boxes sit next to each other *horizontally* on the page (as do the floated boxes shown in Figure 8-9), margins for both boxes are used. If two boxes follow each other *vertically* on the page, the margins between them collapse, and the larger of the two margins is used to separate the two boxes. Figure 8-10 shows the boxes from Figure 8-9 stacked vertically on the page. In this example, the margin for each box is 20 pixels, so 20 pixels of space appear between the boxes. If one box had a 30-pixel margin and the other had 10 pixels, the margin between them would be 30 pixels, the larger of the two margins.

Figure 8-10:
Vertically
stacked
boxes make
margins
collapse.

✔ Microsoft Internet Explorer 5 for Windows incorrectly calculates the box model, by *subtracting* margins and padding from the content width rather than *adding* their values to the content width. Internet Explorer 6 and 7, as well as other browsers, get it right.

Setting CSS box properties in Expression Web

In Figure 8-9, we set the `border`, `margin`, and `padding` properties to the same value all the way around the content area. But you can set individual values for each property and each side, which gives you a lot of control when tweaking the individual items on your page.

Measuring up

You may be wondering why so many measurement values are used for setting style properties, and which ones to use. The answer is — it depends. Remember that your Web visitors have a lot of control over how they view your page: They set their computer monitor's resolution and the size of their Web browser's window. They can also change the default text size. When specifying properties values that relate to text, such as font size, line height, line spacing, and even the width and height of content areas that *contain* text, you should use *relative* value measurements as much as possible. The most common relative measurements for text and text content areas are

✔ **Percent (%):** Increase or decrease size by a percentage value. For example, specifying `font-size: 150%` means "increase the font size 1½ times." Percentages are also useful for specifying the width of certain areas of the Web page that you want to adjust to the width of the browser window, such as a main content area.

✔ **em:** The relative measurement value *em* is the approximate width of the lowercase letter *m* of a font. One em is the starting point from which you decrease or increase (.5 em means "decrease by one-half," and 1.5 em means "increase by one-half"); *ex*, the approximate height of a font's lowercase letter *x*, is less commonly used.

Use **pixels** (px) to specify *exact* width and height. Always use pixels to specify the width and height of images that appear in the content (not as part of the background). Pixels are often used for border widths and for parts of the page that you don't want to change when the browser window is resized (such as a side column for navigation, news, ads, or announcements, for example). If you use pixels for font size, however, the pixel value freezes the text at that size and prevents the Web visitor from changing the text size if necessary.

Other measurement values are used, such as inch (in), pica (pc), point (pt), centimeter (cm), and millimeter (mm), but these should be used only when creating style sheets for printing.

CSS box properties (margins, padding, and borders) for each individual side of the CSS box are written in style rules in this order: top, right, bottom, left. Think of it as moving clockwise around the box, starting at the top. For example, the style property `margin: 5px 10px 15px 20px;` sets the top margin to 5 pixels, the right margin to 10, the bottom to 15, and the left to 20.

In the New Style and Modify Style dialog boxes and in the CSS Properties task pane, use options in these categories to control the CSS box model properties:

- **Box:** Set width values for padding and margins, either the same for all sides or individually. (Figure 8-11 shows the Box category settings in the Modify Style dialog box.)

- **Border:** Set the border style (solid or dotted, for example), width, and color, either the same for all sides or individually for each side.

- **Background:** Set options for the content area's background color. If you place a picture in the content area's background, set options for whether it repeats or scrolls or appears in a specified horizontal or vertical position.

- **Position:** Set options for the content area's width and height (`width` and `height` properties).

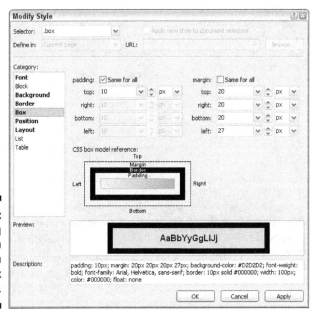

Figure 8-11: Set padding and margin properties in the Box category.

Changing margins and padding in Design view

You can adjust the width of margins and padding for each individual side of an element in Design view by dragging with the cursor. Although this method is a bit tedious for changing all four sides of an object (because you have to change each side individually), it's useful for small adjustments and design tweaks. As you drag the cursor, Expression Web tells you which side you're changing and the width, as shown in Figure 8-12. The picture on the left shows you what you see as you change the *margins* for one of the element's sides; the picture on the right shows *padding*.

Figure 8-12:
Drag a side
to change
margin and
padding
width.

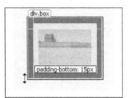

This technique works for block-level elements only (paragraphs, lists, `<div>` elements, headings — anything that forces a line break after it; see Chapter 14 for a quickie list of block and inline elements).

To change a margin width by dragging, follow these steps:

1. **In Design view, select the object whose margins you want to change.**

   Click the object once, and then click the little tab containing the object's tag in the upper-left corner of the blue box that surrounds it, or click the tag on the Quick Tag Selector bar.

   Pink, diagonal line shading appears around the object, indicating current margins (see Figure 8-12).

2. **Hover the cursor over the solid pink horizontal or vertical line corresponding to the side whose margin you want to change and, when the cursor becomes a two-sided arrow, click and drag.**

   A box pops up, telling you the margin width as you drag.

3. **When the margin is the desired size, release the mouse button.**

    This technique is a little tricky at first. If you don't get it right the first time, you can drag again or use the Undo command (Edit➪Undo or Ctrl+Z) to go back to the original size and start over.

To change the *padding* width, follow the instructions just given but press and hold down the Shift key while you drag. Padding lines are light blue.

Changing width and height in Design view

You can change the width or height of an element's *content area* by dragging with the mouse in Design view. You can change either width or height or both at the same time. To do so, follow these steps:

1. **Click the element whose content area you want to change.**

   A blue line appears around it, and the tag name appears on a little tab in the upper-left corner.

2. **Move the cursor over the right or bottom border or the lower-right corner until tiny, rectangular handles appear and the cursor becomes a two-sided arrow.**

3. **Click and drag, and then release the mouse button when the object is the desired size.**

   A box pops up with a message telling you the dimensions as you drag.

   If you want to change both the width and the height while keeping the dimensions in proportion, hold down the Shift key while you drag the lower-right corner's handle.

Document Flow and Positioning

To understand how to get page part boxes (`<div>` elements) to go where *you* want them to go, it's important to grasp how they naturally land on the page in the absence of any marching orders. In Figure 8-13, we gave each of the four parts of our Web page a different-colored 1-pixel border (but no other formatting) so that you can picture each `<div>` element as a CSS box and see the natural flow, width, and position of each one. In the absence of any positioning styles, each box stretches horizontally across the width of the browser window. Each `<div>` box stacks vertically, one on top of the other, down the page in the order they appear in the document. There's nothing sexy about this page, but it has good "bones" — a logical structure, well-defined page parts, and hierarchical headings.

You have as many ways to create CSS-based layouts as you have to cook a Thanksgiving turkey, and all Web designers keep a favorite arsenal of styles tucked in their style sheets for this purpose. In this section, we show you a *few* ways to achieve a *few* positioning effects so that you can get used to using the positioning properties in Expression Web. See the CSS resources we list in Chapter 7. Chapter 16 offers many more CSS positioning and formatting resources.

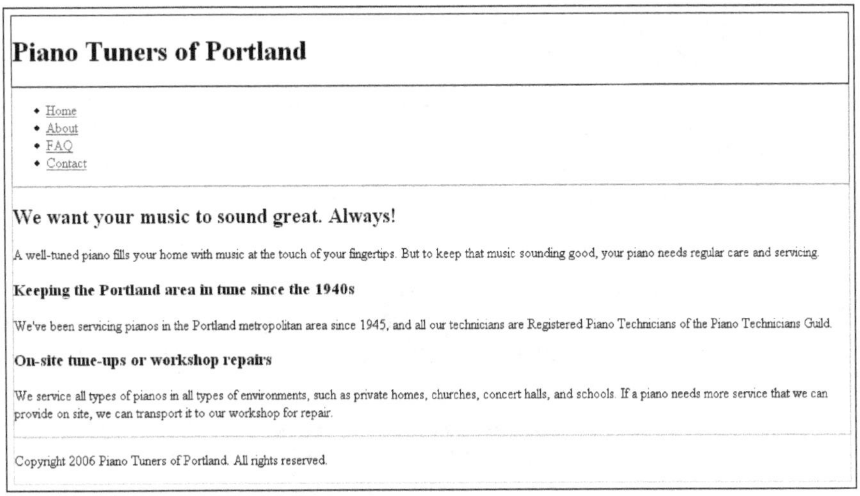

Piano Tuners of Portland

- Home
- About
- FAQ
- Contact

We want your music to sound great. Always!

A well-tuned piano fills your home with music at the touch of your fingertips. But to keep that music sounding good, your piano needs regular care and servicing.

Keeping the Portland area in tune since the 1940s

We've been servicing pianos in the Portland metropolitan area since 1945, and all our technicians are Registered Piano Technicians of the Piano Technicians Guild.

On-site tune-ups or workshop repairs

We service all types of pianos in all types of environments, such as private homes, churches, concert halls, and schools. If a piano needs more service that we can provide on site, we can transport it to our workshop for repair.

Copyright 2006 Piano Tuners of Portland. All rights reserved.

Figure 8-13: Each `<div>` element follows the natural document flow.

Ready, set, layout

Before you start applying CSS positioning properties to your `<div>`-divided page parts, here are a couple of get-ready tips that make laying out your page in Expression Web easier and save you time and work down the road:

✔ **Change the Expression Web CSS sizing, positioning, and floating option:** By default, Expression Web writes style information for dimensions (width and height), positioning, and floating as *inline* styles. (We cover the different types of styles in Chapter 7.) Inline styles cannot be moved to external style sheets. We're pretty sure that you'll want to use your layout on other pages in your Web site after you get it looking the way you want. Why not set it up right in the first place? To change the default layout, choose Tools➪Page Editor Options and then click the CSS tab. For the Sizing, Positioning, and Floating option, select CSS (classes). We talk about external style sheets in Chapter 9.

✔ **Show rulers:** Regardless of whether you choose a fixed- or proportional-width layout, rules give you a helpful visual guide while designing your page. Show rulers (in pixels) by choosing View➪Ruler and Grid➪Show Ruler. You may also want to turn on the page grid by choosing View➪Ruler and Grid➪Show Grid.

✔ **Pick a page size:** Adjusting the page size in Design view to match a common browser resolution helps you design your page so that it looks good at that resolution. Expression Web lets you pick a page size that matches your monitor's current resolution setting and smaller (but not larger) resolution settings. After you pick a page size, Expression Web sizes its Design view to the width and height in available pixels at that resolution. (The browser takes up some width and height to display scroll bars and borders, for example.) To pick a page size, choose View⇨ Page Size and then select a size from the drop-down list. You're welcome to make your layout larger than the page size setting you choose to display in Design view. The page size setting just gives you a rough idea of what your layout looks like at that monitor resolution while you're designing your page.

Keep your audience in mind when designing your page. Although the most common monitor resolution is now 1024 x 768, many people still use 800 x 600, especially those with older computers or less-than-perfect eyesight.

✔ **Create a style rule for the whole page:** To avoid having to specify fonts for each element on the page, create a style rule that uses the `<body>` tag as the selector, and set the "font family" there. All the text on the page uses that font unless you define a more specific rule that overrides the page font. This is also a great place to eliminate the bit of space in the upper-left edge of the browser window that all browsers insert to offset the page content from the top and left edges of the browser window. (Look at Figure 8-13 and notice that the content doesn't sit exactly in the upper-left corner.) Some browsers use margins, and some use padding to insert the space. Set margins and padding for the `<body>` style to 0 to override browser settings. If you want, you can also specify a page background color or image in this style rule, and set the text color to something other than the default black.

Here's an element-based style rule that we set for our sample page. (It uses the `<body>` tag as the selector.) This style rule sets the font family and scales down the overall font size a bit (to .8em, or 80%). It also sets the background color to a very light gray (#EEEEEE) and eliminates the page's default margins and padding by setting them both to 0 (we use this body style in the rest of the screen shots in this chapter):

```
body {
        font-family: Arial, Helvetica, sans-serif;
        font-size: .8em;
        background-color: #EEEEEE;
        padding: 0px;
        margin: 0px;
}
```

Creating and positioning a page content "container"

You probably see Web sites where the page appears to sit on top of a colored (or textured) background and the page content is centered in the browser window. Many Expression Web templates are designed this way. Web designers achieve this effect by wrapping all the individual page parts (the <div> elements that make up each section) in one big "mega-<div>" (often given an ID, such as "container" — <div id="container">). This makes the whole content area of the page into one big CSS box, whose overall width can be set to either an *absolute*, or *fixed,* width (in pixels) or a *proportional* width, specified as a percentage of the browser window. In a *proportional*-width layout, the content width stretches and shrinks as the visitor changes the browser window. Fixed-width layouts set an *absolute* width in pixels that stays the same no matter what size the browser window is.

If you choose to use a fixed-width layout, realize that if your design is too wide for a particular visitor's browser, that visitor is forced to scroll horizontally to read your text. If you ever had to do this, you know how annoying it can be. Pick the lowest common screen width that your visitors are likely to use, and set the width to fit well in that amount of space. (For example, the useable width for an 800 x 600 monitor resolution is 760 pixels.)

When we use the term *content area,* we're referring to all the visual elements of the Web page grouped together as a whole, not just the "content" <div> element.

To wrap container <div> tags around all the other <div> elements in the page, follow the instructions in the section "Wrapping <div> tags around existing page content," earlier in this chapter.

Here's how the page part <div> elements nest inside the mega-<div> for our sample Web page (we replaced each <div> element's content details with a short description for brevity):

```
<div id="container">
        <div id="header">(page heading)</div>
        <div id="navigation">(links)</div>
        <div id="content">(content)</div>
        <div id="footer">(copyright)</div>
</div>
```

After you wrap the container <div> tags around your page content and give it an ID, you're ready to create a style for it that positions the container in the center of the browser window and sets its width. To do so, follow these steps:

1. **Choose Format⇨New Style or, in the Manage Styles or Apply Styles task pane, click New Style.**

   The New Style dialog box appears.

2. **In the Selector box, type #container (or whatever ID you gave the container <div> element).**

   If you didn't yet give the <div> element an id value, cancel the New Style dialog box and select the <div> element in Design view. Then open the New Style dialog box again (refer to Step 1). Type the selector (refer to Step 2) and make sure that you select the Apply the New Style to Document Selection check box.

   No space should appear between the # character and the ID name.

3. **In the Category list, select Box.**

4. **In the margin area, deselect the Same for All check box.**

5. **For right and left margins, select Auto from the drop-down list box.**

   This step centers the container in the browser window.

6. **From the Category list, select Position.**

7. **In the Width text box, enter the container's total width.**

   For a *proportional*-width layout, enter the width value as a percentage (such as **90** for 90 percent) and then select % for the unit of measure, as shown in Figure 8-14.

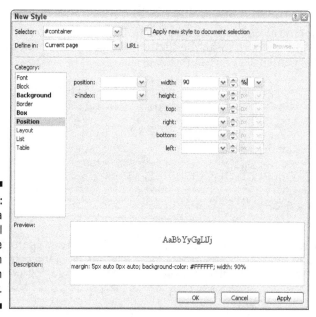

Figure 8-14:
Set a proportional width for the container in the Position category.

For a *fixed*-width layout, enter the width value in pixels.

For both *proportional-* and *fixed*-width layouts, refrain from setting a Height value. This action lets the page get as long as it needs to if the text content and size get bigger (for example, if a near-sighted visitor makes the text really large).

8. **Set any other properties you want for the container.**

   Figure 8-14 shows that we set the container background to white so that the container stands out against the light gray page background (in the Background category). In the Box category, we also set the top margin to 5 pixels, to bring the top of the container down slightly from the top of the browser window. Although Figure 8-14 shows just the Position category, all other properties that we set in other categories appear in the Description area.

9. **When you finish setting properties for your style rule, click OK.**

Figure 8-15 shows our sample page, centered and with a proportional width set to 90 percent.

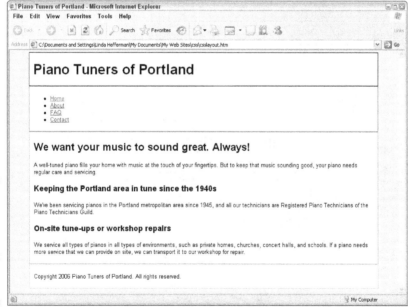

Figure 8-15: Our sample page container, as it appears in a browser.

Here's the style rule for our sample container `<div>`:

```
#container {
        margin: 5px auto 0px auto;
        background-color: #FFFFFF;
        width: 90%;
}
```

Depending on which style properties you set, your style rule may look different from ours. For example, the individual margins for each side may be listed separately (`margin-top: 5px; margin-right: auto; margin-bottom: 0px; margin-left: auto;`).

Obviously, we would need to set many more style properties to make the content of each part look good, but the overall layout is in place, with the main container set to be resized with the browser window. Because each page part `<div>` element gets its width from its containing element (the container `<div>`), all the parts are resized as a whole. It's a simple, functional layout. With a little more work, some background colors, a floated picture, and some styles that format the list of hyperlinks so that it looks like a link bar, our layout is beginning to take shape (although it isn't finished, by any stretch of the imagination). Take a look at Figure 8-16.

Figure 8-16:
Our page
with some
content
areas
styled.

Of the many ways that we could use to format hyperlinks into a horizontal bar, we used the following style rules (for other ways, check out some CSS books and online tutorials, as well as Expression Web template style sheets):

```
#navigation ul {
        padding-left: 0px;
        list-style-type: none;
        width: 100%;
        float: left;
        background-color: #808080;
        margin: 0px;
}
#navigation li {
        display: inline;
}
#navigation ul a {
        display: block;
        float: left;
        padding: .2em 1em .2em 1em;
        text-decoration: none;
        color: #FFFFFF;
        background-color: #808080;
        border-right-style: solid;
        border-right-width: 1px;
        border-right-color: #FFFFFF;
}
#navigation ul a:hover {
        color: #000000;
        background-color: #EEEEEE;
}
```

In these style rules, we bolded a few positioning properties that are useful for styling hyperlinks into navigation bars. The CSS property display: inline changes block-level elements into inline elements so that they appear on the same line. Conversely, display: block changes an inline element into a block-level element, which makes it into a CSS box complete with content, padding, border, and margin possibilities. In these style rules, list items (<li>) are changed from block to inline, and hyperlinks (<a>) are changed from inline to block. See Chapter 14 for more information about block and inline elements. Note that the selector for each of these style rules starts with #navigation. This ensures that these style rules target only the unordered list (<ul>), list items (<li>), and hyperlinks (<a>) that are located inside the navigation <div> element (<div id="navigation">).

Using float to create a two-column layout

The CSS float property is useful for moving CSS boxes (your page part <div> elements) into a side-by-side, two-column layout. When you float a page element, it moves up and over in the direction you tell it, as far as it can go, to either the left or the right. If there's room, the next element in the document flow moves up beside it to "wrap" around it. (We show you how to use float to wrap text around a picture in Chapter 5.) In Figure 8-17, we borrowed some style rules from the Expression Web template Organization 5 to create a fixed-width, two-column layout with our four `<div>` elements (header, navigation, content, and footer) nested inside their container `<div>`. Both the navigation and content `<div>` elements are floated to the left. The footer has the property `clear: both` set in its style rule to force it to fall below the floated elements.

Figure 8-17: A two-column layout with floated navigation and content `<div>` elements.

This layout takes a little math to get it lined up correctly, and you need to call on your CSS box savvy to make sure that you correctly add together all the widths of all the margins, padding, borders, and content areas. The width of the container `<div>` element is set to 700 pixels so that it fits easily in an 800 x 600 browser window. It still centers itself in the browser window, thanks to the left and right margins set to `auto`. The widths of borders, margins, padding, and content areas for the two floated `<div>` elements (navigation and content) are carefully calculated so that the two columns line up perfectly under the page header. To take a closer look at the various style rules and their properties, create a Web site from the Organization 5 template (we tell you how in Chapter 1) and look at the `style3.css` style sheet.

A floated element must have a specified width, although the width can be set to a percentage of the element's containing body — either a containing `<div>` or the browser window — or as a fixed pixel width, as in this example. Pictures have preset widths and heights, so they work as floated elements without using a style rule to specify their width. In Figure 8-17, the piano picture is floated to the left inside the content `<div>` element.

To float a `<div>` element, follow these steps:

1. **Choose Format⇨New Style or, in either the Manage Styles task pane or the Apply Styles task pane, click New Style.**

   The New Style dialog box appears.

   If you already have an ID-based style rule for the <div> element you want to float, in the Apply Styles task pane, click the down arrow next to the style rule and select Modify Style from the drop-down list. The Modify Style dialog box appears. Skip to Step 3.

2. **In the Selector box, type** *#idname* **(where** *idname* **is the id value you gave the <div>).**

   In our example, we floated the navigation and the content <div> elements, so we used #navigation for one style rule and #content for the other.

3. **From the Category list, select Position.**

4. **Set the width for the <div> element you're floating.**

   Remember that this measurement applies to the width that the <div> element's content occupies. Padding, borders, and margins are added to this value.

   In our example, we set the width of the navigation <div> to 148 pixels and the content <div> to 518 pixels.

5. **From the Category list, select Layout.**

6. **From the Float drop-down list, select the desired value. (For example, select Left to float the element to the left.).**

   In our example, we floated both the navigation <div> and the content <div> to the left.

7. **Set any other properties you want for the container.**

   In Figure 8-17, we set the background color for each individual <div> element to white rather than set the background for the container <div> to white. If we had kept the container background white, it would have been shown in the margins between each <div> element. We also changed the borders for each of the four page part <div> elements to dark gray.

8. **When you finish setting properties for your style rule, click OK.**

To force a <div> element to appear below one or more floated elements (as we did for the footer <div>), in the Layout category, set clear to both; clear: both ensures that it appears below all floated elements, whether it's floated to the left or to the right.

It takes time to get the hang of using the `float` property. Check out the excellent online Floatorial by Max Design at `http://css.maxdesign.com.au/floatutorial`.

Here are all the style rules for the page shown in Figure 8-17:

```
body {
        font-family: Arial, Helvetica, sans-serif;
        font-size: .8em;
        background-color: #EEEEEE;
        padding: 0px;
        margin: 0px;
}
#container {
        margin: 10px auto 0px auto;
        width: 700px;
}
#header {
        border: 1px solid #808080;
        text-align: center;
        width: 698px;
        background-color: #FFFFFF;
}
#navigation {
        border: 1px solid #808080;
        background-color: #FFFFFF;
        position: relative;
        float: left;
        width: 148px;
        margin-top: 10px;
        margin-bottom: 10px;
}
#content {
        padding: 10px;
        border: 1px solid #808080;
        float: left;
        width: 518px;
        margin-top: 10px;
        margin-bottom: 10px;
        margin-left: 10px;
        background-color: #FFFFFF;
}
#footer {
        padding: 0px;
        border: 1px solid #808080;
        background-color: #FFFFFF;
        width: 698px;
        clear: both;
        text-align: center;
}
```

```
#navigation ul {
        list-style-type: none;
        width: 100%;
        display: block;
        padding: 0px;
        margin: 0px;
}
#navigation li {
        display: block;
        margin: 0px;
        padding: 0px;
        border: 1px solid #FFFFFF;
}
#navigation a {
        color: #000000;
        text-decoration: none;
        display: block;
        padding: 5px;
        border: 1px solid #FFFFFF;
        background-color: #FFFFFF;
}
#navigation ul a:hover {
        color: #FFFFFF;
        text-decoration: none;
        border: 1px solid #808080;
        background-color: #808080;
}
#footer p {
        padding-top: 0px;
        padding-bottom: 0px;
        margin: 5px 0px 5px 0px;
}
```

Beyond the basics

Here are a few more tips for working with CSS positioning properties:

✔ **You have other ways to achieve multicolumn layouts with CSS positioning** (such as using position: absolute to make columns stay at a specified place on the page). The best way to find out about them is to experiment. Try some of the online tutorials we suggest in Chapter 7 and Chapter 16. Also look through the style sheets that come with the Expression Web templates for layouts that you like, to see how they were done.

✔ **Preview, preview, preview.** Different browsers often display CSS slightly differently, as do the same browsers on different operating systems. Make sure your layout holds up in at least the most popular browsers, but don't neglect a few older browsers, just to see what your page looks like.

✔ **You can use many CSS tricks for creating hyperlink lists that look like horizontal or vertical navigation bars.** Creating the different style rules that format each part of the navigation bar can get tricky. To get started, take a look at the style sheets included with the Expression Web templates. Also, visit the excellent list resource Listamatic at `http://css.maxdesign.com.au/listamatic/index.htm` for all sorts of ways to style navigation bars, both horizontally and vertically.

✔ **When setting styles for content, remember that many elements have defaults already set to make a nonstyled Web page look decent.** For example, headers and paragraphs both have default margins that insert space between the heading or paragraph text and the next element. Any styles you specifically set for the element override the default settings. If you don't want any margins, set the margin property to 0.

✔ **Don't be afraid to make mistakes and muck about, making a mess.** Create a backup of your well-structured raw page content so that you can always revert to a clean copy if you can't find your way out of a snarl. *Remember:* The Undo command is your best friend. Memorize the keyboard command for it (Ctrl+Z), and don't be afraid to call it into service!

Chapter 9

External Style Sheets and CSS Code

*A*n *external* style sheet is a file that contains no content of its own — just a specially arranged list of your site's style rules. When you create an external style sheet to hold your page's formatting instructions, you get to experience the true timesaving benefit of using CSS in your Web site. All of a sudden, your styles have moved beyond the realm of formatting a single page — in a few steps, you can apply these styles to any page in your Web site.

External style sheets are especially useful if more than one author works on a site. Because the site's formatting instructions are stored in the style sheet, individual authors can concentrate on the page's content and can later attach the style sheet to take care of the stylistic details.

In this chapter, we cover what you need to know to create and attach style sheets to your Web pages, as well as some skills for getting comfortable with style sheet code (which is slightly different from HTML). We also help you take a look at some of the style sheets included in one of the Expression Web template Web sites so that you can get an idea of how to organize styles in your own, homemade style sheets.

Using External Style Sheets

The basic process for moving style rules from a Web page to an external style sheet is simple (we cover each of these steps in detail in the sections that follow):

1. **Create a new, blank style sheet file (basically, an empty page with a special extension that identifies it as a style sheet).**

2. **Attach the style sheet file to your Web page (we explain what *attach* means a bit later).**

3. **Move the style rules embedded in the Web page to the style sheet file.**

After you move your styles to an external style sheet, you can continue to perform the following tasks (which we cover in detail in Chapter 7):

- ✔ Apply style rules to content on your Web page
- ✔ Create and save new style rules
- ✔ Change existing style rules

If you already have an existing style sheet and you want to use it in your Web site, import it into your Web site first and then follow the instructions in the "Attaching an external style sheet to a Web page" section, later in this chapter. If you're not sure how to import a file into your site, see the section about adding existing files to a Web site in Chapter 1.

Creating a new style sheet

Creating a new style sheet is easy. To do so, follow these steps:

1. **Choose File➪New➪CSS.**

   Or, on the Common or Standard toolbar, click the New Page down-arrow button and choose CSS.

   A blank CSS file opens in the editing window, with Untitled_1.css displayed on its tab, as shown in Figure 9-1.

Figure 9-1:
New, blank
style sheet
file.

2. **Choose File⇨Save As.**

   The Save As dialog box appears, and `Untitled_1.css` appears in the File Name text box.

3. **In the File Name text box, enter a name for your CSS file.**

   As with other files in your Web site, you should stick to one-word filenames in all lowercase letters. You can cheat a little by using the underscore (_) or hyphen (-) to separate words.

   Make sure that you don't erase the `.css` extension. If you do, Expression Web doesn't know that it's a style sheet file.

4. **Click Save.**

   The style sheet appears in the Folder List task pane with the name you gave it. The name also appears on its tab in the editing window.

Attaching an external style sheet to a Web page

When you *attach* an external style sheet to a Web page, you're basically putting a "note" inside the Web page that tells the browser to look inside the style sheet file for style rules that control the Web page's formatting.

You can attach a style sheet to a Web page in several ways. Attaching an external style sheet to a *single* Web page is a simple drag-and-drop operation. Attaching an external style sheet to more than one Web page is slightly more involved.

To attach a style sheet to a *single* Web page that's located inside the open Web site, follow these steps:

1. **Open the page to which you want to attach the style sheet.**

2. **From the Folder List task pane, drag the icon for the style sheet file into the page's Design view.**

   The style sheet filename appears as a heading in both the Apply Styles and Manage Styles task panes.

   If the style sheet contains predefined style rules, they appear in the Apply Styles task pane, in the Manage Styles task pane (under the style sheet filename), and in the CSS Properties task pane.

3. **Save the Web page to which you attached the style sheet.**

To attach a style sheet to *all* pages in the open Web site, follow these steps:

1. **In the Manage Styles task pane or the Apply Styles task pane (or on the Style toolbar or the Style Application toolbar), click the Attach Style Sheet button.**

   You can also choose Format➪CSS Styles➪Attach Style Sheet.

   The Attach Style Sheet dialog box appears.

2. **In the URL text area, enter the path and filename of the style sheet you want to attach.**

   Or click the Browse button and, in the Locate Style Sheet dialog box, navigate to the location of the style sheet, select it, and click Open. You return to the Attach Style Sheet dialog box. The URL text area shows the path and filename of the style sheet.

3. **To attach the style sheet to all pages in the current Web site, click the All HTML Pages option.**

   Keep the Attach As option set to Link. This option creates a link to the external style sheet in the <head> section of the Web page or pages. (We show you what a link to an external style sheet looks like in Chapter 7.)

4. **Click OK.**

   A message box may appear, warning you that these links will overwrite all the selected pages' style sheet links. Because you're attaching style sheets for the first time, there are no existing style sheet links.

5. **In the message box (if it appears), click the Continue button.**

   The style sheet filename appears as a heading in both the Apply Styles and Manage Styles task panes in all pages in the open Web site.

   If the style sheet contains predefined style rules, they appear in the Apply Styles task pane, in the Manage Styles task pane (under the style sheet filename), and in the CSS Properties task pane.

To attach a style sheet to *selected* pages in the open Web site, follow these steps:

1. **In the Folder List task pane, hold down the Ctrl key and click the page icon of each page to which you want to attach the style sheet.**

2. **In the Manage Styles or Apply Styles task pane (or on the Style or Style Application toolbar), click the Attach Style Sheet button.**

   You can also choose Format➪CSS Styles➪Attach Style Sheet.

   The Attach Style Sheet dialog box appears, as shown in Figure 9-2. The Selected Page(s) option is selected.

Figure 9-2:
The Attach
Style Sheet
dialog box.

3. **In the URL text area, enter the path and filename of the style sheet you want to attach.**

   Or click the Browse button and, in the Locate Style Sheet dialog box, navigate to the location of the style sheet, select it, and click Open. You return to the Attach Style Sheet dialog box. The URL text shows the path and filename of the style sheet.

   Keep the Attach As option set to Link.

   This option creates a link to the external style sheet in the <head> section of the Web page or pages. (We show you what a link to an external style sheet looks like in Chapter 7.)

4. **Click OK.**

   A message box appears, telling you that the files were updated.

5. **In the message box, click the Close button.**

   The style sheet filename appears as a heading in both the Apply Styles and Manage Styles task panes in all pages in the open Web site.

   If the style sheet contains predefined style rules, they appear in the Apply Styles task pane, in the Manage Styles task pane (under the style sheet filename), and in the CSS Properties task pane.

Moving internal (embedded) styles to an attached style sheet

After you attach an external style sheet to a Web page, you can move any internal style rules embedded in the <head> section of the page to the external style sheet. (If you're not sure what an internal style is, see Chapter 7.) Why CSS is such a big deal: If the external style sheet is attached to other pages, those styles become available to the other pages as well.

Searching out style sheets

The Web contains a treasure trove of style sheets you can grab and use in your site. (We list some sources in Chapter 16.) Delving into style sheets created by professional Web designers and CSS experts is a great way to figure out how to use styles to create effects you want to use on your own pages. If you use someone else's style sheet, however, make sure that you're not violating the license agreement under which the style sheet is offered. Many Web sites offer downloadable style sheets as part of their CSS tutorials, and others specify that you can use the style sheets for your own, *noncommercial* use. If you're not sure whether

the way you want to use the style sheet complies with the style sheet creator's intended use, contact the Web site's owner and ask.

Always make sure that the style sheet you use sticks to valid CSS code. Most sites that offer style sheets for download use catch phrases such as "valid" or "code that validates" or "standards-compliant CSS" to state that their style sheets are valid. If you're unsure, you can always run the style sheet through the World Wide Web Consortium's CSS Validation Service at `http://jigsaw.w3.org/css-validator`.

To move an internal style (or styles) to an external style sheet, follow these steps:

1. **In the Manage Styles task pane's CSS Styles list, scroll to the location of the style rule you want to move and click to select it.**

   If the external style sheet already contains styles, the open page's styles are located at the bottom of the list, under Current Page.

   If you want to move more than one style rule, hold down the Ctrl key while you click to select each one.

2. **Drag the styles into the section of the list under the heading for the external style sheet file.**

   A gray line shows the location where the style (or styles) will land when you release the mouse button.

   If the styles aren't in the order you want, drag each style up or down the list until its location suits you.

Some styles need to appear in a particular order in a style sheet (such as hyperlink pseudo classes, which must appear in this order: `a:link`, `a:visited`, `a:hover`, `a:active`). Also, order matters if style rules *collide*; style rules collide when two rules set the same property for the same bit of content, but each style rule's property has a different value. (For example, if one rule sets paragraph text to red, and another one sets it to blue, the style rule farther down in the style sheet, which is closest in the page's code to the paragraphs, wins.) Chapter 7 introduces some of these basics, or check your favorite CSS reference manual for more information.

3. When you're done moving styles, click the Save button.

The Save Embedded Files dialog box appears each time you make changes to the external style sheet. Click Save to save changes to the style sheet file.

TIP

Working with styles stored in external style sheets is exactly like working with internal styles, and the page formatting doesn't change when you move the styles into an external style sheet. Refer to Chapter 7 to find out how to create new styles, modify existing styles, delete styles, or remove styles from content.

Attaching multiple style sheets to Web pages

You can attach more than one style sheet to a page (or pages) in a Web site, and when you do so, the style rules located in all attached style sheets are available to format page elements. The benefits don't come without an extra layer of complication, however. Using multiple style sheets can get tricky if a duplicate style rule exists in both style sheets and must duke it out. For example, what if one style sheet contains a rule that sets all paragraph text to red and the other contains a rule that sets all paragraph text to blue? Which rule wins out?

CSS itself conforms to a set of rules that determine which rules take priority. Sometimes a style rule wins because of where it's located in the "cascade" of style sheets attached to the Web page. This code example shows a Web page with two style sheets attached to it:

```
<link rel="stylesheet" type="text/css" href="styles1.css" />
<link rel="stylesheet" type="text/css" href="styles2.css" />
```

The style sheet listed second is farther down in the cascade of style sheets (and closer to the actual content; remember that browsers are reading the code, and the second line of code is closer to the page's content), so the style rule located in `styles2.css` would win.

The rules of CSS are involved enough that we can't do the topic justice here. Refer to your favorite CSS reference for more information about how style rules interact with one another. We list some of our favorite resources in Chapter 7.

If a style property's value is overridden by another rule, a red line is drawn through the property in the CSS Properties task pane, as shown in Figure 9-3. If you hover your cursor over the crossed-out style property, a helpful tip pops up, telling you what's going on.

Figure 9-3:
Overriding
a style
property.

To attach multiple style sheets to the *current* page or to all pages in the *currently open Web site*, follow these steps:

1. **Choose Format⇨CSS Styles⇨Manage Style Sheet Links.**

   The Link Style Sheet dialog box appears, as shown in Figure 9-4.

Figure 9-4:
The Link
Style Sheet
dialog box.

2. **To link the style sheets to only the current page, select the Current Page option; to link to all pages in the open Web site, select the All Pages option.**

3. **To select a style sheet to attach, click the Add button.**

4. **In the Select Style Sheet dialog box that appears, navigate to the style sheet file, click to select it, and then click OK.**

   The Select Style Sheet dialog box closes, and the style sheet appears on the URL list in the Link Style Sheet dialog box.

5. **Repeat Steps 3 and 4 to add all style sheets you want to attach.**

   Style sheet links appear in the Web page's <head> section in the same order they appear in the URL list. Click the Move Down and Move Up buttons to change the order of individual style sheets.

   To remove a style sheet from the list, click it and then click the Remove button.

6. **After you arrange the style sheets in the order you want them, click OK.**

   If you're attaching the style sheets to *all* pages in the Web site, a message box appears, warning you that these links will overwrite all the selected pages' style sheet links. Because you're attaching style sheets for the first time, there are no existing style sheet links, so it's not a problem.

7. **In the message box, click the Continue button.**

To attach multiple style sheets to *selected* pages, you begin as follows:

1. **In the Folder List task pane, hold down the Ctrl key and click the page icon of each page to which you want to attach style sheets.**

2. **Choose Format⇨CSS Styles⇨Manage Style Sheet Links.**

   The Link Style Sheet dialog box appears. The Selected Pages option is selected.

3. **Now, in the Link Style Sheet dialog box, you can start at Step 3 in the preceding set of steps.**

Detaching a style sheet

If you find that you no longer want to use a style sheet in your Web site or on a particular page, you can detach it. If a page has more than one style sheet attached to it, you can specify which style sheet you want to detach. When you detach a style sheet, it gathers up all its style rules and they disappear from the style-related task panes. Your page elements revert to their original formatting.

To detach an external style sheet from a single page, follow these steps:

1. **In either the Apply Styles or Manage Styles task pane, right-click the name of the style sheet you want to detach.**

2. **From the pop-up menu that appears, choose Remove Link.**

   A message box appears, asking you to confirm deleting the style sheet link.

3. **Click Yes to close the message box and then save your page.**

To detach multiple style sheets or detach a single style sheet from multiple pages, follow these steps:

1. **If you want to detach a single style sheet or multiple style sheets from *selected* pages, in the Folder List task pane, hold down the Ctrl key and click the icon for each page whose style sheet (or sheets) you want to detach.**

   If you want to remove style sheets from a single page or all pages in your site, go on to Step 2.

2. **Choose Format⇨CSS Styles⇨Manage Style Sheet Links.**

   The Link Style Sheet dialog box appears. The URL area lists the style sheets attached to the selected pages.

3. **Choose the option that corresponds to the pages from which you want to detach the style sheet (or sheets).**

   Choose the All Pages option to detach the style sheet or style sheets from all pages in the open Web site.

   Choose the Current Page option to detach the style sheet or style sheets from only the current page.

   If you highlighted pages in the Folder List task pane in Step 1, the Selected Page(s) option is already selected.

4. **In the URL list, click the name of the style sheet you want to detach and then click the Remove button.**

   If necessary, repeat this step to remove other style sheets from the list.

5. **Click OK.**

   If you chose to detach a style sheet (or style sheets) from all pages, a message box appears, warning you that existing style sheet links will be overwritten.

6. **In the message box, click the Continue button.**

Sometimes it's handy to *temporarily* unlink a style sheet from a page. This option is especially useful for troubleshooting page formatting when you have multiple style sheets attached to a page. Unlinking one of the style sheets allows you to see which style sheet is producing which formatting effects on your page. To temporarily unlink a style sheet, in Code view of the Web page, scroll up to the <head> section and locate the style sheet link. Change the style sheet's filename to a bogus filename. For example, if your style sheet is named styles.css, change it to stylesx.css. Save the page and view it without the style sheet. When you're ready to reattach the style sheet, change the style sheet's filename back to its real name.

Attaching a style sheet to another style sheet

Rather than attach multiple style sheets to a Web page, you can attach a style sheet to another style sheet. This option is especially useful if a generic style sheet contains styles you use in all your Web sites and you don't want to retype them each time you start a new site. Attaching the more generic style sheet to a more specific style sheet gives your site access to both sets of styles.

To attach a style sheet to another style sheet, follow these steps:

1. **Open the style sheet to which you want to attach another style sheet.**

2. **Choose Format➪CSS Styles➪Attach Style Sheet.**

   The Attach Style Sheet dialog box appears. Import is selected as the Attach As option. Styles from the attached style sheet are "imported" into the existing style sheet.

3. **In the URL text box, type the name and path of the style sheet you want to attach. Or click the Browse button and, in the Select Style Sheet dialog box that appears, navigate to the style sheet file, click to select it, and then click the Open button.**

   The Attach Style Sheet dialog box appears again, with the style sheet filename and path in the URL text box.

4. **Keep the Attach To option set to Current Page.**

5. **Click OK.**

This code appears at the top of the style sheet, indicating that it is importing styles from the other style sheet:

```
@import url('stylesheet.css');
```

The Web site templates that come with Expression Web all use several layers of style sheets, where a style sheet that defines layout styles is attached to a formatting style sheet that is then attached to a Web page (which happens to be a Dynamic Web Template; we talk about that topic in Chapter 11). Style rules cascade from one style sheet to the next, down to the actual page. We talk about using styles for page layout in Chapter 8.

Working with Style Sheet Code

When you get the hang of style rule syntax, you may start to feel at home in Code view (or at least feel less like an awkward guest). In fact, if you've ever written style sheets, you can create a blank CSS file, write your own style rules, and attach the file to your Web pages. As long as the style rule syntax is correct (and Expression Web lets you know if it's not), it doesn't matter if you write your style rules manually or use the New Styles dialog box.

Expression Web lets you decide how to format your CSS and provides code shortcuts to simplify writing correctly formatted style rules.

Changing style rule formatting

Although Web browsers couldn't care less about how a style sheet looks (as long as the code is valid), a little bit of white space makes it much easier for human eyes and brains to decipher.

Expression Web writes style rules with each property on a separate line. Use the options on the Code Formatting tab in the Page Editor Options dialog box to change the way style rules are formatted, as shown in Figure 9-5 (choose Tools⇨Page Editor Options and then click the Code Formatting tab).

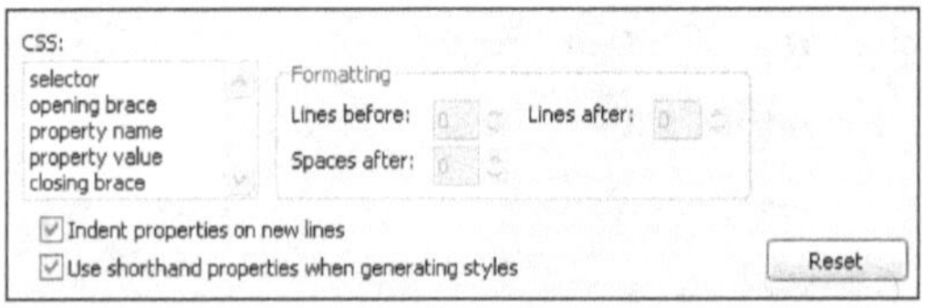

Figure 9-5:
The CSS area on the Code Formatting tab.

In the CSS list, select the part of the style rule you want to change, and in the Formatting section, choose a line break and the number of spaces after it. Also, choose whether to indent style properties and use shorthand properties in generated styles. Not all choices are available for all style rule parts.

Changing style rule defaults

You can change the way Expression Web writes style rules as you format your page elements. You change these options by tinkering with the settings on the CSS tab in the Page Editor Options dialog box, as shown in Figure 9-6 (choose Tools⇨Page Editor Options and then click the CSS tab).

The options in this dialog box tell Expression Web how to write style rules when you format your page's content. If you already used CSS and you're picky about how style rules get written, you may want to tinker with these settings to match the way you prefer to work.

If you're new to using styles for Web page formatting, the Expression Web default style rule settings are probably fine for you. As you get more comfortable working with styles, you can experiment with changing these settings. We talk about changing a few of these options in Chapter 8.

Figure 9-6:
The CSS tab
in the Page
Editor
Options
dialog box.

Using CSS IntelliSense

CSS IntelliSense combines code autocompletion and syntax checking. IntelliSense pops up to help when you're writing CSS style rules, either inside a Web page's code or in an external style sheet. The CSS Properties task pane also uses IntelliSense for entering or editing property values. Figure 9-7 shows the pop-up list of CSS properties that appears when you're writing a style rule in Code view.

Figure 9-7:
IntelliSense
for CSS
style rules.

Some tips for working with CSS IntelliSense:

- ✒ To scroll through a pop-up menu of properties, use the up- and down-arrow keys or the PgUp and PgDn keys to scroll a block at a time. Or type the beginning letters of the property to jump to that property.

- ✒ To insert a property from the IntelliSense pop-up menu, double-click the property or select it and press the Tab or Enter key.

- ✒ The Value icon indicates a predefined property value. Click to insert the value.

- ✒ Click the Pick icon to select or enter a custom value (such as a color value).

The Microsoft Expression Web Help system contains more information about IntelliSense. To get help, press F1.

Adding comments to external style sheets

Use comments to add explanatory text and reminders to your external style sheets. Comments in style sheets are particularly useful for explaining what different groups of style rules are used for. Figure 9-8 shows a style sheet file with comments. CSS comments have a different syntax than HTML comments do. (We show you HTML comments in Chapter 14.)

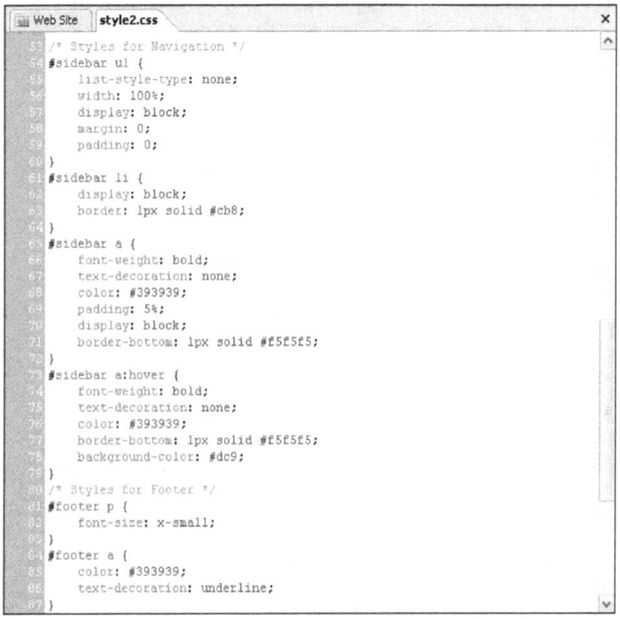

Figure 9-8:
Comments
in a CSS
style sheet.

```
/* Styles for Navigation */
#sidebar ul {
    list-style-type: none;
    width: 100%;
    display: block;
    margin: 0;
    padding: 0;
}
#sidebar li {
    display: block;
    border: 1px solid #cb8;
}
#sidebar a {
    font-weight: bold;
    text-decoration: none;
    color: #393939;
    padding: 5%;
    display: block;
    border-bottom: 1px solid #f5f5f5;
}
#sidebar a:hover {
    font-weight: bold;
    text-decoration: none;
    color: #393939;
    border-bottom: 1px solid #f5f5f5;
    background-color: #dc9;
}
/* Styles for Footer */
#footer p {
    font-size: x-small;
}
#footer a {
    color: #393939;
    text-decoration: underline;
}
```

To insert a comment, follow these steps:

1. **Open the CSS style sheet file.**

2. **Click in the style sheet where you want to insert the comment.**

   To create a new, blank line, place your cursor at the end of a style rule's curly bracket (}) and press Enter.

3. **Type /* and then press the spacebar once to insert a space.**

4. **Type the comment, press the spacebar once, and type */ to end the comment.**

5. **Save the style sheet by clicking the Save button on the Common or Standard toolbar.**

To delete a comment, select the comment along with its opening and closing characters (/* comment */) and press the Delete key.

Comments are useful tools for troubleshooting CSS styles. You can comment-out a style rule, which allows you to see what effect removing it has on your Web page's formatting without *actually* deleting it from the style sheet. Here's what a commented-out CSS style rule looks like:

```
/*
p {
        font-size: large;
        color: #008000;
}
*/
```

Running CSS Reports

Use the Expression Web CSS reports to find out more about your Web site's styles. In this section, we tell you about the three main types of CSS reports you can run in Expression Web and what they tell you about your styles.

CSS Errors report

The CSS Errors report finds mistakes in your Web site's CSS. It checks for these boo-boos:

✔ **Unused styles:** Any element-, class-, or ID-based style rules that aren't applied to any page elements. Honestly, nothing is *wrong* with having a few unused styles in your CSS. In fact, if you're using a style sheet that someone else created, that person may have included styles that you haven't used but may find a use for later. But if you have a lot of obsolete styles cluttering your style sheet, you may want to remove them, just to keep your CSS lean and tidy.

✔ **Undefined classes:** Classes that are assigned to page elements but have no style rules that target them. Although your Web site's CSS doesn't break if you have a few wayward classes loitering around, you should remove any you don't need, to keep your page's code to a minimum.

✔ **Mismatched case:** Class- and ID-based styles where the style rule selector uses a different case than the class or id attribute value. For example, if you have a class attribute in a page element whose value is SmallText and the style rule's selector is .smalltext, the style rule shows up in the CSS Errors report. This type of error is one that you need to fix. Style rules are case sensitive, and the selector must match the value exactly. Keep all your class and id values lowercase, and you won't run into this problem.

Always use lowercase letters for your class and id values, and you will never run into a mismatched case!

To run a CSS Errors report, follow these steps:

1. **Open the Web site for which you want to run the CSS Errors report, and decide whether you want the report to check all pages or only certain pages.**

   Your choices are all pages, open pages, selected pages, and the current page.

   To run the report for open pages, in the editing window, open the pages you want the report to check.

   To run the report for selected pages, in the Folder List task pane, hold down the Ctrl key and click the page icon for each page you want the report to check.

   To run the report on the open page only, make sure that it's the active page.

   To run the report for all pages, go to Step 2. You set this option in the dialog box.

2. **Choose Tools⇨CSS Reports.**

   The CSS Reports dialog box appears, with the Errors tab open, as shown in Figure 9-9.

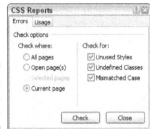

Figure 9-9:
The Errors
tab.

3. **In the Check Where area, choose the option for which pages you want the report to check.**

   The Selected Pages option is available only if you selected pages in the Folder List task pane before you opened the CSS Reports dialog box (refer to Step 1).

4. **In the Check For area, select the type of errors you want the report to check your pages for.**

5. **Click the Check button to run the report.**

   The CSS Reports task pane appears at the bottom of the editing window, listing any errors it found, as shown in Figure 9-10.

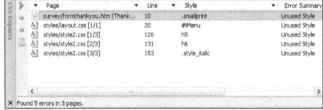

Figure 9-10:
The CSS
Errors
report.

6. **Make use of the reporting tools to find and fix these errors:**

   • To go to the CSS error in your Web page, double-click the error listing.

   • To run the report again, click the CSS Reports button in the upper-left corner of the task pane. This action opens the CSS Reports dialog box.

   • Click the Next and Previous buttons to scroll through the pages containing the errors. Expression Web highlights each error for you.

   • Click the Style Sheet Links button to show the Style Sheet Links report in the upper part of the editing window. (We talk about this report later in this chapter.)

You can specify filter criteria on the CSS report by clicking the down-arrow button in one of the report columns and choosing a filter criteria from the drop-down list that appears. Refer to Microsoft Expression Web Help for instructions on how to filter reports.

CSS Usage report

Want to take a look at a list of the style rules that are being used? Run the CSS Usage report for all pages in your Web site, or select one or more pages. You can limit the report to a particular type of style rule (element-, class-, or ID-based style rules) or list all types.

To run a CSS Usage report, follow these steps:

1. **Open the Web site for which you want to run the CSS Usage report, and decide whether you want the report to check all pages or only certain pages.**

   Your choices are all page, open pages, selected pages, and current page.

   To run the report for open pages, in the editing window, open the pages you want the report to check.

   To run the report for selected pages, in the Folder List task pane, hold down the Ctrl key and click the page icon for each page you want the report to check.

   To run the report on only the open page, make sure that it's the active page.

   To run the report for all pages, go to Step 2. You set this option in the dialog box.

2. **Choose Tools⇨CSS Reports.**

   The CSS Reports dialog box appears, with the Errors tab open.

3. **Click the Usage tab.**

4. **In the Check Where area, choose the option for which pages you want the report to check.**

   The Selected Pages option is available only if you selected pages in the Folder List task pane before you opened the CSS Reports dialog box (refer to Step 1).

5. **In the Check For area, select the type of style rules you want the report to check your pages for.**

6. Click the Check button to run the report.

The CSS Reports task pane appears at the bottom of the editing window, listing the styles of the type you selected, as shown in Figure 9-11.

Style	Usage Location	Line	Definition Locatio
.regsymbol	default.htm	65	style2.css
.regsymbol	default.htm	67	style2.css
.regsymbol	default.htm	74	style2.css
#masthead h1	default.htm	23	style2.css
#masthead h3	default.htm	24	style2.css
#navigation ul	default.htm	29	style2.css
#navigation li	default.htm	30	style2.css

X Found 73 styles used in 1 page.

Figure 9-11: The CSS Usage report.

For each style, the report lists these items:

- The page on which it's used (in the Usage Location column)

- The Code view line number

- The style sheet filename, for external style rules, or Web page, for internal style rules (in the Definition Location column)

7. Make use of the reporting tools to review the styles:

- To go to the CSS style in your Web page, double-click the style rule listing.

- Click the Next and Previous buttons to scroll through the Web pages containing the styles. Expression Web highlights each HTML element that the style targets.

- To view the style in the style sheet, click the style sheet or page link in the Definition Location column.

- To run the report again, click the CSS Reports button in the upper-left corner of the task pane. This action opens the CSS Reports dialog box.

- Click the Style Sheet Links button to show the Style Sheet Links report in the upper part of the editing window. (We talk about this report later in this chapter.)

You can specify filter criteria on the CSS report by clicking the down-arrow button in one of the report columns and choosing a filter criteria from the drop-down list that appears. Refer to Microsoft Expression Web Help for instructions on how to filter reports.

Style Sheet Links report

The Style Sheet Links report shows you all the pages in your Web site that link to or import external style sheets. Use this report if you changed the style sheet that is attached to some of your pages and you want a quick look to make sure all the style sheet links are working properly.

To run the Style Sheet Links report, choose Site➪Reports➪Shared Content➪ Style Sheet Links. The Style Sheet Links report appears on the Web Site tab in the editing window, as shown in Figure 9-12.

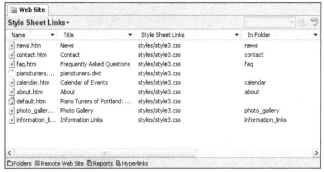

Figure 9-12:
The Style
Sheet Links
report.

If you have a CSS report open in the editing window, you can also run this report by clicking the Style Sheet Links button.

Understanding Expression Web Template Style Sheets

Creating a "sandbox" Web site to play with based on one of Expression Web's Web site templates is a great way to practice tinkering with styles. (We tell you how to create a new Web site from one of the Expression Web templates in Chapter 1.)

In this section, we take you on a brief tour of the Web site template named Organization 4. Here's why: Sometimes a guided walk through an already completed CSS-based site is easier than learning CSS from the ground up.

The Organization 4 template uses two style sheets to define formatting, one of which is attached — or *imported into* — the other one, which is then attached to the content pages by way of a Dynamic Web Template. (See Chapter 11 for more information about Dynamic Web Templates.)

Figure 9-13 shows what the home page (`default.htm`) for this Web site template looks like in a browser.

Navigation   Masthead

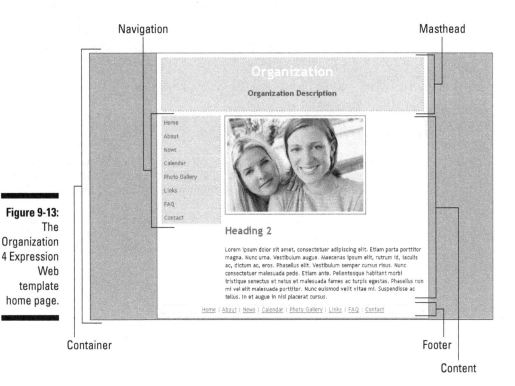

Figure 9-13:
The
Organization
4 Expression
Web
template
home page.

Container   Footer

                                                             Content

The Manage Styles task pane, shown in Figure 9-14, shows the two style sheets that format the content on the page — `style1.css` and `layout.css` — and lists all their style rules. The style rules contained in `layout.css` are listed first, slightly indented, indicating that these styles cascade into the `style1.css` style sheet.

Figure 9-14:
The
Manage
Styles task
pane.

Although this two-style-sheet scenario is standard practice in the Expression Web templates, you don't have to use this setup in your Web sites. These two style sheets can easily be combined into one. Here's the advantage of using more than one style sheet: If you use style rules common to all Web sites you create, you can keep them in a separate style sheet file and then attach the file to the more specific Web site style sheet (in this case, style1. css). This strategy saves you the trouble of retyping these styles for each new Web site.

The layout style sheet

First, take a look at the style rules in layout.css. This style sheet contains a style rule for the <body> element and for each of the five <div> elements that define the main areas of the page. (Figure 9-13 shows which part of the page each <div> element defines.) Each <div> tag contains an id value — container, masthead, navigation, content, footer — to identify it as a unique page element. If you look at the HTML code for the page, you see that the <div> tags look like this: <div id="container">, <div id="masthead">, and so on.

```
body {
        margin: 0;
        padding: 0;
        border: 0;
}
#container {
        margin: 0;
        padding: 0;
        border: 0;
}
#masthead {
        margin: 0;
        padding: 0;
        border: 0;
}
#navigation {
        margin: 0;
        padding: 0;
        border: 0;
}
#content {
        margin: 0;
        padding: 0;
        border: 0;
}
#footer {
        margin: 0;
        padding: 0;
        border: 0;
}
```

Each of these styles is an ID-based style rule that sets the margins, padding, and border properties to 0 for all four sides of each unique <div> element. By default, browsers put a little space between page content and the edge of the browser window. Some browsers use padding, and some use margins. These style rules override browser settings so that only formatting specified by the style sheet apply to the page's content. They say to the browser, "If you have default margins set, I'm setting margins to 0; if you have padding values set, I'm setting those to 0, too. And while I'm at it, no borders either." After these styles get applied to the page's <div> elements, the content of each <div> extends all the way out to the edge without any space.

The values in these style rules for the properties margin, padding, and border are good examples of CSS shorthand. The style declaration for margins could also be specified as margin: 0 0 0 0; or, even longer, margin-top: 0; margin-right: 0; margin-bottom: 0; margin-left: 0;.

The formatting style sheet

Now look at the other style sheet this Web site uses — style1.css — which has the layout.css style sheet attached to it. The style rules in layout.css cascade into the style sheet style1.css:

```
@import url("layout.css");
```

The next style rule sets properties for the page's font family, font size, and background:

```
body {
        font-family: "Trebuchet MS", Arial, Helvetica,
         sans-serif;
        font-size: 0.8em;
        background-image:
         url("../images/background.gif");
        background-repeat: repeat;
        background-attachment: scroll;
}
```

Text that isn't affected by a more specific style rule farther down in the style sheet appears in Trebuchet MS (or Arial or Helvetica or sans serif), scaled down a bit (0.8 em; see Chapter 8 for information on the value settings you can use in CSS). The background settings control the background pattern image (background.gif) and tell the browser to repeat it and let it scroll with the content.

Style rules for each <div> element

This part of the style sheet explanation requires a bit of math and a solid understanding of the CSS box model, which we explain in Chapter 8.

For this template, all the content of the page is nested inside a main <div> element named *container* (<div id="container">). (Refer to Figure 9-13.) All the other <div> elements (such as masthead and content) get some properties right from the start (such as width) from the style rules that are set for the container <div> element:

```
#container {
        width: 620px;
        margin: 0 auto;
        padding: 10px;
        border-right: 2px solid #725972;
        border-bottom: 2px solid #725972;
        border-left: 2px solid #725972;
        background-color: #fff;
}
```

The first property sets the width of the container's contents to 620 pixels. This layout is a fixed-width layout. None of the other <div> elements nested inside the container can be wider than 620 pixels, in order to fit inside the container <div>. The next property, margin: 0 auto, sets two values for margins: 0 sets top and bottom margins and auto sets right and left margins. Using auto as a value for the right and left margins centers the container in the browser window. The padding property inserts 10 pixels all the way around the container's content so that any element inside the container <div> has 10 pixels of breathing room between it and the container's borders.

Border sizes, style, and color are set for three sides (but not for the top because the container sits against the top of the browser window). The last property, background-color: #fff; sets the container's background to white. The container for the content now sits like a white place mat on top of the patterned tablecloth that is the page's background.

The next rule in the style sheet sets properties for the next <div> element, the masthead (<div id="masthead">), which holds the text *Organization* as a first-level heading and *Organization Description* as a third-level heading (refer to Figure 9-13):

```
#masthead {
        text-align: center;
        width: 600px;
        padding: 10px;
        border: 1px dotted #725972;
        background-image: url("../images/masthead.gif");
        background-repeat: repeat;
        background-attachment: scroll;
}
```

The two headings are centered (text-align: center). The masthead's content area is set to a width of 600 pixels. The next property, padding: 10px, ensures that the *masthead* content has 10 pixels of elbow room around all sides so that it doesn't butt up against the masthead's border. A dotted, 1-pixel, colored border around all sides of the masthead is specified, and the masthead has a repeated background image (masthead.gif) that scrolls with the masthead, like the page background. The masthead image is the same pattern as the page background image; it's just a lighter color. Figure 9-15 shows both images, side by side. The page background image is on the left, and the masthead image is on the right.

Figure 9-15:
Page and
masthead
background
images.

The next style rule sets properties for the navigation <div> element (<div id="navigation">), which contains the Web page's list of hyperlinks:

```
#navigation {
        position: relative;
        float: left;
        width: 139px;
        margin-top: 10px;
        margin-bottom: 10px;
        border-right: 1px dotted #725972;
}
```

The first two properties tell the navigation menu (<div id="navigation">) where to go inside the container <div>. The navigation <div> element's position is relative to its containing body, the container <div> (rather than fixed to a set place on the screen) and it floats to the left side. The navigation <div> element has a fixed width of 139 pixels plus a 1-pixel border (dotted, with a color specified) on the right, making the navigation <div> element 140 pixels wide. It also has top and bottom margins of 10 pixels each, so that the navigation <div> has 10 pixels of space between it and the element above it (the masthead) and 10 pixels of space between it and the element below it (the footer). None of these properties sets styles for the actual hyperlinks — just their containing element, the navigation <div>.

The next style rule controls the main content area of the page, the content <div> (<div id="content">):

```
#content {
        float: left;
        width: 470px;
        margin-top: 10px;
        margin-bottom: 10px;
        margin-left: 10px;
}
```

The content <div> also floats to the left, which places it next to the navigation <div>. The margin-left property inserts 10 pixels of space between the content <div> and the navigation <div>. The content <div> is 480 pixels wide (470 width + 10 margin-left = 480). Add that amount to the navigation width of 140 pixels, and you get 620 pixels, the same width as the masthead. (The masthead content area is 600 pixels wide plus 10 pixels on both the left and right sides: 600 + 10 + 10 = 620). The navigation and content elements align correctly underneath the masthead. Like the navigation <div>, the content <div> has top and bottom margins set to 10 pixels, to bump it down from the masthead and provide space between the content and the footer.

The next style rule sets properties for the last <div> element, the footer (<div id="footer">):

```
#footer {
        text-align: center;
        clear: both;
        width: 618px;
        border: 1px dotted #d8bfd8;
}
```

Footer text is center aligned, and the total width of the footer is 620 pixels (618 content + 2 pixels left and right borders). The property clear: both ensures that the footer always appears below the navigation and content elements that precede it. The property clear: both is often used after floated elements to ensure — absolutely and positively — that this element (the footer) always lands below the floated elements (in this case, the navigation and content).

Style rules for content inside the masthead

The next set of style rules get more specific about how the masthead should look. Notice that the author of the style sheet inserted a comment:

```
/* Masthead Styles */
#masthead h1 {
        color: #fff;
}
#masthead h3 {
        color: #402640;
}
```

These style rules both use contextual selectors, which set the text color for
<h1> and <h3> elements, but only <h1> and <h3> elements inside the mast-
head (<div id="masthead">).

Style rules for the navigation<div>

The next few style rules control the navigation element, which is an unordered
list of hyperlinks. There are many different ways to use CSS properties to style
lists into navigation menus of hyperlinks. This style sheet shows you one way
and one style sheet author's preference. Every CSS author has a favorite set of
properties to achieve the desired look. You will most likely run into other ways
to get the same effect as the author of this style sheet, in books on CSS, in
online list tutorials, and in classes that offer CSS instruction. Find the method
that makes the most sense to you and gives you the results you want. Also
understand that different browsers interpret CSS properties slightly differently,
and some property settings appear in style rules to make elements behave
correctly across multiple browsers.

Notice that the author inserted a helpful comment to let the user know which
element these style rules target. Look at the first style rule:

```
/* Navigation Styles */
#navigation ul {
        list-style-type: none;
        width: 100%;
        display: block;
        margin: 0;
        padding: 0;
}
```

This style rule uses the contextual selector #navigation ul, which tells the
browser to apply these style rules to the <ul> (unordered list) element, but
only if it appears inside the navigation element (<div id="navigation">).
If a <ul> shows up somewhere else in the page's content area, these styles
don't affect it. The margin and padding properties (both set to 0) remove
the default left indentation that browsers set for lists (some use the padding
property others use margin), and set all margins and padding to 0 on all sides.
The property list-style-type: none removes the bullets from each list
item. The property width: 100% means that the list fills the containing element (the navigation <div>) entirely. And display: block ensures that the
unordered list is treated as a block-level element.

Look at the next style rule, which controls each list item element (<li>) — in
this case, each separate hyperlink:

```
#navigation li {
        display:block;
        margin: 0;
        padding: 0;
        border: 1px dotted #dfb8df;
        background-color: #dfb8df;
}
```

The style rule uses the contextual selector #navigation li to tell the browser that this rule set controls only the list items found in the navigation <div>. The property display: block is used again, to treat each list item as a block-level element. Margins and padding are set to 0 on all sides, and a 1-pixel dotted, lavender border appears around each list item. The background color for each list item is set to the same color.

The next set of rules set properties for the navigation-menu hyperlinks themselves:

```
#navigation a {
        color: #402640;
        text-decoration: none;
        display: block;
        padding: 5px;
        border-bottom: 1px dotted #fff;
        background-color: #dfb8df;
}
#navigation a:hover {
        color: #402640;
        text-decoration: none;
        background-color: #fff;
}
```

The first style rule sets general properties for all link states (but only those within the navigation <div> because it's a contextual selector, #navigation a). The color property sets the link text color; text-decoration: none removes the default underlining; and display: block treats each hyperlink as a block-level element. Making each hyperlink into a block-level element creates the possibility of setting properties (padding, borders, and margins) for the CSS box model. The padding: 5px property provides 5 pixels of space between the hyperlink text and the hyperlink border, to spread the list out a bit. Each hyperlink has a 1-pixel dotted white border on the bottom, and background-color is set to the same lavender color.

The second style rule uses a contextual selector and pseudo class, to target hyperlinks within the navigation <div>, but only in its hover state (when the visitor's cursor moves over it): #navigation a:hover. In this state, the hyperlink color changes to a dark purple color and the background color changes to white; `text-decoration: none` removes underlining. Any hyperlink state not targeted by a specific rule (active or visited, for example), use the properties set by the `#navigation a` style rule.

Note: Some redundancies occur in these style rules for the navigation menu. One example is the `text-decoration: none` property in `#navigation a:hover`. Underlining for all navigation menu hyperlinks is already turned off in the style rule `#navigation a`. Why the redundancies? Our guess is that in order to help CSS beginners understand which properties control which formatting, the author of this style sheet repeated properties in a few rules.

Style rules for the content <div>

Two styles are set for the content element. (Note the comment introducing this section of the style sheet.) This one sets the heading color for all headings in the content `<div>`:

```
/* Content Styles */
#content h1,h2,h3,h4,h5,h6 {
        color: #503750;
}
```

The style rule uses a contextual selector that affects all headings within the content `<div>` (`<div id="content">`). If you want to change the color of all headings in this element, you need to change only this color value.

The second content rule targets any pictures (`<img>`) inside the content `<div>`:

```
#content img {
        padding: 5px;
        border: 1px solid #402640;
}
```

It places 5 pixels of padding all the way around the picture and then places a solid, 1-pixel colored border around the picture. You can see the effects of this style rule's properties on the home page's picture (`default.htm`) in Figure 9-16.

Figure 9-16: The picture with 5 pixels for padding and a border around it.

Style rules for the footer <div>

The next set of style rules target content inside the footer <div> element
(<div id="footer">). Note the comment that introduces these rules. The
first style rule sets the text color for any paragraph elements inside the
footer element, with the contextual selector #footer p:

```
/* Footer Styles */
#footer p {
        color: #808080;
}
```

The next style rule controls hyperlinks inside the footer element by setting
the text color and specifying that they're underlined:

```
#footer a {
        color: #503750;
        text-decoration: underline;
}
```

This style rule specifies properties for hyperlinks in the footer element in
their hover state, changing the color and removing the underline set by the
previous style rule:

```
#footer a:hover {
        color: #402640;
        text-decoration: none;
}
```

Setting other styles for page elements

The last four styles in this style sheet set styles for specific elements that
aren't located in a particular <div> element. The first two rules set properties for page hyperlinks, such as the ones that would appear in the page's
content text:

```
a {
        color: #402640;
        text-decoration: underline;
}
a:hover {
        color: #dfb8df;
        text-decoration: underline;
}
```

The first rule sets the color value and specifies underlining for all page hyperlinks. The second rule sets a different color for hyperlinks in their hover state (another redundancy — the `text-decoration: underline` property, which is already set by the `a` rule).

Hyperlinks that appear in the navigation and footer `<div>` elements have their own style rules that override these hyperlink properties.

The last two styles are class-based style rules:

```
.style_bold {
        font-weight: bold;
}
.style_italic {
        font-style: italic;
}
```

You can use these style rules in place of the HTML tags `<strong>` and `<em>` by assigning a class attribute to a chunk of text using the `<span>` tag (`<span class="style_italic">`) or adding a class attribute to a whole paragraph (`<p class="style_italic">`) or heading (`<hx class="style_italic">`). Using these class-based styles rather than their HTML equivalents removes all formatting from your page's content and puts it in the style sheet.

Chapter 10

Tables for Data (And Layout, If You Must)

In This Chapter

▶ Deciding whether to lay out your web pages by using CSS or tables

▶ Creating and formatting a data table

▶ Using the Expression Web table layout tools

▶ Deleting a data table or a layout table

*B*efore CSS, designers had to use tables if they wanted to arrange chunks of text, pictures, and even other tables in a graphically pleasing way. (For an example of a Web page laid out with tables, see Figure 10-9, later in this chapter.)

By the time CSS made its debut on the Web-design stage, table-based layout was well established as the method that consistently delivered a solid performance. When you take a peek at the source code behind some of the biggest and longest-standing sites on the Internet, you notice that tables are holding all those fancy bits in place.

For the past few years, however, the move has been toward using tables mostly for data and letting CSS do the formatting. Several reasons are driving this shift:

✔ Build a Web site with tables for layout, and your HTML code clogs up with a tangle of code bits that tell the browser not only *what* to display but also *how* and *where*.

✔ With Web content moving beyond the Web browser to other viewing devices, CSS builds a strong case for keeping formatting information out of content.

✔ Another problem is accessibility. Screen readers (devices that make Web pages readable for people who can't view Web pages in standard browsers) stumble awkwardly through pages laid out using tables.

✔ Table-based page layout violates a fundamental goal in the push for Web standards: to separate content from formatting.

Web design practices now stand at a crossroads. CSS is no doubt the future, and it will eventually replace table layout as surely as the automobile replaced the horse and buggy. Even so, you may still need to understand table layout if you're working with an older site and don't have time to bring it up to CSS standards. Tables continue to be a useful way to present data. And, if you have a fairly simple site and you know that problems accessing your site with a Web-enabled phone, screen reader or other device won't be issues for your audience, table-based layout is also, frankly, easier to master than CSS layout, so you can get your site up much more quickly.

In this chapter, we cover how to build and format tables, for both data and Web page layout. Yes, you *should* lay out your Web pages by using CSS, just as you *should* floss your teeth every night. But CSS positioning isn't something that you can get up to speed on in an hour. Take a look at the next section for some guidelines for deciding which layout technique you should use.

When we say *data table* in this chapter, we mean a grid of static information lined up in rows and columns, not a data-driven Web site.

Table Layout versus CSS Positioning

Even with relatively good browser support for CSS by the *majority* of browsers used by the *majority* of Web visitors (with some annoying exceptions), the debate over tables versus CSS still rages. (If you want to know more about it, type **table layout versus CSS positioning** in your search engine, pull out your reading glasses, and cozy up to your computer screen for some interesting reading.) To determine which layout method is best for you, ponder these considerations:

✔ If you're accustomed to building sites by using table layout and to maintaining a number of sites that are laid out using tables, you may want to stick with tables for your existing sites but make a vow to try your hand at using CSS positioning in your new sites.

✔ If you're using a table for layout, try to make it as simple as possible and use as much CSS as possible. You may want to try building a CSS-positioned mock-up along with it so that you can start transferring your skills from table building to CSS. To find out more, take a look at `www.sitepoint.com/article/tables-vs-css`. In this article, the author steps you through the process of building a site by using both table-based and CSS-based design techniques and discusses the advantages and disadvantages of both methods.

✔ If you're new to Web design and have never used tables, don't start. Spend the time you have to invest anyway into getting up to speed with CSS. Expression Web, with its full CSS integration, is a perfect tool to help you do that. We include many resources for helpful books and online tutorials throughout this book.

✔ If a table is just the best darn way to present a block of data, by all means, add a table to your page. You use a table for its original intention: to present data in a row-and-column format.

Taming tables with CSS styles

Regardless of whether you add a table to your Web page to organize data or to hold its parts, you can control many aspects of a table's appearance with CSS styles. In fact, using CSS styles for as much formatting as possible helps keep your table code to a minimum so that pages load faster. Here are some tips for using CSS with tables:

✔ If you're going to use CSS to fine-tune the appearance of a table, consult some good CSS books and Web sites on the topics to get a grasp on the subtleties of table parts and the CSS properties that control them. *Cascading Style Sheets: Separating Content from Presentation*, Second Edition, by Owen Briggs and others (published by Friends of ED), covers tables in detail. To dive deep into table formatting minutiae, consult the World Wide Web Consortium CSS specification for tables at `www.w3.org/TR/REC-CSS2/tables.html`.

✔ By default, Expression Web writes sizing values (width and height) for all HTML elements as *inline* styles, including the `<table>` element. Because inline styles can't be moved to external style sheets, you should change this setting to write class-based styles. Choose Tools⇔Page Editor Options, and then click the CSS tab. Change the Sizing, Positioning, and Floating option to CSS (Classes).

✔ Look for table-specific CSS properties in the Tables category in the New Style or Modify Style dialog boxes and in the CSS Properties task pane.

✔ Be sure to preview your tables in numerous browsers because not all browsers support all table CSS properties exactly the same way.

Creating Tables of Data

Tables are useful for cordoning off individual bits of data into *cells*, which are little boxes arranged in horizontal rows and vertical columns. Figure 10-1 shows a data table in the Expression Web Design view.

Figure 10-1:
Data table
in Design
view.

Tree	Vine Maple
Shrub	Red Twig Dogwood
Perennial	Sedum 'Autumn Joy'

Inserting a data table

Expression Web has several methods for creating a data table. This one is the easiest and fastest:

1. **Place the cursor in the page where you want the table to appear.**

2. **On the Common toolbar, click the Insert Table button.**

   A grid of white boxes representing table rows and columns appears underneath the button.

3. **Click and drag your cursor on the grid until the number of high-lighted boxes equals the number of rows and columns you want your table to contain (see Figure 10-2).**

   As you highlight boxes, the number of rows and columns appears at the bottom of the grid.

   If you don't know exactly how many rows or columns you need, just pick something close. You can add or delete rows and columns later.

Figure 10-2:
Using the
Insert Table
button.

3 by 2 Table

4. **Release the mouse button.**

   A new, empty table appears in your page, indicated by gray dotted lines.

Scrunching existing text into a data table

If you already have text that you want to format into a data table, either in Expression Web or in a word processing program, you can convert text separated with commas or another character into a table. To do so, follow these steps:

1. **In your word processing program (or a text editor, such as Notepad), type the text for your table. If the text is already in Expression Web, skip to Step 5.**

   Separate each line of text that you want to appear in its own *row* by placing the text inside its own paragraph. Section each row into "columns" by separating the text with commas or some other character. *Do not* apply any formatting to the text.

   Don't worry if the spacing is uneven — everything lines up nicely when you convert the text into a table.

    We don't recommend using tabs to separate bits of data. Expression Web interprets them as nonbreaking spaces, which makes a mess in your code. Use commas or some other character, and refrain from putting spaces between the characters and the chunks of data so that no extra spaces end up in your table that you later have to delete.

2. **Select and copy all the text to the Windows Clipboard.**

   Use your word processing program's Edit➪Copy command or Ctrl+C.

3. **In Design view, insert your text on the page by pressing Ctrl+V, or choose Edit➪Paste.**

   The text appears on the page, with the Paste Options button next to it. Some programs, such as Notepad, don't cause the Paste Options button to appear.

4. **Click the down arrow next to the Paste Options button and select the Remove Formatting option.**

   This step removes all coding from the text carried over from the word processing program. If you don't see a Paste Options button, ignore this step.

5. **Highlight the text and then choose Table➪Convert➪Text to Table.**

   The Convert Text to Table dialog box appears.

6. **Select the option next to the text separator that you want Expression Web to recognize when it creates columns.**

   If the text separator in your page isn't a comma, select the Other option and then, in the accompanying text box, type the text separator character.

7. **Click OK.**

   The dialog box closes, and a table materializes around the selected text, indicated by gray dotted lines.

You can copy a data table from Excel, and Expression Web already recognizes it as a table, preserving row heights and column widths.

Inserting stuff into a table

After your table is on the page, you can insert anything into a table cell that you can insert into a regular paragraph: text, pictures, and even other tables. Just click inside a cell and proceed as usual. By default, the cell height and width stretch to accommodate whatever you place inside, so don't be alarmed if your table cells grow and shrink as you type and insert stuff. The table settles down and behaves itself after you get all its cells filled.

Text entered into a cell *wraps* as you type, which means that, when the text reaches a cell boundary, the word being typed jumps down to a new line. You create line breaks by pressing Enter or Shift+Enter.

A block of text that you enter within a table cell is not by default a paragraph (<p>). If you want to format the cell as a paragraph, select the text and, on the Common toolbar, select Paragraph <p> from the Style drop-down list. We talk about how to format text in Chapter 3. Defining text as a paragraph allows you to create a style rule that specifies how the paragraph looks.

If you're ready to type text in another cell, press Tab until the cursor ends up in the destination cell, and then type away. If you press the Tab key when the cursor is sitting in the last cell in the bottom row of the table, a new table row appears, and the cursor jumps to the first cell in that new row so that you can continue to add to the table. To move the cursor backward through a table, press Shift+Tab.

Take a look at the code for an inserted table that we typed some text into:

```
<table style="width: 100%">
<tr>
        <td>Tree</td>
        <td>Vine Maple</td>
</tr>
<tr>
        <td>Shrub</td>
        <td>Red Twig Dogwood</td>
</tr>
<tr>
        <td>Perennial</td>
```

```
        <td>Sedum &#39;Autumn Joy&#39;</td>
  </tr>
  <tr>

        <td>Annual</td>
        <td>Sunflower</td>
  </tr>
  </table>
```

Notice that the first tag is `<table>`, which tells the browser to expect a table. The matching closing tag, `</table>`, tells the browser that the table is done. The opening tag contains an inline style rule (`<table style="width: 100%">`) that tells the browser to make the table as wide as the browser window (or other containing element, such as a `<div>`; we talk about `<div>` elements in Chapter 8). This property value is the default width for a new, unformatted table.

If Expression Web is set to write width as a class-based style rather than inline (see the earlier sidebar "Taming tables with CSS styles"), the width is written in a style rule rather than inside the table tag, like this:

```
.stylex {
        width: 100%;
}
<table class="stylex">
```

Next comes the data itself. Each *row* of data opens with the `<tr>` (table row) tag that tells the browser where a new row of cells starts. The closing tag `</tr>` indicates where each table row ends. Nested within each set of `<tr></tr>` tags, each chunk of data (in this case, text) appears between its own set of `<td></td>` (table data) tags. Each set of `<td></td>` tags represents a single *cell* in the table. The following line of code shows the nesting order of table tags:

```
<table><tr><td>data in a single cell</td></tr></table>
```

If you insert a *blank* table, each `<td></td>` tag set looks like this:

```
<td> </td>
```

The ` ` "character" is a *nonbreaking space*. (If you press the spacebar while typing in Design view, you get these, too.) Expression Web uses nonbreaking spaces as placeholders until you insert something else in the table's cells.

Whew! Aren't you glad that Expression Web takes care of adding all those HTML tags?

Selecting table parts

This section's heading sounds like something you do at a hardware store. But we're talking about how to select different parts of your table in order to format them in some way. Here's how you select the following table parts:

- **Cells:** To select a single cell, click inside the cell and then choose Table⇨ Select⇨Cell. Or, on the Quick Tag Selector bar, click the `<td>` tag. To select more than one cell, select the first cell and then press and hold down the Ctrl key as you click each cell. Or, right-click and, from the pop-up menu that appears, choose Select⇨Cell.

- **Columns:** To select a column, click inside the topmost cell in the column and then choose Table⇨Select⇨Column. Or, right-click and, from the pop-up menu that appears, choose Select⇨Column. Or, pass the cursor over the table until the cursor hovers just above a column. The cursor turns into a stubby downward-pointing arrow. Click once to select the column. To select more than one column, select the first column and then drag until you highlight the area you want.

- **Rows:** To select a row, place your cursor in the leftmost cell and choose Table⇨Select⇨Row. Or, right-click and, from the pop-up menu that appears, choose Select⇨Row. You can also pass the cursor over the left side of the table until the cursor hovers just to the left of a row. The cursor turns into a stubby arrow pointing to the right. Click once to select the row. To select more than one row, select the first row and then drag until you highlight the area you want. Or, on the Quick Tag Selector bar, click the `<tr>` tag.

- **Entire table:** Choose Table⇨Select⇨Table. Or, right-click the table and, from the pop-up menu that appears, choose Select⇨Table. Or, on the Quick Tag Selector bar, click the `<table>` tag.

Changing a data table's dimensions

You have two options for controlling the dimensions of your table: Give the table *absolute* measurements (a fixed size) or *proportional* measurements (the particulars of which are based on the size of the visitor's browser window).

You may be tempted to opt for *absolute* measurements so that you can retain control over the table size. Consider, however, the unfortunate visitor who must view your page inside a small or low-resolution monitor. That visitor may need to scroll all over the place to see the table in its entirety and may curse the inconsiderate person who created such a table. By using *proportional* measurements, you enable the visitor's browser window to determine the dimensions of the table. You give up precise control, but your visitor gets to see the entire table, no matter what the monitor or window size.

Another option is to forgo specifying the table's height and width altogether. If you do this, the table stretches to accommodate the dimensions of whatever sits inside the table's cells, and no more.

A good middle ground is to specify widths for *columns* rather than the dimensions of the table as a whole, and to let the content determine the height. In this way, you can give some columns an absolute width and give others a proportional width, creating a more flexible table. In the "Changing cell, row, and column dimensions" section, later in this chapter, we show you how to change column dimensions.

To reduce the *overall percentage width* of your table, hover the cursor over the little round handle in the middle of the table's right border until the cursor turns into a two-sided arrow. A tip pops up, telling you the percentage width of the table. (If you inserted a table and didn't fiddle with it yet, the width is 100 percent.) Click and drag the mouse to the left until the width matches the desired percentage. This action maintains the table's proportional dimensions, but changes its width in proportion to the page or its containing element (such as a <div>; we talk about <div> elements in Chapter 8).

Don't get frustrated if it takes a few tries to get what you want. When you're trying to select exactly what you want with the cursor, it can be a little squirrelly.

If you want to *fine-tune* your table's dimensions, follow these steps:

1. **Right-click the table and, from the pop-up menu that appears, choose Table Properties.**

   The Table Properties dialog box appears, as shown in Figure 10-3.

2. **In the Table Properties dialog box, select the Specify Width check box and, in the corresponding text box, type the width of the table.**

   To specify a *proportional* width, type the width of the table as a percentage of the width of its containing element (such as the browser window or <div>). For example, if you type **50**, Expression Web sets the width of the table at 50 percent, or half the width of the browser window or containing element. To specify an *absolute* width, type the table width in pixels. To turn off table width specifications, deselect the Specify Width check box.

3. **Select the option that corresponds to the measurement you specified in Step 2.**

   If you specified a proportional width, select the In Percent option. If you specified an absolute width, select the In Pixels option.

4. **If you want to specify a table height, select the Specify Height check box; in the corresponding text box, type the table's height in pixels or as a percentage value, and then select the corresponding option.**

5. **Click OK to close the dialog box and change the table size.**

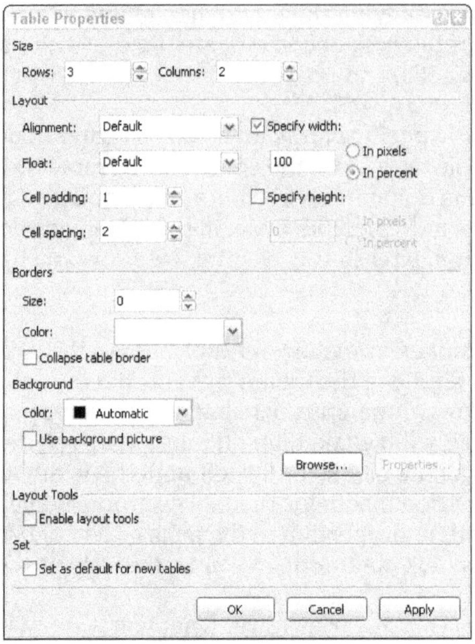

Figure 10-3:
The Table
Properties
dialog box.

Aligning a table

You can left-align, right-align, or center a table on the page or inside its containing element. Just follow these steps:

1. **Right-click the table and, from the pop-up menu that appears, choose Table Properties.**

   The Table Properties dialog box appears.

2. **In the dialog box, choose an option from the Alignment list box.**

   Your choices are Default, Left, Right, and Center. The Default option uses the visitor's default browser-alignment setting, which is left aligned.

3. **Click OK.**

   If you want to preview the table's alignment before saving changes, click the Apply button.

When you specify alignment for the table, Expression Web inserts the `align` attribute in the table's opening tag, like this:

```
<table align="center">
```

Wrapping text around a table

Similar to a picture, adjacent text can wrap around the right or left side of a table. This effect is referred to as *floating* the table. To make your table float, do the following:

1. **Right-click the table and, from the pop-up menu that appears, choose Table Properties.**

   The Table Properties dialog box appears.

2. **In the dialog box, choose an option from the Float list box:**
   - *Default:* Creates no floating effect
   - *Left:* Causes the table to float over to the left margin, with adjacent text wrapping around its right side
   - *Right:* Causes the table to float over to the right margin, with adjacent text wrapping around its left side

3. **Click OK to close the dialog box and change the table's floating setting.**

Expression Web uses the CSS property `float` to align the table with its surrounding elements, which it inserts in the table's opening tag as an inline style or into an existing or new class-based style. (See the earlier sidebar "Taming tables with CSS styles.") Here are the two style properties (inline is listed first):

```
<table style="float: left;">
.stylex {
        float: left;
}
```

Inserting blank space inside or between table cells

Adding space between the contents of table cells and their cell borders is known as *cell padding*. Padded cells open a table by placing white space around the contents of each cell. Figure 10-4 illustrates the difference a little padding makes. The table on the left contains no cell padding, and the table on the right has 5 pixels of cell padding applied. (We made the cell borders gray so that you can see them.)

Figure 10-4:
The difference that cell *padding* makes.

Tree	Vine Maple
Shrub	Red Twig Dogwood
Perennial	Sedum 'Autumn Joy'

Tree	Vine Maple
Shrub	Red Twig Dogwood
Perennial	Sedum 'Autumn Joy'

Cell spacing determines how much space exists *between* cells and also affects the appearance of table and cell borders. Figure 10-5 illustrates how changes in cell spacing affect a table. The table on the left contains no cell spacing, and the table on the right has 5 pixels of cell spacing applied to it.

Figure 10-5:
The difference that cell *spacing* makes.

Tree	Vine Maple
Shrub	Red Twig Dogwood
Perennial	Sedum 'Autumn Joy'

Tree	Vine Maple
Shrub	Red Twig Dogwood
Perennial	Sedum 'Autumn Joy'

To change cell padding or spacing, follow these steps:

1. **Right-click the table and, from the pop-up menu that appears, choose Table Properties.**

2. **To enlarge the area between cell contents and their borders (cell padding), in the Cell Padding text box in the dialog box, type the desired amount of padding (in pixels). To add space between the cells, in the Cell Spacing text box, type the desired amount of spacing (in pixels) separating table cells.**

3. **Click OK to close the dialog box and change the cell padding and spacing settings.**

When you change a table's cell padding or cell spacing, Expression Web inserts these attributes in the opening table tag:

```
<table cellpadding="2" cellspacing="5">
```

You can specify cell padding with the CSS `padding` property (`padding-top` or `padding-right`, for example), which allows you to set padding differently around each side of the cell (create a style rule that targets the `<td>` tag). You can also use CSS in different ways to control the space between cells, rows, and columns. See the earlier sidebar "Taming tables with CSS styles" for more information.

Adding borders to data tables

In Expression Web, tables are born naked, without *visible* borders, although you can see them in Design view — light gray dotted lines, dutifully holding your data in tidy rows and columns. Figure 10-6 illustrates what a default table looks like in a browser.

Figure 10-6:
A
borderless
table in a
browser.

Tree	Vine Maple
Shrub	Red Twig Dogwood
Perennial	Sedum 'Autumn Joy'

Tables have two types of borders:

- ✔ **Cell border:** Surrounds individual *cells*
- ✔ **Table border:** Surrounds the entire table

You set cell and table borders separately.

Expression Web controls both cell and table borders by creating CSS style rules, which gives you a lot of control over the border line style (solid, dotted, or dashed, for example), width, and color. You can have Expression Web write style rules for you as you format the borders, or you can write your own style rules by using the border properties. (We tell you how to create new styles in Chapter 7.)

To add *cell* borders, follow these steps:

1. **Select all the cells in the table.**

   For tips on how to select cells in a table, see the section "Selecting table parts," earlier in this chapter.

2. **Right-click the table and, from the pop-up menu that appears, choose Cell Properties.**

   The Cell Properties dialog box appears, as shown in Figure 10-7.

3. **In the Size text box in the Cell Properties dialog box, enter the desired border thickness in pixels.**

   The number you type refers to the thickness of the border surrounding the table. (Typing 0 in the Size text box makes borders invisible.)

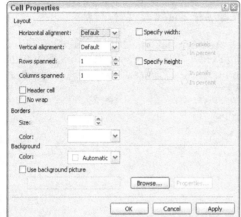

Figure 10-7:
The Cell
Properties
dialog box.

4. **To change the border color, from the Color list box, choose the color you like.**

5. **Click OK to close the dialog box.**

This example shows you how Expression Web sets borders for table cells by writing a class-based style rule:

```
.stylex {
        border: 1px solid #008000;
}
<td class="stylex">cell contents</td><td
        class="stylex">cell contents</td>
```

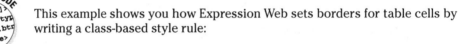

Notice that Expression Web inserts the class in each cell by inserting class="stylex" in each <td> tag, which means that you have to select each cell that you want formatted. (See the section "Selecting table parts," earlier in this chapter.)

To add *table* borders, follow these steps:

1. **Right-click the table and, from the pop-up menu that appears, choose Table Properties.**

2. **In the Size text box in the Table Properties dialog box, enter the desired border thickness in pixels.**

    The number you enter refers to the thickness of the border surrounding the table. (Entering 0 in the Size text box makes borders invisible).

3. **To change the border color, from the Color list box, choose the color you like.**

4. **If you prefer to put a single line between cells (rather than outline each individual cell with a box), select the Collapse Table Border check box.**

   This setting turns borders into thin lines.

5. **Click OK.**

This example shows you how Expression Web sets table borders and collapses cell borders by writing a class-based style rule that targets the table:

```
.stylex {
        border: 1px solid #008000;
        border-collapse: collapse;
}
<table class="stylex">
```

You can also control which table and cell borders appear by experimenting with the Borders button on either the Common or Formatting toolbar. To do so, select the part of the table you want to affect (or select the entire table), and then click the arrow button next to the Borders button to display a menu of options. Choose the option you want and see how your table changes.

Because table and cell borders are controlled by class-based CSS style rules, using the options available through the Borders button can cause Expression Web to generate a ridiculous number of styles, all of which set a border on one side or another of a cell. Unless you *need* to set borders for a particular cell or set of cells separately, select the cells you want to format all at one time and display the Cell Properties dialog box, which applies the same class-based style to the selected cells.

Another option is to use the AutoFormat function to slap a predefined set of attractive colors, border styles, and alignment options onto your table. To do so, click anywhere inside the table, and then click the Table AutoFormat button on the Tables toolbar (choose View➪Toolbars➪Tables). In the Table AutoFormat dialog box that appears, choose a table style from the list and adjust individual options until you like what you see. Click OK to close the dialog box and apply the format. Expression Web writes all the accompanying CSS styles needed to display the table in the format you choose.

Tweaking the table with the Tables toolbar

The Tables toolbar, shown in Figure 10-8, contains tools that give you precise control over your table's individual cells, rows, and columns. Select the cells, rows, or columns you want to change, and then click one of the buttons. Table 10-1 gives you the lowdown about what each button does.

Figure 10-8:
The Tables
toolbar.

Table 10-1	Table Options on the Tables Toolbar	
Button	*Button Name*	*What It Does*
	Column To the Left, Column To the Right	Inserts a column of cells to the left or right of the selected cell.
	Row Above, Row Below	Inserts a row of cells above or below the selected cell.
	Delete Cells	Deletes the selected cells.
	Merge Cells	Removes the borders between selected cells, creating one big combined cell.
	Split Cells	Creates multiple cells from one cell; you pick options in the Split Cells dialog box that appears.
	Align Top, Center Vertically, Align Bottom	Aligns the contents of the selected cells vertically inside the cells. See the Cell Properties dialog box for additional alignment options (explained elsewhere in this chapter).
	Distribute Rows Evenly, Distribute Columns Evenly	Makes each cell in the selected row or column an equal width.
	AutoFit to Contents	Adjusts the dimensions of columns and rows in the whole table to fit their contents precisely.

Button	Button Name	What It Does
	Fill Color	Adds a background color to selected cells.
	Table AutoFormat	Applies a variety of predefined table styles and customizes individual options when you select a table style from the drop-down list or click the button to display the Table AutoFormat dialog box.
	Show Layout Tool	Displays the table layout visual guides (explained later in this chapter).
	Draw Layout Table	Draws a custom-size layout table (explained later in this chapter).
	Draw Layout Cell	Draws a individual cell in a layout table (explained later in this chapter).

In addition to the alignment options available on the Tables toolbar, the Cell Properties dialog box gives you more options for aligning content vertically and horizontally within cells. To access the Cell Properties dialog box, right-click the selected cells and choose Cell Properties from the pop-up menu that appears.

Adding a single cell

You can use the options on the Tables toolbar to add entire rows and columns. But if you want to add a single cell rather than an entire row or column, follow these steps:

1. **Click inside the cell next to where you want the new cell to appear.**

2. **Choose either Table⇨Insert⇨Cell to the Left or Cell to the Right.**

   A new cell appears.

When you insert a single cell, the cell dislocates the other cells in the row, creating a somewhat lopsided table. That's not a problem if that's the effect you're looking for. However, if you want to add a cell to a table and maintain the table's gridlike structure, consider splitting an existing cell in two (see Table 10-1).

Adding a background picture

You can add a background picture that sits behind the contents of a single cell, a selected group of cells, or the whole table. (We show you how to change your Web page's background in Chapter 5.)

To add a background picture to a table, follow these steps:

1. **Select the cells, columns, or rows you want to change. (If you're not sure how, read the section "Selecting table parts," earlier in this chapter.) To change the background settings for the entire table, right-click the table and choose Table Properties from the pop-up menu that appears.**

   If, instead, you're changing the background of selected cells, choose Cell Properties from the pop-up menu. Depending on your choice, the Table Properties or Cell Properties dialog box appears.

2. **Select the Use Background Picture check box and, in the accompanying text box, type the location of the background image.**

   If you don't remember the file's location, click the Browse button to display the Select Background Picture dialog box. After you select the file, the dialog box closes, and the picture's location appears in the text box of the Table Properties (or Cell Properties) dialog box.

3. **Click OK to close the dialog box and apply the background setting.**

Expression Web uses CSS style properties for cell and table background colors and pictures; it either creates new class-based rules or adds background properties to existing style rules. Here's an example of how Expression Web adds a background image to the whole table:

```
.stylex {
          background-image: url('leaves.jpg');
}
<table class="stylex">
```

Changing cell, row, and column dimensions

Controlling the dimensions of table cells (and by extension, columns and rows) is similar to working with table dimensions because you can set an absolute size in pixels or a proportional size based on the size of the entire table. If you want to use absolute measurements, the easiest way to adjust the dimensions of cells, rows, and columns is to click a border and drag it to a new position.

To use proportional measurements to adjust the height or width of a cell, column, or row (or for more control over the absolute dimensions), follow these steps:

1. **Select the cells, columns, or rows you want to format.**

2. **Right-click the selection and choose Cell Properties from the pop-up menu that appears.**

   The Cell Properties dialog box appears (refer to Figure 10-7 earlier in this chapter).

3. **In the Specify Width text box, enter the desired width.**

   (If the text box appears dimmed, be sure that the Specify width check box is selected.)

   If you're specifying a proportional width, type the width of the cell or column as a percentage of the width of the table. For example, if you type **50**, Expression Web sets the width of the cell or column at 50 percent, or half the width of table.

   If you're specifying an absolute width, type the width in pixels.

   To turn off width specifications, click to deselect the Specify Width check box. (If you do this, the size of the selected area is determined by the size of its contents.)

4. **Select the option that corresponds to the measurement you specified in Step 3.**

   If you're specifying a proportional width, select the In Percent option. If you're specifying an absolute width, select the In Pixels option.

5. **Select the Specify Height check box; in the corresponding text box, type the desired height in pixels or as a percentage value, and then select the corresponding option.**

   To turn off height specifications, deselect the Specify Height check box.

6. **Click OK to close the dialog box and change the dimension settings.**

Depending on which way you have Expression Web set up to write styles for width and height, cell width (and/or height) is specified in each cell's `<td>` tag as an inline style or as a class-based style rule. (See the sidebar "Taming tables with CSS styles," earlier in this chapter.) Columns are nothing more than a set of cells in a particular location in the table (`<td>cell contents</td>`). When you change the width of a column, Expression Web figures out which cells you selected and adds the necessary inline styles or class-based style rules to just those cells that make up the column.

To distribute the rows and columns equally in the table, or to adjust the dimensions of columns and rows to fit their contents precisely, see the Tables toolbar options, explained in Table 10-1.

Expression Web contains a quirk that makes it possible to set the width of table columns to a number not equal to the total width of the table. For example, if you set the width of a two-column table to 100 pixels, you can also set the width of the table's columns to a number totaling more or less than 100. Things also get funky if you set different widths for individual table cells (as opposed to entire columns of cells), especially if the table is complex. The solution is to keep your tables relatively simple. At a minimum, preview your page in several Web browsers to see how your table looks to your visitors.

Deleting a data table

Building the perfect table takes some work, but deleting a table is effortless. You can either preserve the table's contents by converting the contents to regular paragraphs, or you can erase the table and its contents completely.

To convert the contents of a table into regular paragraphs, click inside the table and then choose Table⇨Convert⇨Table to Text.

To *really* delete a table, select the table by choosing Table⇨Select⇨Table (or click the <table> tag on the Quick Tag Selector bar), and then press the Backspace or Delete key.

Laying Out Pages with Tables

As far as Expression Web is concerned, data tables with their borders turned off are *layout tables*. Layout tables create a framework into which you place chunks of text, pictures, and even other tables. By changing the table's layout and dimensions, and the alignment of page content, you change how content is arranged inside the page. Figure 10-9 shows a page layout using a table to hold the different parts.

The easiest way to work with a layout table is to use it as the starting point for a new, empty page and then insert content into the layout table. You can certainly add a layout table to an existing page, but the operation requires some cutting and pasting to get the content already sitting in the page into the new layout table.

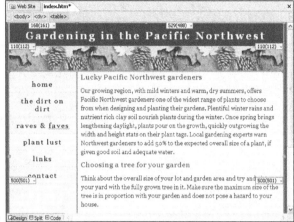

Figure 10-9:
This page uses a layout table to give it structure.

Although, on the HTML level, layout tables and data tables are technically the same (and use the same HTML tags — `<table>`, `<tr>`, and `<td>`), Expression Web treats these two table varieties as fundamentally different animals. Therefore, creating and working with layout tables involves using a distinct set of tools. Layout table tools live inside the Layout Tables task pane, as shown in Figure 10-10. To display the task pane, choose Task Panes➪Layout Tables.

Figure 10-10:
The Layout Tables task pane.

Using a "canned" table layout

The easiest way to add a layout table to your page is to choose one of the layouts Expression Web provides. To do so, place the cursor in your page where you want the layout table to appear. In the Table layout box of the Layout Tables task pane, scroll until you see a format you like, and then click it. Just like that — a layout table appears inside your page. (If none of the layouts looks exactly like what you want, just pick the closest approximation — you can change the table setup later.)

The table's green outside border displays pixel measurements for each row and column in the table. If you click one of the blue interior borders inside the table, measurements for the selected cell appear. (By the way, these borders are visible only in Design view. When you see the table in a Web browser or in Preview view, the borders are invisible.)

Drawing a layout table from scratch

After you're familiar with how layout tables work, you may find it easy to draw your own. Expression Web gives you two methods for creating new layout tables; here's our take on the easiest method:

1. **Place the cursor in your page where you want the layout table to appear, and then, in the Layout Tables task pane, select the Insert Layout Table option.**

    An empty layout table, measuring 450 x 450 pixels, appears inside the page.

    You may find it easier to draw your table with Expression Web rulers and grids visible; to show rulers or grids, choose View➪Ruler and Grid➪Show Ruler or View➪Ruler and Grid➪Show Grid.

2. **To add cells to the table, in the Layout Tables task pane, click the Draw Layout Cell button.**

    After you click this button and move the cursor over the layout table, the cursor turns into a little drawing tool.

3. **Click inside the layout table and, while holding down the mouse button, drag the cursor diagonally to draw a rectangle the size and shape of your desired cell.**

    To create a simple row or column, click one of the green table borders, and then drag the cursor to the opposite corner of the table. Or, click anywhere inside the table and draw a rectangle that's any size or shape.

4. **Release the mouse button to create the cell.**

   The layout cell you drew appears inside the table, surrounded by a blue border. Depending on how you drew the cell, other placeholder cells may appear inside the table to fill out the table's structure.

You can fill a layout table with as many layout cells as you like (within reason, of course). Drawing layout table cells takes a bit of practice, so don't be afraid to press Ctrl+Z to undo your changes if you don't like the results. You can always try again, or you can tweak the measurements of the cells later.

Turning a data table into a layout table

If you're more comfortable using the data table tools to build tables, that's no problem. You can easily transform filled grid tables into layout tables. To do so, follow these steps:

1. **Create the data table and insert the content of your choice. (We tell you how earlier in this chapter.)**

   If you're working with an existing table, skip this step.

2. **Right-click the table, and from the pop-up menu that appears, choose Table Properties.**

   The Table Properties dialog box appears.

3. **In the dialog box, select the Enable Layout Tools option.**

4. **If you haven't already, turn off table borders by entering 0 in the Size text box.**

5. **Click OK.**

   The Table Properties dialog box closes.

Although the table looks no different than before its transformation, Expression Web now considers the table a layout table. (You can tell because when you pass the cursor over the table, its outer border turns green, and its inner borders turn blue.) You can now use the Expression Web layout table tools to play with how the table looks.

Changing a layout table's width, height, and alignment on the page

You can change the layout table's dimensions to keep everything visible within the browser window. If you're not sure how wide or tall to make your layout table, Expression Web can give you some ballpark numbers. In the lower-right part of the Expression Web status bar, click the Page Size box. (You see two numbers separated by an *x*, such as 760 x 420.) The menu that appears shows you, in pixels (width x height), the amount of page space that appears inside common browser window sizes at different monitor resolutions, ranging from your monitor's setting down to lower resolutions. (Resolutions higher than your monitor's setting aren't available.) If you want to design your pages so that they look good when viewed at 800 x 600, your layout tables should be no wider than 760 pixels. (They can be taller, however, because visitors are more willing to scroll up and down than they are to scroll from side to side.)

The ruler and grid may make it easier for you to eyeball the dimensions of your table. To turn on the ruler and the grid, choose View➪Ruler and Grid➪Show Ruler and View➪Ruler and Grid➪Show Grid.

To specify a fixed width for the layout table, and to specify the layout table's alignment on the page, follow these steps:

1. **In Design view, click anywhere inside the layout table.**

2. **In the Layout Tables task pane's Width text box, enter a number of pixels and then press the Tab key.**

3. **To set or change the table's height, in the task pane's Height text box, enter a number of pixels and then press the Tab key.**

By default, the layout table's height equals the height of the page, which is ultimately determined by the size of the table's contents. You can generally leave the table height as it is, unless you specifically want to control the table height.

4. **To change the dimensions of the cells inside the table to maintain the table's proportion, select the Auto-Scale Cells with Table check box.**

5. **To change the table's alignment on the page, in the task pane, click the Align Left, Align Center, or Align Right button.**

By default, layout tables are left aligned.

Changing row and column dimensions

Although it's perfectly acceptable to set a layout table's overall dimensions, you gain more control by changing the dimensions of the individual rows and columns inside the table. For example, you can set one column to a fixed width and another one to stretch automatically so that it resizes according to the visitor's Web browser (also known as *autostretch*).

Here's how to change the dimensions of individual columns and rows in your layout table:

1. **In Design view, move the cursor over the layout table's outer border until it turns green, and then click the outer border.**

   The table's row-and-column pixel dimensions become visible. Column widths are visible in little boxes along the table's top and bottom borders, and row heights are visible in little boxes along the left and right borders.

2. **To change a column's width, click the down arrow inside the column's width box, and choose an option from the menu that appears:**

   • **Change Column Width:** Choose this option to change the column's width (in pixels). In the Column Properties dialog box that appears, enter a number of pixels in the Column Width text box, and then click OK to close the dialog box.

   • **Make Column Autostretch:** Choose this option to cause the column to automatically stretch to fill the available space in the browser window. This option is most often used in the rightmost column in layout tables so that the column's contents can stretch as a visitor widens or narrows the browser window.

   • **Use Column Spacer Image:** Choose this option to insert an invisible spacer image (a transparent 1-pixel GIF) into the column to maintain the column's width in older browsers. This option is generally used in empty columns that exist only to add space between two columns filled with content.

3. **To change a row's height, click the down arrow inside the row's height box, and choose an option from the menu that appears.**

   (The options on this menu work just like the options for column width, which we describe in Step 2.)

Adding and deleting rows and columns

To add a new row or column to your layout table, follow these steps:

1. **Place the cursor inside the layout table next to where you want the new row or column to appear.**

2. **Choose Table⇨Insert⇨Rows or Columns.**

   The Insert Rows or Columns dialog box appears.

3. **Select the Rows or Columns option button (depending on what you want to create).**

4. **In the Number of Rows/Columns box, enter the number of rows or columns you want to create.**

5. **In the Location section of the dialog box, select the option corresponding to where you want the new rows or columns to appear.**

   Your choices are Above Selection or Below Selection (for rows) or Left of Selection or Right of Selection (for columns).

6. **Click OK.**

   The dialog box closes, and the new rows or columns appear.

To delete a row, column, or cell, click inside the row, column, or cell you want to delete and then choose Table⇨Delete⇨Row, Column, or Cell.

Filling layout tables with content

You can insert into a layout table any elements that you can insert into a regular page (such as headings, paragraphs, or pictures). Just click inside a cell and proceed as usual. If you add a layout table to a page that already contains text, pictures, and other content, simply cut and paste the content into the appropriate places in the table.

Keep in mind that you don't have to fill *every* cell in your layout table. Because the table is ultimately invisible to your visitors, you can leave some rows and columns blank to act as spacers between rows and columns filled with content (although you should keep your layout table as simple as possible).

Adding borders and backgrounds to layout table cells

You have the same options available for adding borders and backgrounds to layout table cells as you have for data table cells. Expression Web uses CSS styles to control borders and backgrounds, which gives you a lot of control over the line style, width, and color. To take full advantage of the stylish properties you can apply, create a class- or ID-based style that targets the cell.

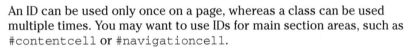

We cover creating class- and ID-based styles in Chapter 7, but here's a brief rundown for creating a style rule for a layout table cell:

1. **Select the cell for which you want to create a style rule.**

2. **Choose Format⇨New Style.**

   The New Style dialog box appears.

3. **In the Selector box, type** .stylename **to create a class-based style rule or** #stylename **to create an ID-based style rule.**

    An ID can be used only once on a page, whereas a class can be used multiple times. You may want to use IDs for main section areas, such as #contentcell or #navigationcell.

4. **Select the Apply New Style to Document Selection check box.**

   When Expression Web creates the style rule, it also adds the class or ID to the layout table cell.

5. **Use the options in the Border and Background categories to add borders and background colors or pictures to the selected cell.**

6. **Click OK.**

 The options in this section apply to individual layout cells. If you want to apply effects to more than one cell at a time, you need to select those cells first. (If you're applying a style to multiple cells, create a class-based style rather than an ID-based style.)

Like data table cells, you can also use the options in the Cell Properties dialog box to set options for selected layout table cells by right-clicking in the cell and, from the pop-up menu that appears, choosing Cell Properties. The options for borders are more limited because you can only specify a solid line-style border around all sides of the cell.

Deleting a layout table

If you change your mind about using a layout table in your page (which we hope you won't), you can easily delete the table. The problem is that all the table content goes, too.

To preserve the table content, you must first cut all the table content and paste it elsewhere in the page, outside the table. (Oy, what a pain.)

To delete the layout table, choose Table⇨Select⇨Layout Table, and then press the Backspace or Delete key.

Chapter 11

Streamlining Sites with Dynamic Web Templates

In This Chapter

▶ Simplifying building large-scale Web sites with Dynamic Web Templates

▶ Working with Dynamic Web Templates (from creation to updates and detachment)

*S*trangely enough, as your site grows in size beyond a handful of pages, you may find yourself doing more and more repetitive work, especially when you're expanding your site. If your pages' layout and design are consistent, creating new pages generally involves copying and pasting material from old pages and then inserting new content. The job isn't necessarily difficult, but it's certainly not exciting, and it's definitely time consuming.

Expression Web cuts out some of the drudgery with Dynamic Web Templates. In this chapter, we demonstrate how *Dynamic Web Templates* simplify creating and maintaining a Web site (especially large sites or those with more than one author). We also show you how to create Dynamic Web Templates and how to put them to work in your site.

Introducing Dynamic Web Templates

Before you jump into using Dynamic Web Templates, you should understand what you're getting yourself into. Dynamic Web Templates can save you a lot of time, but can also cause unnecessary hassle when used for the wrong type of site. Read on for details about what Dynamic Web Templates do, and for advice about how (or whether) to use them in your site.

Separating fixed and unique content

Dynamic Web Templates enable you to place all the stuff that stays the same across pages (*fixed content*) into a template. Typical bits of fixed content include logos, page banners, copyright notices, and navigation. You then attach the template to separate pages containing *unique content*, and the fixed content appears in the page automatically.

Think of Dynamic Web Templates as your site's "letterhead" — a set of standard elements that appear in several pages, independently of the pages' content.

Dynamic Web Templates versus regular page templates

Dynamic Web Templates differ from regular page templates in three important ways. With dynamic templates, you can

✔ **Keep several templates on hand.** You can create several Dynamic Web Templates and then radically change the look of a page by switching the Dynamic Web Template attached to that page. (You can use a regular page template only as a page's starting point; you can't later "detach" a regular page template.)

✔ **Update several pages at a time.** You can attach a single Dynamic Web Template to several pages and then change the fixed content in *all* the pages by simply updating and saving the Dynamic Web Template. (Regular page templates can only be used individually.)

✔ **"Lock" fixed content so that other authors can't edit it.** When you attach a Dynamic Web Template to a page, you (and other site contributors) can type only inside the areas of the page that you define in the template as editable regions. The rest of the page is "locked," and its content can't be edited. In this way, you can rest assured that the page's layout and design remain consistent, even when several people work on the site.

Editable regions are simply empty spaces inside the Dynamic Web Template that act as placeholders for each page's unique content. After you apply a Dynamic Web Template to a page, you can place any type of content you like (text, graphics, headings, tables, form elements — anything) into the page's editable regions.

Deciding whether you should use Dynamic Web Templates in your site

To figure out whether Dynamic Web Templates would cut your workload or add to it, you must step back and take a look at your site's content. Sites that are good candidates for Dynamic Web Templates contain several pages with a consistent design and layout.

For example, if most or all of the pages in your site use the same background graphic, have a page banner or company logo at the top of the page, and use the same layout, it makes sense to place those fixed elements inside a Dynamic Web Template so that you don't have to rebuild these elements each time you add a new page to the site. With the help of the Dynamic Web Template, creating a new page becomes a matter of attaching the Dynamic Web Template to a new, blank page, filling the new page's editable regions with unique content, and then formatting that content however you like.

For a simple site, you might use only a single template for most or all of your pages. For a more complex site with different sections, each with its own design, you may want to use more than one Dynamic Web Template.

Creating a Dynamic Web Template

Creating a Dynamic Web Template involves three steps: Build the template itself, define the editable regions inside the template, and then save the template. The following sections walk you through each part of the process.

Building the template

To create a Dynamic Web Template, take a look at your site's design and identify the elements that remain the same in several pages in your site. These elements are the ones you want to place inside the Dynamic Web Template. Figure 11-1 illustrates elements that a typical Dynamic Web Template might contain.

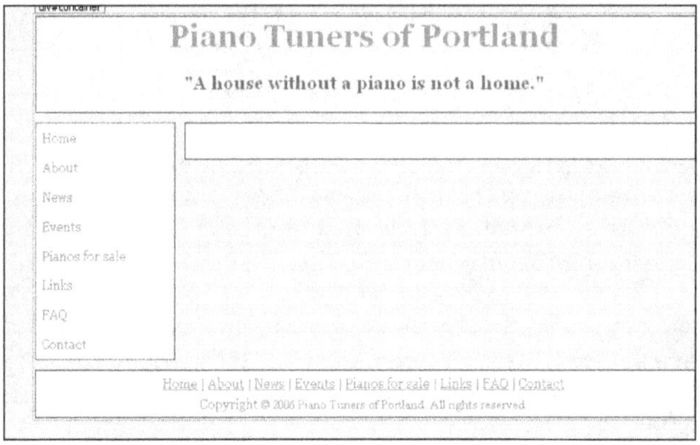

Figure 11-1:
The
beginning of
a typical
Dynamic
Web
Template.

To build a Dynamic Web Template, follow these steps:

1. **Create a new, blank Web page.**

   Create the page as though you're creating a regular page.

2. **In the new page, add the elements that you want to appear inside your Dynamic Web Template.**

   For example, insert the logo, page banner, navigation, copyright information — anything you want to appear in each of your content pages later on.

   You can create styles for positioning and formatting the various elements right in the template or attach an external style sheet, just as with any other Web page.

3. **Save the page as a Dynamic Web Template by choosing File⇨Save As.**

   The Save As dialog box appears.

4. **In the dialog box's Save As Type list box, choose Dynamic Web Template.**

5. **In the dialog box's File Name list box, enter a one-word filename.**

   Expression Web automatically adds the `.dwt` filename extension to the end of the filename after you save the page.

6. **In the dialog box, click the Save button.**

   The Save As dialog box closes, and Expression Web saves the Dynamic Web Template.

If you already have a page in your site that contains all the elements that you want to appear inside your Dynamic Web Template, a quicker course of action may be to create a new page based on that existing page, and, in that new page, to delete whatever content you *don't* want to appear inside the template. We explain in Chapter 2 how to create a new page based on an existing page.

Defining editable regions inside the template

After you build your Dynamic Web Template, you must tell Expression Web which areas inside the template are editable. That is, you must define spaces in the template into which you (or other site authors) can later plop content after the template is attached to a regular Web page.

To define the Dynamic Web Template's editable regions, follow these steps:

1. **With the Dynamic Web Template open in Design view, place the cursor in the page where you want the editable region to appear.**

2. **Right-click the page, and from the pop-up menu that appears, choose Manage Editable Regions.**

   The Editable Regions dialog box appears (see Figure 11-2).

Figure 11-2:
The Editable
Regions
dialog box.

3. **In the dialog box's Region Name text box, enter an identifying label for that region.**

   Give the region a logical name that prompts the page's author to fill the region with the appropriate content. Good examples are Page Content and Product Image.

4. **In the dialog box, click the Add button.**

   The region name appears inside the Other Regions on This Page box. The region also appears in the template as a rectangular box with a small name label attached to its upper-left corner and a text placeholder inside it.

5. **In the dialog box, click the Close button.**

   The dialog box closes. Figure 11-3 shows what a Dynamic Web Template with one editable region named Page Content looks like.

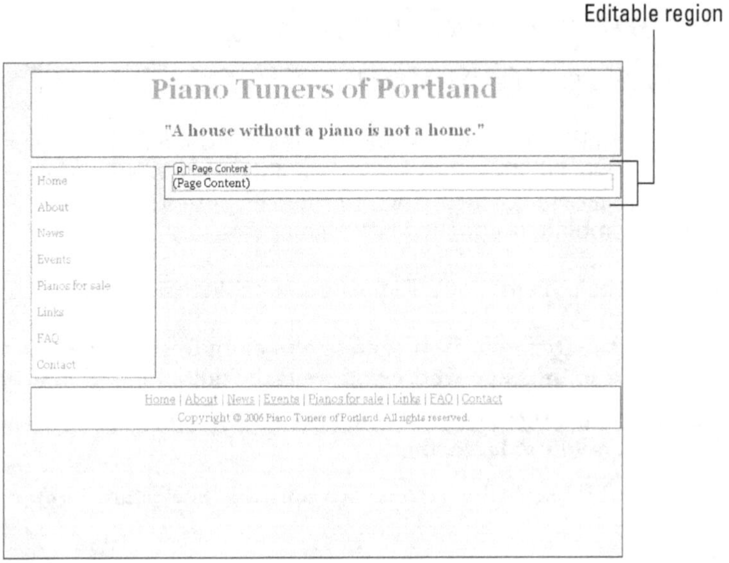

Editable region

Piano Tuners of Portland

"A house without a piano is not a home."

Home
About
News
Events
Pianos for sale
Links
FAQ
Contact

p | Page Content
(Page Content)

Home | About | News | Events | Pianos for sale | Links | FAQ | Contact
Copyright © 2006 Piano Tuners of Portland. All rights reserved.

Figure 11-3:
Adding an editable region to a Dynamic Web Template.

Insert as many editable regions as you like into your Dynamic Web Template. To add another editable region, click elsewhere in the page and follow the steps in this section again.

If you're not sure where the editable region should be placed, just remember that these areas eventually become the places where you add new stuff to a page formatted with this template. Place the editable region wherever you want the unique content to appear. It's as easy as that.

Editable regions contain a basic text placeholder: the region name inside parentheses (refer to Figure 11-3). You can replace the placeholder with standard content (so that the page looks good whether or not it's edited), or you can add your own placeholder text to indicate to page authors what type of content you expect. Chapter 2 offers tips about placeholder text you might put into a template.

Saving the template

After you add editable regions to your Dynamic Web Template, save the page as you normally would (press Ctrl+S). If you created the Dynamic Web Template by using an existing Web page, when you attempt to save the page, Expression Web pops open a dialog box reminding you that you're saving the page as a Dynamic Web Template. That's okay: Just click OK to close the dialog box, and then proceed as usual to save the page.

After you save the template, you're not stuck with it — you can edit Dynamic Web Templates just as you edit regular Web pages. Just make whatever changes you want, and then save the file again.

Take a look at the code for editable regions in a Dynamic Web Template:

```
<!-- #BeginEditable "Page%20Content" -->(Page Content)<!--
     #EndEditable -->
```

When you define a region in your Web page as editable, Expression Web surrounds it with HTML comments that show where the editable region begins and ends. In this case, the comment `<!-- #BeginEditable "Page%20Content" -->` defines the start of the editable region Page Content, and the comment `<!-- #EndEditable -->` defines where it stops. The placeholder text `(Page Content)` appears on the page in the editable region. (`%20` indicates a space between words, in this case, between `Page` and `Content`).

Comments are special HTML tags that you can insert anywhere in your code as notes to yourself or other authors; Web browsers know not to display the comments on the screen. We talk more about comments and how to insert your own comments in Chapter 14.

Attaching a Dynamic Web Template to a Web Page

After you create and save a Dynamic Web Template in your site, you *attach* it to a regular Web page. (We call this regular page the *content page.*) The content page you choose can be full of text and graphics, or it can be empty. Either way, after you attach a Dynamic Web Template to the content page, all the elements in the template appear automatically inside the content page.

If your page *contains* content, Expression Web can put the existing content into only one editable region, even if your Dynamic Web Template contains several editable regions. Be sure to read these instructions carefully and thoroughly because some of the steps can seem a bit confusing.

To attach a Dynamic Web Template to a content page, follow these steps:

1. **Open (or create) the content page to which you want to attach the Dynamic Web Template.**

   Figure 11-4 illustrates a simple content page. This page contains only text, but keep in mind that content pages can contain anything, from text and pictures to tables, form fields, and anything else a Web page can hold. Content pages can also start out empty.

Figure 11-4:
A typical
content
page.

2. **In the Folder List task pane, click to select the icon for the page you want to attach the Dynamic Web Template to.**

   If you want to attach the Dynamic Web Template to multiple Web pages, hold down the Ctrl key and click each page.

3. **Choose Format⇨Dynamic Web Template⇨Attach Dynamic Web Template.**

   The Attach Dynamic Web Template dialog box appears.

4. **Click the filename for the Dynamic Web Template and then click Open.**

   If the page or pages you're attaching the template to contain content, a message warns you that content outside the <html> tag will be erased. Because your content is safely nested inside the page's <html> tags, click Yes.

   Keep these considerations in mind when you attach the Dynamic Web Template:

   • If the content page is empty, the elements inside the Dynamic Web Template appear inside the content page automatically.

   • The filename of the attached template appears in the upper-right corner of the page. (This notation is only a reminder for you; it doesn't appear when the page is viewed with a Web browser.) Also, the cursor blinks inside the content page's editable region (the first region in the page if the page has more than one), prompting you to add some content to the page. Do so by typing some text, adding a graphic, or inserting whatever content you want. (You can skip the rest of the steps in this section.)

   • If the content page already contains text, graphics, or other content, the Match Editable Regions dialog box appears, as shown in Figure 11-5.

Figure 11-5:
The Match
Editable
Regions
dialog box.

- The first time you attach a Dynamic Web Template to a content page, you must tell Expression Web which editable region should hold the page's existing content (even if the page contains only a single editable region).

- The Dynamic Web Template column lists the name of the first (or only) editable region in the page.

- The Current Page column lists Expression Web's best guess about which existing content on the content page should be placed in the editable region displayed in the Dynamic Web Template column.

5. **Choose an editable region to hold the page's existing content by clicking that region's name in the dialog box.**

Existing content can be funneled only into a single editable region, even if the template contains more than one region.

If you're happy with the Expression Web default choice (the first editable region in the template), or if the template contains only one editable region, click OK. The Match Editable Regions dialog box closes, and a Microsoft Expression Web dialog box appears, confirming that the content page has been updated. (Click the Close button to close the dialog box.) You're done!

If you're not happy with the default choice, read on.

6. **In the main area of the Match Editable Regions dialog box, click the name of the editable region you want to change, and then click the Modify button.**

The Choose Editable Region for Content dialog box appears.

7. **From the New Region list box, choose the name of the region you want, and then click OK.**

The Choose Editable Region for Content dialog box closes, and the Match Editable Regions dialog box becomes visible again.

8. **In the dialog box, click OK.**

The Match Editable Regions dialog box closes, and a Microsoft Expression Web dialog box appears, confirming that the content page has been updated. (Click the Close button to close the dialog box.) The finished page appears, as shown in Figure 11-6.

Figure 11-6: How the content page looks with the Dynamic Web Template attached.

You can attach the same Dynamic Web Template to as many content pages in your site as you like. The more pages you format by using the templates, the more pages you don't later have to edit by hand when you simply want to change a single element that appears in all the pages (such as a new logo, a page banner, or an updated copyright notice).

After you attach a Dynamic Web Template to a page, Expression Web inserts a comment with the template name near the top of the page, like this:

```
<!-- #BeginTemplate "pianotuners.dwt" -->
```

An ending comment is inserted at the bottom of the page:

```
<!-- #EndTemplate -->
```

Other than that, the code for a page with a Dynamic Web Template attached looks almost exactly like the code for the Dynamic Web Template, except that the page's unique content, rather than the placeholder text, appears between the comments. All non-editable regions (the fixed content areas from the Dynamic Web Template) have a light orange background. Here's what the first line or two of our content page example looks like:

```
<!-- #BeginEditable "Page%20Content" --><h2>We want your
        music to sound great. Always!</h2>
<p>A well-tuned piano fills your home with music...</p>
        <!-- #EndEditable -->
```

After you attach a Dynamic Web Template to a content page, you can type or insert content only into the page's editable regions; the rest of the page is "locked." If this isn't okay, and you need to make a change to a part of the page that lies outside an editable region, you can either detach the content page from the Dynamic Web Template (making the entire page editable) or add more editable regions to the attached template and then save the template's changes (automatically updating any attached pages). We explain how to update a site based on Dynamic Web Templates in the next section.

Here are a few considerations to keep in mind when working with Dynamic Web Templates:

- ✔ When a page with a Dynamic Web Template attached to it is open in the editing window, Expression Web shows you what you can and cannot edit by graying out the fixed, "locked" content in Design view. Also, when you pass your cursor over one of these regions, it changes to a circle with a slash through it. If elements in the non-editable region have a light background color, this highlighting makes them look different in Design view (for example, white turns gray). To see what your page will look like to your Web visitors, preview it in a browser. (We tell you how in Chapter 2.) In Code view, locked code is highlighted in light orange.

- ✔ You can combine the power of Dynamic Web Templates and Cascading Style Sheets in your Web site by attaching an external style sheet containing all positioning and formatting to the Dynamic Web Template. Not only do your content pages contain the fixed content from the Dynamic Web Template, they also already have the style sheet attached. All the Web site templates provided with Expression Web use style sheets and Dynamic Web Templates in this combination. Create a new Web site from your favorite Expression Web template (we tell you how in Chapter 1) and take a look around to see how the different pieces fit together.

- ✔ Although Dynamic Web Templates are powerful creatures, they don't play well with each other. Each page can have only one Dynamic Web Template attached to it at a time.

Creating a New Page from a Dynamic Web Template

Creating new Web pages based on Dynamic Web Templates is a snap. To do so, follow these steps:

1. **Choose File⇨New⇨Create from Dynamic Web Template.**

   The Attach Dynamic Web Template dialog box appears.

2. **Click the Dynamic Web Template you want to use and then click Open.**

   A Microsoft Expression Web dialog box appears, confirming that the file has been created.

   The page appears in the editing window, with the filename `Untitled_x.htm`.

3. **Save the page. (We tell you how in Chapter 2.)**

   You're ready to add content to the page's editable regions.

Updating a Site That Uses Dynamic Web Templates

Here's where all your work of creating templates and attaching them to content pages pays off.

After your site's fixed content and unique content are neatly divided among Dynamic Web Templates and attached to content pages, updating your site becomes a piece of cake. Depending on how you want to change your site, you can do so in one of three ways: Make and save changes to the Dynamic Web Template itself; attach a different Dynamic Web Template to a content page; or detach the Dynamic Web Template from the content page altogether.

Updating the template itself

If you want to change any of the fixed elements in your content pages, you simply need to open the attached Dynamic Web Template file, make whatever changes you want to that file, and then save it. Expression Web keeps track of which pages the template is linked to and automatically reflects the changes inside those pages (after checking with you first to make sure that you want to update them all).

For example, you may have attached a Dynamic Web Template to 20 content pages in your site. The Dynamic Web Template contains a number of fixed design elements that form the visual backbone of your site's pages, including a rather dated logo that was designed in the early 1980s. You decide to overhaul the company image by designing a new logo. To update all 20 pages in one attempt, you simply open the Dynamic Web Template file, replace the old logo with the new logo, and save the page. The new logo appears automatically in all the linked content pages.

You can change the template in any way you want. You can add or delete elements, and you can move, add, or remove editable regions.

To open a Dynamic Web Template, you can either double-click its icon in the Folder List task pane, or, with a linked content page open in Design view, choose Format➪Dynamic Web Template➪Open Attached Dynamic Web Template.

If your site uses several Dynamic Web Templates and you can't remember which is linked to what, take a look at the Dynamic Web Template report, which rounds up all the information in a useful table. To view this report, choose Site➪Reports➪Shared Content➪Dynamic Web Templates.

All Dynamic Web Templates must contain at least one editable region. If you delete an editable region in a template that, in linked pages, is filled with content, when you save the template's changes, Expression Web prompts you to move the content from the old region (the one you're deleting) to a different region in the page. If the region you're moving the content to already contains its own stuff, the two chunks of content merge and share that region.

Swapping Dynamic Web Templates

For a more radical change of image, rather than make piecemeal changes to the attached template, you may want to create an entirely new template and swap it for the old one. Like changing outfits in a dressing room, changing Dynamic Web Templates enables you to "try on" different looks for a page without affecting the page's core content.

To swap Dynamic Web Templates, follow these steps:

1. **Create a new Dynamic Web Template (follow the steps we provide earlier in this chapter).**

   Ideally, the new Dynamic Web Template should contain editable regions *with the same names as the old template.* That way, when you swap templates, Expression Web automatically funnels the content from the XYZ editable region in the old template to the XYZ region in the new template.

If the new template contains regions that are named differently, or if the template contains a different number of regions, the swapping process becomes slightly more complicated.

2. **In the Folder List task pane, select the file or files to which you want to attach the new Dynamic Web Template.**

   To select more than one file, while holding down the Ctrl key, click the files' icons.

3. **With the file icon or icons selected, choose Format⇨Dynamic Web Template⇨Attach Dynamic Web Template.**

   The Attach Dynamic Web Template dialog box appears.

4. **In the dialog box, double-click the new template's icon.**

   One of the following three events then occurs:

   • *The old and new templates contain equivalent editable regions:* The Attach Dynamic Web Template dialog box closes, Expression Web attaches the selected template, and a Microsoft Expression Web dialog box pops up, letting you know that all is well. Click the Close button to close the dialog box. You're done!

   • *The old and new templates contain different numbers of editable regions, or the regions are named differently:* The Match Editable Regions dialog box appears, prompting you to map the regions between the current page and new Dynamic Web Template. If the regions correspond properly, click OK. The Match Editable Regions dialog box closes, and a Microsoft Expression Web dialog box appears, confirming that the content page has been updated. Click the Close button to close the dialog box. You're done!

   • *The regions don't correspond properly:* You must manually map the regions listed in the Match Editable Regions dialog box. Proceed to Step 5.

5. **In the main area of the Match Editable Regions dialog box, click the name of the editable region that doesn't match correctly and then click the Modify button.**

   The Choose Editable Region for Content dialog box appears.

6. **From the New Region list box, choose the name of the region you want, and then click OK.**

   The Choose Editable Region for Content dialog box closes, and the Match Editable Regions dialog box becomes visible again.

7. **In the dialog box, click OK.**

   The Match Editable Regions dialog box closes, and a Microsoft Expression Web dialog box appears, confirming that the content page has been updated. Click the Close button to close the dialog box.

Detaching a page from a Dynamic Web Template

If you decide that a content page no longer benefits from its association with a Dynamic Web Template, detach the template. The good news is that all the fixed content contributed by the template stays inside the content page and is now completely editable, so you don't have to rebuild the entire page to have it match up with all the other pages in your site. The bad news is that if you later change the Dynamic Web Template (thereby updating all attached pages in the site), you must update the detached pages by hand.

Detaching a Dynamic Web Template is a one-way operation. The page inherits all the content from the Dynamic Web Template and continues its life as a normal page without any content provided from elsewhere. Make sure this is what you want before detaching a Dynamic Web Template from your page.

To detach a content page from a Dynamic Web Template, do this:

1. **Open the content page that you want to detach from the Dynamic Web Template.**

2. **Choose Format⇨Dynamic Web Template⇨Detach from Dynamic Web Template.**

   Expression Web unlinks the two files, and a Microsoft Expression Web dialog box appears, confirming the action.

3. **In the dialog box, click the Close button.**

Part IV
Going Live and Keeping House

The 5th Wave   By Rich Tennant

"You're not going to believe this, but I'm standing in front of a 56 k chimney. I'll be here all night downloading this stuff."

In this part . . .

Ready, set, GO! Follow the instructions in Chapter 12 to get your beautiful site out on the Web for everyone to ooh and ahh over. And although keeping everything in good working order isn't nearly as glamorous, we tell you how to do it in Chapter 13. Chapter 14 gives you an overview of the Expression Web code tools and gets you up to speed on some basic HTML concepts.

Chapter 12

Making Your Worldwide Debut

Drum roll, please! It's the moment of truth — time to unveil your painstakingly prepared, lovingly built Web site and make it visible to the world.

In this chapter, we show you how to put your site through its paces to get it ready to send out onto the World Wide Web. We also give you tips on how to update your site to keep it fresh and interesting.

Determining What "Publishing Your Web Site" Means

Publishing your Web site means making the site visible on the World Wide Web for all to see (or, in the case of a smaller-scale intranet site, visible to members of that intranet). For your site to be accessible to visitors, you must copy all the site's files and folders from your computer to a Web server. A *Web server* is a computer running special software that maintains a high-speed, round-the-clock connection to the Internet or to an internal network.

A typical Web-hosting service provider offers storage space on its Web server for a monthly fee, although you can also find Web hosting for free. The amount of storage space varies, ranging from 100MB free sites to sites that offer 200 gigabytes and charge a monthly fee.

✔ A *shared* Web server means the server that holds your Web site also holds other Web sites. This option works well for all except the largest and most complex Web sites, which benefit from dedicated servers.

✔ A *dedicated* Web server holds only one Web site. The service fee for a dedicated server is therefore significantly higher.

If you're not sure which option is best for you, check the different plans and the storage space available at different price levels, and talk to the Web host's customer service personnel before you sign up for a Web hosting service.

If you're not sure how much file space your Web site takes up, try this: In the Folder List task pane, right-click the site's top-level folder and then choose Properties from the pop-up menu. The dialog box that appears displays the Web site's total file size. (The file size shown there doesn't include the size of any subsites; you must open subsites separately to check their sizes. For more information about what subsites are and do, see Chapter 13.)

If I created my site in FrontPage, do I still need FrontPage Server Extensions?

The answer is . . . it depends. A Web site built from scratch with Expression Web can be hosted on any Web server. But if you originally created your site by using FrontPage, *and* the site contains features that require FrontPage Server Extensions to be able to work, you still need to host the site on a server with FrontPage Server Extensions installed. Be aware that many Web hosts will likely stop offering and supporting FrontPage Server Extensions because Microsoft no longer builds software that require them. Chapter 15 lists alternatives to popular FrontPage Web components that require FrontPage Server Extensions. Chapter 16 also lists online sources for getting help from masterminds who are dedicated to helping former FrontPage users make the transition to Expression Web.

Here are the FrontPage features that need the help of FrontPage Server Extensions to display properly in your site:

✔ Nested subsites (subsites within subsites)

✔ The following Web components: Confirmation field, Web search, hit counter, table of contents based on categories, and Top 10 list

✔ FrontPage workgroup features, including source control (as set up in FrontPage)

✔ FrontPage discussion groups

✔ FrontPage user-registration systems

✔ Usage reports

✔ File-upload form field

✔ Custom link bars

✔ Shared border and background properties

✔ Permissions and security (as set up in FrontPage)

If your site uses forms built in FrontPage, you can adjust the form handler to work on any Web server with a form handler installed. See Chapter 6 for details.

If you're in the market for Web hosting, check out www.freewebspace.net. This search tool helps you compare free and subscription-based Web hosting services.

If you're building an intranet site, your company maintains its own Web server and network connection. Speak to your company's system administrator for details about your network setup.

Testing, Testing, and More Testing

Before you publish your site, you need to give it the white-glove treatment. Expression Web comes with two built-in tools that make testing easy.

The Expression Web Accessibility Checker scans your site to make sure that it complies with accessibility guidelines so that visitors with impaired vision or other disabilities can use the site. The Compatibility Checker looks for any problems in the code. Both tools mark the spots in your pages where guidelines aren't met or lines of code are below par. Each tool then offers its advice for fixing the problems.

Expression Web also comes with a number of reports that help you find other faults *before* you go live, such as broken hyperlinks (which go nowhere) and unlinked (*orphan*) pages.

Here's a dress-rehearsal checklist for preparing your Web site for its big debut:

- ✔ Run the Accessibility Checker. (We tell you how later in this chapter.)
- ✔ Run the Compatibility Checker. (We tell you how later in this chapter.)
- ✔ Run a CSS report to check for errors in your external style sheets. (We tell you how in Chapter 9.)
- ✔ Verify your hyperlinks to make sure they work properly. (We tell you how in Chapter 4.)
- ✔ Run other problem-oriented reports, such as these:
    - Slow Pages report (choose Site➪Reports➪Problems➪Slow Pages)
    - Unlinked Pages report (Site➪Reports➪Problems➪Unlinked Pages)
- ✔ Check for spelling errors (choose Tools➪Spelling➪Spelling) and proofread all your pages.
- ✔ Preview your site in a number of Web browsers at different screen resolutions (and, ideally, on more than one operating system platform) to catch problems caused by inconsistencies in the way browsers interpret CSS styles. (We tell you how in Chapter 2.)

The impotence of proofreading

We had you there for a moment, didn't we? As much as it pains our copyeditor to leave that typo in the sidebar title, we felt that it best illustrates the *importance* of proofreading. Nothing is more damaging to a beautifully designed Web site's reputation than a page full of full of typos. And as the previous sentence demonstrates (take a second look at it), spell checkers can do only so much. One unconventional-but-effective way to proofread your pages is to detach their style sheets temporarily (we show you a quick way to do that in Chapter 9) and then print their content. Words on paper simply look different from words on the screen, and you're more likely to catch errors when you read your text in stark black and white. Or, you can enlist a picky friend to proofread your site. Nothing works like a fresh pair of eyes to ferret out errors you overlooked.

Checking Your Site against Accessibility Guidelines

When your site is *accessible,* it recognizes visitors to your site who have disabilities or speak different languages. Although it's nearly impossible to accommodate 100 percent of your visitors, familiarizing yourself with accepted accessibility guidelines helps a lot.

Both the World Wide Web Consortium (W3C) and the U.S. government have come up with guidelines. The *W3C,* a consortium of Web-savvy organizations and businesses, creates universal standards for Web content and design. The W3C Web Content Accessibility Guidelines (WCAG) explain how to make Web sites understandable to the majority of Web visitors. These guidelines are mainly geared toward people with hearing, visual, or mobility challenges, but they effectively make Web sites more usable for everyone. The guidelines are divided into priorities:

- ✔ **Priority 1:** The most important guidelines to follow

- ✔ **Priority 2:** Still important but less so than Priority 1

- ✔ **Priority 3:** A good idea, but certainly not as important as the first two groups

The Access Board, an agency of the federal government of the United States, has also created accessibility standards specifically for Web sites (and other information technology resources) that are developed, used, or maintained by a U.S. federal agency. These standards fall under Section 508 of the Rehabilitation Act, passed by the U.S. Congress in 1988.

We recommend perusing the guidelines so that you can keep them in mind as you design your site. These documents are meaty, but a look-through can save you lots of time as you consider how to design your site. The WCAG is available at

```
www.w3.org/TR/WAI-WEBCONTENT/
```

For more about Section 508 standards, see

```
www.access-board.gov/sec508/summary.htm
```

Expression Web knows about both sets of accessibility standards, and can sift through your site to make sure it conforms to one or both sets. After Expression Web has scanned your Web site, it then proposes design changes based on what it finds.

To check your Web site against accessibility standards, do this:

1. **With a Web site open, choose Tools⇨Accessibility Reports.**

   The Accessibility Checker dialog box appears.

2. **In the Check Where section of the dialog box, select the radio button next to the group of pages that you want Expression Web to check.**

   You can check the entire site in one pass, or you can select specific pages.

3. **In the Check For section of the dialog box, select the check boxes next to the accessibility standards you want to use.**

   We suggest checking all three, for good measure.

4. **In the Show section of the dialog box, select the check boxes next to the types of information that you want to appear in the report.**

   You can check for these types of information:

   - **Errors:** Select this check box if you want the report to show items that are considered errors according to the accessibility standards you're using.

   - **Warnings:** Select this check box if you want the report to include items that may not technically be errors but may need to be adjusted according to the standards.

   - **Manual checklist:** If you select this check box, you can check your pages manually against the accessibility guidelines. Expression Web includes items on the report that are proverbial red flags for accessibility — but which you may have handled correctly already — such as a link in a page to an external style sheet. The accessibility guidelines state that the content of a page should be readable without the style sheet attached (as shown in Figure 12-1). Most likely, you already took care of that.

Figure 12-1:
Suggestions
and changes
based on
accessibility
guidelines.

	Page	Line	Issue Type	Checkpoint	Problem Summary
	calendar/calendar.htm (Calendar ...	11	Warning	WCAG 6.1	Verify that this document can be read with sty
	contact/contact.htm (Contact Us) ...	44	Warning	WCAG 3.5	Use header elements to convey document stru
	contact/contact.htm (Contact Us) ...	11	Warning	WCAG 6.1	Verify that this document can be read with sty
	site_map/site_map.htm (Site Map)...	44	Warning	WCAG 3.5	Use header elements to convey document stru
	site_map/site_map.htm (Site Map)	11	Warning	WCAG 6.1	Verify that this document can be read with sty
	default.htm (Home) [1/2]	45	Warning	WCAG 3.5	Use header elements to convey document stru
	default.htm (Home) [2/2]	11	Warning	WCAG 6.1	Verify that this document can be read with sty
	employees/employees.htm (Emplo...	44	Warning	WCAG 3.5	Use header elements to convey document stru

✕ Found 30 accessibility problem(s) in 15 page(s).

5. Click the Check button.

Expression Web checks the selected documents against the accessibility standards you chose and opens the Accessibility task pane (refer to Figure 12-1) below the editing window.

Each problem is identified by page name and by line number, which refers to the page's HTML. (You can see the HTML line numbers by looking inside the document's Code view, which we talk about in Chapter 14.)

To read the specific guideline that pertains to the problem, click the link in the Checkpoint column. This action opens a Web browser, showing the exact guideline in the Web Content Accessibility Guidelines document so that you can read it and decide whether you need to make any changes.

To save the results of the Accessibility Checker, in the Accessibility task pane, click the Generate HTML Report button. After the dialog box closes, a new page is visible in Expression Web. Save the report just as you save any other Web page. (We show you how in Chapter 2.)

The Accessibility Report lists the filenames of the documents that Expression Web checked, along with a description of each potential problem. Some of these descriptions point out problems with the HTML code and others propose easy content or formatting changes. Make whatever changes you can, and then generate the report again to see how your site checks out.

If an issue continues to pop up and you don't know how to fix it, you may want to post your question on an online user group. To find the Microsoft Expression Web public newsgroup, go to the main Microsoft Expression Web site: www.microsoft.com/products/expression/en/expression-web/ default.mspx. Then, in the Knowledge Center area, click the Join a Discussion link.

Running a Compatibility Report

Expression Web knows right out of the box how to write clean Web pages that comply with the standards set by the World Wide Web Consortium. The Compatibility Checker goes over your Web pages' code to make sure that everything is A-OK under the hood.

 The Compatibility Checker is a useful tool for bringing an older site up to today's Web standards because it can check for nonstandard ways of specifying formatting. It can also check for missing or deprecated tags (tags that still work but have been replaced by newer tags). We talk about updating old sites in Bonus Chapter 18. (To find Bonus Chapter 18, go to www.dummies.com, use the search box to navigate to this book's Web page, and then click the Bonus Chapters link.)

To run a compatibility report on your Web site, follow these steps:

1. **With a Web site open, choose Tools⇨Compatibility Reports.**

   The Compatibility Checker dialog box appears.

2. **In the Check Where section of the dialog box, select the radio button next to the group of pages you want Expression Web to check.**

   You can check the entire site in one pass, or you can select specific pages.

3. **In the Check HTML/XHTML Compatibility With list box, choose the version of code rules you want to check your code against.**

   This option defaults to the document type declaration (doctype) specified on the Authoring tab in the Page Editor Options dialog box. (Choose Tools⇨Page Editor Options, and then click the Authoring tab.) It basically means "Which brand of HTML coding do you want to check your page's compatibility against?" By default, Expression Web writes your pages' code in XHTML Transitional, so you can just let Expression Web pick this option for you.

   If you need to know more about document type declarations, we explain them in a sidebar in Chapter 14.

4. **Unless you're sure that you want to check your Cascading Style Sheet code against an earlier version, leave the Check CSS Compatibility option set to CSS 2.1.**

   The Compatibility Checker checks only internal Cascading Style Sheets styles that are embedded in your Web pages. To check external style sheets, you need to run a CSS report. (We tell you how in Chapter 9.)

5. **Leave the Run Check Based On Doctype Declaration in Page If Available check box selected.**

If your page doesn't have a doctype declaration, the checker uses the code version specified in the Check HTML/XHTML Compatibility With list box.

We talk about doctype declarations in Chapter 14.

6. **Click the Check button.**

Expression Web checks the selected documents' code against the rules for the code version you chose, and opens the Compatibility task pane (see Figure 12-2) below the editing window.

Figure 12-2:
Identifying problems in your pages' HTML and CSS code.

Each problem is identified by page name and line number, which refers to the page's HTML, and a summary of the problem. (You can see the HTML line numbers by looking inside the document's Code view, which we talk about in Chapter 14.)

To open the page and find the problem, double-click the problem. The page opens and Expression Web highlights the renegade code problem in your page's Code view. If you know how, you can fix the problem directly in Code view. If you're not comfortable with HTML, read Chapter 14. We talk about basic HTML concepts and working in the Expression Web Code view in that chapter.

HTML 4 For Dummies, 5th Edition, by Ed Tittle and Mary Burmeister (Wiley), is a great HTML reference. If you're still stumped, visit the Microsoft Expression Web newsgroup. To find the Microsoft Expression Web public newsgroup, go to the main Microsoft Expression Web site at `www.microsoft.com/products/expression/en/expression-web/default.mspx`. Then, in the Knowledge Center area, click the Join a Discussion link.

To save the results of the Compatibility Checker, in the Compatibility task pane, click the Generate HTML Report button. After the dialog box closes, a new page is visible in Expression Web. Save the report just as you save any other Web page. (We show you how in Chapter 2.)

After fixing the problems, run the Compatibility Checker again to see how your site checks out.

Going Public

After you build your site and comb through it using the testing checklist given earlier in this chapter, you're ready to take your show on the road. Here's how to publish your Web site (finally!).

Excluding unfinished pages from publishing

If some of the files on your site (Web pages, graphics, or any other files) aren't yet ready for public viewing, you can tell Expression Web to hold those files back while publishing the rest of the site. To do so, follow these steps:

1. **In the Folder List task pane, right-click the file you want to hold back.**

   You can select multiple files by pressing the Ctrl key while clicking icons, and then right-clicking the selection.

   A pop-up menu appears.

2. **Choose Don't Publish.**

   A red X appears next to the file icon, letting you know that the file won't be published the next time you publish the site.

For an overview of your site's publish status, take a look at the Publish Status report by choosing Site⇨Reports⇨Workflow⇨Publish Status.

If you exclude a page from being published and it's linked to another page in the site, that link doesn't work properly in the live version of the site. Therefore, before you publish, be sure to dismantle any hyperlinks that lead to unfinished pages. (For instructions on how to do this, see Chapter 4.)

Publishing your Web site

The next step is to find out your publishing address. Most servers use FTP, or *File Transfer Protocol*, to transfer files between computers on the Internet. Even though the address your visitors eventually type to view your published Web site begins with `http://`, your publishing address most likely begins with `ftp://`.

You must have the correct publishing address in hand in order to publish your Web site. If you're in doubt, your Web host customer service (or system administrator, if you're publishing on an intranet) can tell you your publishing address.

To publish your Web site for the first time, follow these steps:

1. **In Expression Web, open the Web site you want to publish.**

   If the site is already open in Expression Web, be sure to save any changes you have made to the site's pages. (To do so, choose File⇨Save All.)

2. **Activate your Internet connection.**

3. **Choose File⇨Publish Site.**

   Expression Web switches to Remote Web Site view, and the Remote Web Site Properties dialog box appears. You use this dialog box to tell Expression Web where you want to publish your Web site.

4. **In the dialog box's Remote Web Server Type area, select the option that corresponds to the type of host Web server that your ISP uses.**

   It's most likely FTP.

5. **In the Remote Web Site Location text box, type your publishing address.**

6. **If the Web site contains subsites and you want to publish the subsites and the parent Web site at the same time, at the top of the dialog box, click the Publishing tab, and then select the Include Subsites check box.**

7. **If you want Expression Web to clean up your site's HTML code before publishing, click the Optimize HTML tab (at the top of the dialog box), select the When Publishing check box, and then select the check boxes next to items you want Expression Web to remove.**

   For example, you can tell Expression Web to strip the published site of all HTML comments (most of which were probably meant for the site's authors, not its visitors). You can also have Expression Web tidy the code by removing unnecessary white space between HTML tags or Expression Web-specific code that's no longer necessary now that the site is heading off to the host server. When you do so, the look of your pages doesn't change — just the look of the HTML code for those visitors who care to check it out. (And they do, believe it or not.)

8. **In the Remote Web Site Properties dialog box, click OK.**

   The Remote Web Site Properties dialog box closes, and Expression Web contacts the server at the publishing address you specified. If the server contains security features (most do), the Name and Password Required dialog box appears.

It may not be necessary to enter a name and password each time you publish your site to your Web address. Expression Web is supposed to remember login information for FTP sites between publishing sessions (although it occasionally gets amnesia).

9. **If necessary, in the Name and Password text boxes, enter the user-name and password that you chose when you established your account, and then click OK.**

The dialog box closes, and Remote Web Site view becomes visible with the contents of the open (local) Web site displayed on the left side of the view and the contents of the publish destination displayed on the right side, as shown in Figure 12-3.

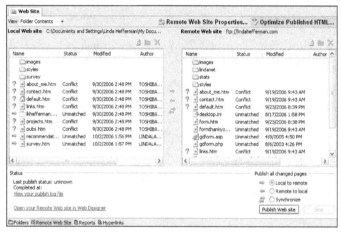

Figure 12-3: Remote Web Site view.

10. **In the lower-right corner of the Expression Web window, click the Publish Web Site button.**

Expression Web copies all your Web site files to the remote server. Depending on the size of your Web site and the speed of your Internet connection, this process may take a few minutes.

A status indicator appears at the bottom of the Web Site view to tell you what's going on.

After the work is done, an encouraging note appears at the bottom of the view, saying that your Web site was published successfully.

Congratulations — your site is now visible to the world!

Letting the World Know That You're Ready for Visitors

Pass the bubbly! Your Web site has joined the Internet community, and you can now call yourself a true-blue Web publisher. Using your Web browser, visit your live Web site at its new URL and, just to be safe, give the site one last check. (Don't forget to test those hyperlinks.) If all is well, heave a sigh of relief and enjoy a moment of satisfaction.

You may even want to line up a group of sympathetic testers who use different types of computers and browsers and ask them to give your site a run-through. Even if everything works perfectly when viewed with your computer and browser, a glitch can pop up when your site is viewed on a different platform, especially for designs built with complex CSS styles. Now that your site is live, look at it with every browser you can get your hands on, and bug your friends who have Macs or use other browsers to take a look.

If something doesn't work properly, fix the problem on the *local* copy of your Web site — the copy stored on your computer — and publish your Web site again. (We show you how later in this chapter, in the "Keeping Your Web Site Fresh" section.)

Now that your Web site is open to the public, you need to let everyone know that you're accepting visitors. If you want your site to benefit from publicity, the following list gives some suggestions on how you can promote your site:

- ✔ **Search services:** List your site with popular search services, such as Yahoo! (`www.yahoo.com`) and Google (`www.google.com`). Each search service posts listing instructions on its Web site. Even if you don't actively list your site, many search engines use automated programs (called such creepy names as *spiders, webcrawlers,* or *bots*) to index the Web automatically, but doing a little legwork on your own never hurts.

- ✔ **E-mail signature:** Include your Web site address in the signature line of your e-mail messages. Most e-mail programs enable you to append a few lines of text to the bottom of every message.

- ✔ **Newsgroups and blogs:** Post discreet announcements to newsgroups and as comments in blogs related to your topic. Keep your announcement low key and respectful. If you blanket a newsgroup or a blog with advertising hype, not only do you irk the other participants (and invite bad word-of-mouth), but your publicity campaign will also probably backfire.

✔ **Traditional print advertising:** Add your Web site address to business cards, letterhead, and print advertising.

✔ **Word-of-mouth:** Your best bet is to invite your friends and colleagues (especially those who blog) to visit your Web site and, if appropriate, provide a link to your site from their Web sites and blogs. And, of course, talk it up on your blog if you have one. Word-of-mouth is a powerful and effective way to spread the word.

Check out *Web Marketing For Dummies*, by Jan Zimmerman (Wiley), for more ideas on how to maximize your World Wide Web presence.

Keeping Your Web Site Fresh

Stagnant Web sites are as appealing as day-old pastry. With doughnuts and Web pages, freshness counts — so keep your site vital by changing its content, updating its graphics, and adding new features regularly.

To update your site (or to correct any mistakes you find), you make changes on the local copy of your Web site and then publish the Web site again. To update the site's changed pages, a single button-click does the trick:

1. **In Expression Web, open the Web site you want to update, and make (and save) whatever changes you want.**

2. **Activate your Internet connection.**

3. **Choose File⇨Publish Site.**

4. **If necessary, reenter your username and password.**

   Note: If you update your site several times during a single Expression Web session, this dialog box appears only the first time you publish or update the site.

   The dialog box closes, and Expression Web copies the changed pages to the host Web server. Your site is now fresh as a daisy.

If you prefer to choose which pages and files to update (as opposed to letting Expression Web simply publish all files that have changed), here's the procedure:

1. **In the Folder List task pane, right-click the file or folder you want to publish, and then right-click the selection.**

   You can select multiple files and folders by pressing the Ctrl key while clicking icons.

2. **Choose Publish Selected Files from the pop-up menu that appears.**

   The Remote Web Site Properties dialog box appears with the site's publishing address visible in the Remote Web Site Location text box.

3. **Click OK to close the dialog box and publish the selected files.**

To republish the entire Web site (not just the changed pages) or to publish the Web site to a different location, follow the steps in the earlier section "Publishing your Web site."

If you want to know about what kind of visitors you're getting and how many, check with your Web hosting service. Most services offer detailed reports on all your stats.

Chapter 13

Web Site Management

*U*sing Expression Web, you can do just about anything to change, update, or repair your Web site (assuming that something needs repairing).

In this chapter, you delve into the site-management capabilities of Expression Web. You become familiar with the four Expression Web site-management views. You also discover how to use Expression Web to manage the files that make up your Web site.

Taking In the Views

No doubt you have wondered about that mysterious Web Site tab lurking at the top of the Expression Web design window. The Web Site tab is your doorway to the Expression Web site-management *views*. Expression Web contains four such views, each of which illuminates your site in a different way.

To switch between views, click the Web Site tab, and then click the appropriate icon at the bottom of the window (see Figure 13-1). Or, choose from the View menu the name of the view you want to see.

Folder List task pane   Web Site tab in Folders view

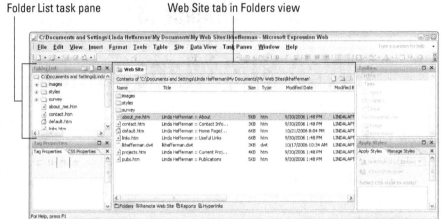

Figure 13-1:
The
contents of
the Web
Site tab.

Folders view

Folders view of the Web Site tab, shown in Figure 13-1, displays your Web site as a group of files and folders to help you manage and organize your Web site's file system. This view serves the same purpose for your Web site as Windows Explorer serves for the files stored on your hard drive and local network.

The Web Site tab Folders view is similar to the Folder List task pane in that it lists files and folders in your Web site. However, Folders view shows only those files and folders contained in the folder that's *selected* in the Folder List task pane. If you select the top-level folder in the Folder List task pane, Folders view displays all files and folders in the site. If you select a subfolder in the Folder List task pane, Folders view shows only the files and folders located inside that folder. Think of the Folder List task pane as the macro view of your Web site, and think of Folders view of the Web Site tab as the micro view.

Folders view looks and works much like Windows Explorer:

✔ Click a folder in the Folder List task pane to display its contents in the Folders view Contents area.

✔ To sort the list of files and folders in the Contents area, click the header label of your choice.

✔ To move a page into a folder, click the page icon, drag it on top of the folder, and then release the mouse button. Expression Web updates the page's hyperlinks to reflect its new location. (We talk about how hyperlinks work in Chapter 4.)

Folders with globe icons denote *subsites,* which are complete Web sites that live inside a folder of the main, or *parent,* Web site. To view the contents of a subsite in Folders view, double-click the subsite's folder to open the subsite in a new Expression Web window. We talk more about subsites in the "Working with subsites" section, later in this chapter.

Reports view

Reports view tells you all sorts of interesting things about your Web site, as shown in Figure 13-2. For example, the Slow Pages report helps you monitor your site's estimated download speed, and the Older Files report reminds you which pages may benefit from an update.

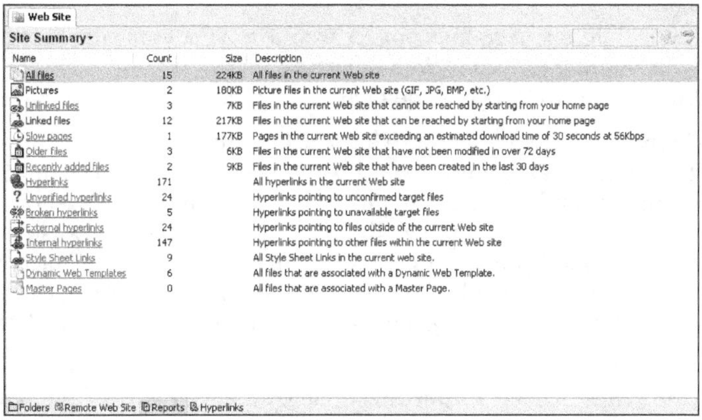

Figure 13-2: Site Summary report in Reports view.

When you first display Reports view, you're greeted by the Site Summary report. This report rounds up useful tidbits of information — including how many hyperlinks and pictures the site contains, how many pages can (and cannot) be reached by following a link from the home page, and how many pages contain broken hyperlinks. This report contains much more information than we list here — see for yourself!

You can click any of the Site Summary report titles that are in blue and underlined to perform a relevant task or to display a more detailed report. Or navigate to the report you want by choosing Site➪Reports.

Another way to switch between the reports in Reports view is to select the category and name of the report you want to see from the drop-down menu in the upper-left corner of Reports view. To return to the Site Summary report, in the upper-left drop-down menu, select Site Summary.

Most of the reports contain helpful information, but here are the reports we find most useful:

- **Problems/Unlinked Files:** This report lists files that don't contain hyperlinks to them.

  Take a close look at the pages listed in this report. They may be strays that can be safely deleted because they're effectively cut off from the rest of the site. We show you how to delete pages later in this chapter (although you can probably guess how to do it — select the page and then press the Delete key).

  One exception is a confirmation page for a form that pops up after a Web visitor clicks the Submit button on a form. (We talk about forms in Chapter 6.) This page doesn't need any other links *to* it (although it should contain a link back to some logical place in your Web site — most likely, the site's home page.)

  If you delete a page by using Expression Web, you can't later change your mind. Expression Web-deleted pages don't end up in the Recycle Bin — they go to Web-page heaven. If in doubt, leave the page alone.

- **Problems/Slow Pages:** Web surfers hate to wait for pages to download. This report helps you keep track of potential slowpokes in your site. The report lists pages that take more than an estimated 30 seconds to load at a connection speed of 28.8 Kbps. We say *estimated* because download speed depends on several factors, only one of which is page content. (Other factors include the speed of the host Web server, the amount of network traffic at that given moment, and the state of the data lines that make up the Internet, to name a few.)

- **Problems/Broken Hyperlinks:** Use this report to test the hyperlinks in your Web site between pages and to verify external links to Web pages on the World Wide Web. We tell you how to use this report in Chapter 4.

Hyperlinks view

The links between the pages in your Web site create a path that visitors follow when they explore the site. Hyperlinks view shows you a road map of the different links in your Web site and how they link to each other.

When you click a page in the Folder List task pane, an icon representing that page appears in the Hyperlinks area of the view. Figure 13-3 shows how a Web site looks in Hyperlinks view.

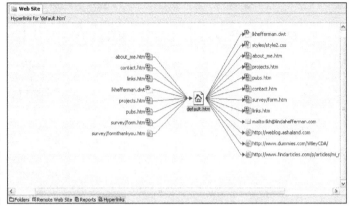

Figure 13-3:
Hyperlinks
view.

Small icons with blue arrows pointing to the central page icon illustrate *incoming hyperlinks* — pages that contain hyperlinks leading to the selected page. Small icons to the right of the central page icon illustrate *outgoing hyperlinks* — the destinations of the hyperlinks inside the selected page. Broken hyperlinks appear as broken gray lines rather than blue arrows. (We show you how to find and repair broken hyperlinks in your site in Chapter 4.) If the selected page contains no hyperlinks and isn't linked to from any other page in the site, the page icon appears in the Hyperlinks area all by itself.

Weird Expression Web folders

If you view the contents of your Web site folder in Windows Explorer, no doubt you notice some unfamiliar folders hanging about. All Web sites created with Expression Web contain a standard set of folders that Expression Web uses to store *metadata* — that is, information about the structure and workings of the site itself. Metadata is the Expression Web way of keeping everything about your site tidy, such as hyperlink information and other page settings so that everything continues to work when you move files around in your Web site. Metadata also keeps your links working when you publish your Web site on the Internet. (We talk about publishing in Chapter 12.) To keep these folders from getting accidentally deleted, moved, or changed, they're hidden inside your Web site and don't show up in Web Site view. Here are the mystery folders and what they keep track of (fret not; you don't need to understand or even open these folders):

✔ **_vti_cnf:** Expression Web uses this folder to store information about each file, such as hyperlinks and page settings.

✔ **_vti_pvt:** This folder stores configuration information about the site itself.

Follow this good general rule: If the folder name begins with an underscore character (_), leave it alone. Folders that Expression Web generates for its own purposes are earmarked with this character.

Using Expression Web as a workgroup tool

Few Web sites are one-person operations. Even if you're the lucky staff member who got tapped to put together the company Web or intranet site, you probably need input and cooperation from other members of your team. If those team members are sitting in an office 500 miles away, collaboration can be tricky.

Expression Web comes with some handy tools for managing team collaboration:

Document check-in/check-out: You can set up this option for a Web site on a remote or local site. Choose Site➪Site Settings and, on the General tab, select the Use Document Check-In and Check-Out check box to make the options available.

Page-level categories, assignments, and status tracking: To access these options, right-click a page in the Folder List task pane and choose File➪Properties, and then click the Workgroup tab.

If you're looking for a software tool designed exclusively for helping workgroups and teams collaborate via an intranet, Microsoft SharePoint may be the tool for your company. (Find out more at `www.microsoft.com/sharepoint/default.mspx`.) Microsoft Office SharePoint Designer 2007 (`http://office.microsoft.com/en-us/sharepointdesigner/FX100487631033.aspx`), the intranet cousin of Expression Web, helps users custom design their SharePoint sites.

You can modify the Hyperlinks view diagram by right-clicking anywhere inside the view and then choosing one of the following options from the pop-up menu that appears:

- ✔ **Show Page Titles:** By default, Hyperlinks view displays the page's filenames. Choose this option to display the page's titles instead.

- ✔ **Hyperlinks to Pictures:** Choose this option to display links to picture files.

- ✔ **Repeated Hyperlinks:** If the page contains more than one hyperlink to the same destination, Hyperlinks view displays only one instance of the link. Choose this option to make repeated hyperlinks visible.

Remote Web Site view

When you're ready to publish, back up, or move your Web site, you do it in Remote Web Site view. It contains all the tools you need to transfer your Web site's files and folders to a different location — whether it's a host Web server, another computer on your network, or other backup media you choose. We touch on the workings of this view later in this chapter, in the "Backing up and moving a Web site" section, and in Chapter 12, when we show you how to publish your site on the World Wide Web.

Working with Web Site Files and Folders

It's best to do all site-related tasks inside Expression Web, such as creating new pages and adding files from outside your Web site, shifting files between folders, and renaming pages. We show you how to do most tasks related to Web *sites* in Chapter 1 and to Web *pages* in Chapter 2. In this section, we tell you about a few more useful housekeeping duties, especially as the size of your site grows.

Renaming files and folders

If, for any reason, you need to change the name of a file or folder in your Web site, Expression Web automatically updates all the file's associated hyperlinks. This is a big deal. Back in the days of hand-coding HTML, changing a file or folder name without updating associated links throughout the site resulted in broken hyperlinks. Not so with Expression Web! The program is smart enough to search your site for links containing the old file or folder name and to update the references for you.

You can rename a file or folder in several ways, but the easiest is by following these steps:

1. **In the Folder List task pane, or in any Web site view except Tasks view, right-click the icon for the file or folder you want to rename and, from the pop-up menu that appears, choose Rename.**

   A box appears around the filename, and the filename is highlighted.

2. **Highlight the part of the name to the left of the extension (.htm) and type a new name.**

   Be sure to maintain the same filename extension so that Expression Web knows what kind of file you're renaming. Also, choose either one-word names or short words separated by a hyphen (–) or underscore character (_). You should also use only lowercase letters.

3. **Press Enter.**

   If the file contains associated links, the Rename dialog box appears, asking whether you want to update the links to reflect the new name.

4. **In the dialog box, click Yes.**

   The dialog box closes, Expression Web updates the links, and all is well.

Renaming the home page

Renaming the home page involves extra consideration. The home page *must* be named `index.htm`, `index.html`, `default.htm`, or `default.html` (or whatever name the host Web server recognizes as the site's default page), or else your site doesn't work properly. If you're not sure which home page filename your host Web server recognizes, give the customer service staff a call.

To make a page the home page, follow these steps:

1. **In the Folder List task pane, right-click the icon for the file you want to make the home page.**

   The home page must be located in the top level of your Web site folder.

2. **From the pop-up menu that appears, choose Set As Home Page.**

   If your site already contains a home page named either `default.htm` or `index.htm` (or either one with the extension `.html`), the Confirm Rename dialog box appears.

   Expression Web just wants to make sure that you know what you're doing. If you click Yes, Expression Web renames the previous home page `default_old` (or `index_old`). Don't worry. Expression Web doesn't destroy your old home page — it just renames it. You can still open, edit, and rename the old home page, just as you can any other Web page. It has, however, lost its former status as the top dog in your Web site.

   If you click No, the dialog box closes and nothing changes.

Renaming a Web site

Need to change the name of a Web site? No problem. You can change it at any time.

A Web site name is simply a glorified folder name that Expression Web uses to identify that folder as a Web site because it contains a collection of inter-related Web pages. Your Web visitors never see the site name. Renaming a Web site is a housekeeping matter for you.

To rename a Web site, follow these steps:

1. **Choose Site➪Site Settings.**

   The Site Settings dialog box appears.

2. **In the Web Name text box, type the new name.**

3. **Click OK.**

Really. It's that easy.

To rename a subsite, follow these steps, but do so in the subsite's workspace window. (We tell you how to work with subsites next.)

Working with subsites

Small, straightforward Web sites are easy to maintain in Expression Web. As the Web site grows or the number of people involved in the site's creation and maintenance increases, keeping track of the Web site's exploding number of pages can turn into a major pain.

If your Web site is starting to resemble an ever-expanding amoeba, consider breaking the Web site into a core *parent* Web site with second-level tiers of information called subsites. A *subsite* is a complete Web site that lives in a folder inside the parent Web site.

The parent Web site/subsite setup works well when you're creating a large network of interrelated Web sites — for example, a main company site with subsites for each of the company's different products. The Microsoft Web site offers a good example; check out the Microsoft parent Web site at www.microsoft.com and the Expression Web subsite at www.microsoft.com/products/expression (dedicated to the Expression family of products).

Another example is a companywide intranet site, to which members of different departments contribute material. The entire operation exists inside a single parent Web site, but each department works on its own subsite. In this situation, you can take advantage of Expression Web workgroup features. (See the sidebar "Using Expression Web as a workgroup tool," earlier in this chapter.)

A subsite is a complete Web site in its own right. You can therefore open a subsite in its own Expression Web workspace window and manage the Web site as you see fit. This is a good way to break an overwhelmingly big Web site into easy-to-manage chunks.

You have two choices for creating a subsite: Either convert a folder inside an existing Web site into a subsite, or create a new subsite from scratch or by using a Web site template.

To convert a folder into a subsite, follow these steps:

1. **With the parent Web site open in Expression Web, right-click the folder you want to convert into a subsite, and then, from the pop-up menu that appears, choose Convert to Web.**

   The Microsoft Expression Web dialog box appears, warning you that pages inside the folder will be affected by the conversion. If you change your mind and decide to maintain the status quo, click No. Otherwise. . . .

   The page changes relate mainly to features that only pages formerly created in FrontPage would contain (such as include files, link bars, and themes.)

2. **In the dialog box, click Yes.**

   The dialog box closes, and Expression Web converts the folder into a subsite. If the folder contains lots of files, the conversion may take a few moments. You can tell that the conversion has taken place because a little globe appears on top of the folder icon.

If you change your mind and want to consolidate a parent Web site and its sub-sites back into a single Web site, you can convert subsites into regular folders.

To convert a subsite into a folder, with the parent Web site open in Expression Web, right-click the subsite's folder, and then choose Convert to Folder from the pop-up menu that appears. The Microsoft Expression Web dialog box appears, listing the changes that will occur in the subsite's pages as a result of the conversion. If the changes are okay with you, click Yes to close the dialog box and convert the subsite into a folder.

To create a new subsite from scratch, follow these steps:

1. **With Expression Web running, choose File⇨New⇨Web Site.**

   The New dialog box appears, with the Web Site tab open.

2. **In the New dialog box, choose the desired options for creating a new site or creating a site from one of the templates.**

   We talk about how to create a new, blank site or a site from a template in Chapter 1.

3. **In the Specify the Location of the New Web Site text box, change the path so that the subsite folder is *inside* the parent Web site folder.**

   For example, if the parent Web site folder is `C:\Documents and Settings\Your Name\My Web Sites\nwgardening`, the path for the subsite should look like this: `C:\Documents and Settings\Your Name\My Web Sites\nwgardening\subsitename`.

   The subsite folder name you choose should include all lowercase letters and only one word or short words separated by a hyphen (-) or underscore (_).

4. **After you specify the Web site's location, in the New dialog box, click OK.**

   The dialog box closes, and Expression Web creates the new subsite. The subsite appears in a new Expression Web workspace window. In the parent Web site, the subsite's folder appears in the Folder List task pane with a globe icon on top, as shown in Figure 13-4.

Figure 13-4:
A parent
Web site
with a single
subsite,
named
plants.

You can now update and work with the subsite just like you would any other Web site.

Try to maintain a unified design or include common design elements across your subsites to help them blend with their brethren. Although a few subsites can help make a large site workable, too many can turn into a mishmash of styles that can dilute your company's cohesive look and feel.

Deleting files and folders

If your Web site contains a file that has outlived its usefulness or is otherwise cluttering your Web site, you can boot the file out with one swift click. To delete a file or folder, do the following:

1. **In the Folder List task pane or in any Web Site view, click the file or folder you want to delete.**

   To select multiple files or folders, hold down the Ctrl key while you click each file.

2. **Press the Delete key.**

   The Confirm Delete dialog box appears, making sure that you want to delete the files or folders.

3. Click Yes.

If you're deleting more than one file, click Yes to All to delete them all in one step (rather than have the Confirm Delete dialog box pop up before deleting every single file). If you change your mind, click No or Cancel to close the dialog box without deleting the file.

Be careful: After you delete a file or folder by using Expression Web, you can't change your mind and bring it back into existence later.

Also, if you delete a file that's the destination of a link from elsewhere in your Web site (whether that file is a Web page or a picture file), the link breaks. The damage isn't irreparable; you can always use Expression Web to find and fix broken hyperlinks. You should be aware of the problem all the same.

Backing up and moving a Web site

Expression Web enables you to copy your Web site to other locations. By backing up your Web site, you not only have a clean copy in the event of a computer glitch, but you can also maintain a working copy to use as a scratchpad so that you avoid making permanent changes to the original. You can also use this method to transfer your Web site from one computer to another, if the need arises.

To back up your Web site, you follow similar steps to the ones you would follow if you were publishing your Web site:

1. With the Web site open in Expression Web, choose File⇨Publish Site.

The Remote Web Site Properties dialog box appears. You use this dialog box to tell Expression Web where you want to back up or copy your Web site files.

If you already published your Web site on a host Web server, you can still follow these steps to back up or copy your site's files. By doing so, you don't affect the files already sitting on the host server's hard drive.

2. On the Remote Web Site tab, select the File System option.

3. In the Remote Web Site Location text box, type the path to the location to which you want to back up the Web site.

Alternatively, you can click the Browse button to display the New Publish Location dialog box and either navigate to a folder already located on your computer or network or create a new folder by clicking the New Folder button in the upper-right corner of the dialog box.

Do not type anything in the Site Name box. Just use the New Publish Location dialog box to navigate to a folder location. When you have located or created the folder to which you want to back up your Web site, click the Open button to return to the Remote Web Site Properties dialog box.

4. **Click the Publishing tab and, in the Publish area, choose from these options:**

   - *Changed Pages Only:* If you already backed up your Web site to this location and you want to back up only *changed* pages, choose this option.

   - *All Pages, Overwriting Pages Already on Destination:* Choose this option if you want to back up the whole Web site, regardless of whether you previously backed it up to this location.

5. **If the Web site contains subsites and you want to back up the subsites at the same time, select the Include Subsites check box.**

6. **In the Remote Web Site Properties dialog box, click OK.**

   If the path you entered into the Remote Web Site Properties dialog box doesn't yet exist, Expression Web first prompts you to create a new folder there. Click Yes.

   The Remote Web Site Properties dialog box closes, and Remote Web Site view becomes visible again. The contents of the open Web site are displayed on the left side of the view, and the contents of the publish destination are displayed on the right side, as shown in Figure 13-5.

   If Expression Web created a new folder in Step 6, the Remote Web Site area is blank.

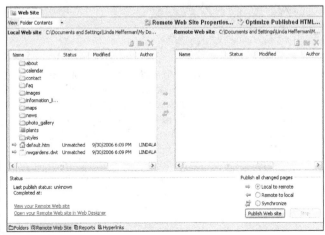

Figure 13-5: Backing up a Web site.

7. **Click the Publish Web Site button.**

A status indicator appears at the bottom of Web Site view to tell you what's going on.

After the work is done, an encouraging note appears at the bottom of the view, saying that your Web site was published successfully. Don't be misled: Your Web site *isn't* live yet. This is just the way Expression Web lets you know that the copy process went smoothly.

To close the Remote Web Site view and return to the Folders view, click Folders in the lower-left corner of the editing window. To move your Web site to a different computer that's not connected to yours by way of a local network, follow the steps in this section to copy the Web site to an archive media (such as a USB flash drive). From the destination computer, launch Expression Web and follow this process, but specify your local computer as the *remote Web site* and *publish* the Web site from the archive media to the destination computer's hard drive.

When you publish your site on the Internet for real, follow the instructions in Chapter 12 and, in the Remote Web Site Properties dialog box, choose the option button that corresponds to the way you transfer files to your Web server (for example, FTP).

An alternative to this method is to use Windows Explorer to copy your Web site folder to a backup device. Make sure that you copy the *entire* folder so the hidden metadata files also get backed up. (See the sidebar "Weird Expression Web folders," earlier in this chapter, for information about metadata folders.)

Importing and Exporting Personal Web Packages

Expression Web allows you to package and export all or part of a Web site as a Personal Web Package. *Personal Web Packages* are useful for copying particular files and folders within a Web site into another Web site. For example, if you have a particular set of files that you always start with when building a new Web site, you can export them as a Personal Web Package and then import them into a new site, to give yourself a head start. Or, you may have a site that has a file structure and pages that you want to expand on to either build a new site or reuse in slightly different form. You can think of Personal Web Packages as a simple way of creating your own, personal Web site template.

To create and export a Personal Web Package, follow these steps:

1. **With the Web site open that you want to export as a Personal Web Package, choose File⇨Export ⇨Personal Web Package.**

   The Export Web Package dialog box appears. The Files in Web Site area shows all the files and folders in the Web site, as shown in Figure 13-6. The top-level folder is selected.

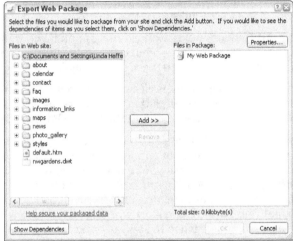

Figure 13-6:
The Export
Web
Package
dialog box.

2. **To add all files and folders in your Web site to the Personal Web Package, click the Add button.**

   To select particular files and folders, hold down the Ctrl key and, in the Files in Web Site area, click to select each file or folder you want to include. When you've selected the files and folders you want to include, click the Add button.

   If you add a folder that has files in it to the Files in Package list, a message appears, asking whether you want to add the contents of the folder. Click Yes to add the folder and its contents; click No to add just the folder.

   You may notice that when you add a particular file or folder to the Personal Web Package, a bunch of other files are added along with it. Most likely, the file or folder you added is dependent on those other files or folders for some of its content. For example, it may need an associated image file or a Dynamic Web Template that supplies some of its content. For the file to work in its new home, it needs to bring its buddies (known as its *dependencies*) along with it.

You can take a look at a file's dependencies by clicking the Show Dependencies button, which pops open another section of the dialog box. Click a file or folder in the Files in Web Site list to see any other files and folders it needs. Control the criteria that Expression Web uses to pick which files or folders need to go along by selecting an option in the Dependency Checking list box (if you change the option, click the file or folder again to force the list of dependencies to refresh):

- **Check All Dependencies, Except Hyperlinks:** Choose this option if you want to include files and folders that the selected file needs, but *not* pages that it links to or that link to it.

- **Check All Dependencies:** Choose this option if you want to include *all* dependencies — image (or other) files, folders, and pages that link to and from the selected page.

- **Do Not Check Dependencies:** Choose this option if you don't want to include the files or folders that the selected file depends on. Just the file or folder itself is added to the Files in Package list.

Even the simplest Web site can be a quagmire of dependencies, and trying to sort them out and figure out what to include and what not to is confusing. If you're not sure, err on the side of including all dependencies rather than excluding them. You can always delete the ones you don't need when you import the Personal Web Package and start working on it as a new Web site. (You also have the chance to say yea or nay to the files in the Personal Web Package when you import it.)

To remove a file or folder from the Files in Package list, click the file or folder and click the Remove button.

3. After you add all the files and folders you want included in the Personal Web Package, click OK.

The File Save dialog box appears. The name `My Web Package.fwp` appears in the File Name text box.

4. Using the options in the File Save dialog box, navigate to the location and folder where you want to save your Personal Web Package and, in the File Name text box, type a new name for the file.

Unlike with Web folders and files, you're not limited to lowercase filenames with no spaces. You should still keep your filenames short, however; there's no use in wearing out your typing fingers.

5. Click Save.

Expression Web shows you an encouraging dialog box which says that your Web Package was saved successfully.

6. Click OK to close the dialog box.

When you're ready to import your Personal Web Package, launch Expression Web and create a new Web site (or open the Web site into which you want to import the Personal Web package).

If your Personal Web Package already contains a home page, you can create a new, blank Web site and simply pull in all the files and folders from your Personal Web Package. In a few clicks of a mouse, you have a brand-new Web site up and running with all its content in place.

To import a Personal Web Package into an open Web site, follow these steps:

1. **Choose File ⇨Import ⇨Personal Web Package.**

   The File Open dialog box appears.

2. **Navigate to the folder containing the Personal Web Package you want to import, and then click to select it.**

   A Personal Web Package's file icon looks like a little file cabinet, and the filename has the extension .fwp.

3. **Click the Open dialog box.**

   The Import Web Package dialog box opens, listing the items included in the Personal Web Package.

4. **To import all items, click the Import button.**

   If you want to exclude an item from importing, click its check box to deselect it. You can include or exclude any files or folders. Then click the Import button, watch what happens, and respond accordingly:

   • Depending on your computer's settings, a Security Warning may pop up. Don't be alarmed. Just click the Run button.

   If the site into which you're importing the Personal Web Package contains a duplicate filename (such as the default or index home page), a Confirm Save dialog box appears, asking whether you want to overwrite the file. This situation can happen if your open Web site contains a home page named default.htm or index.htm. (You can avoid this problem by importing the Personal Web Package into a new, blank Web site).

   • Click Yes to *overwrite* the file in the open Web site with the file in the Personal Web Package. Click No to stop the duplicate file in the Personal Web Package from importing.

   When the file is done importing, Expression Web pops open a dialog box telling you that the Personal Web Package import process is complete.

5. **Click OK to close the message.**

   The files and folders from the Personal Web Package appear in the Web site's Folder List task pane.

Chapter 14

Getting Cozy with Code

. . . .

In This Chapter

▷ Finding out why HTML knowledge is worthwhile

▷ Getting a grasp on HTML basics

▷ Working with the Expression Web code tools

▷ Letting Expression Web clean up your page's code

▷ Inserting comments in your HTML and CSS style sheets

. . . .

*W*hen it comes to Web publishing, there are two types of people: those who like to poke around "under the hood" to see how things work and those who are either worried that they'll break something or just want everything to work without needing to know *how*.

If you're in the first group, more power to you. You'll find it easy to work in the Expression Web Design and Code views — you may even enjoy moving between the two views as you build your site.

If you're in the second group, you're not alone. HTML may seem intimidating at first, but with a little guidance, you'll find that it's not all that complicated. Expression Web already gives you a sturdy leg up on the process — the code that Expression Web creates is clean, correct, and by the book. So, for you, finding out about HTML will be a matter of tagging along with Expression Web while it serves as your tutor of sorts.

If you're new to HTML, read the first part of this chapter, which introduces some basic HTML concepts that help you understand your HTML pages. If you've never looked at a Web page's underlying code, this section gives you an idea of what's going on. Later sections of this chapter cover the special Expression Web tools and features for working in Code view and with HTML tags. Along the way, you pick up a few tricks for making a page's HTML code or CSS easier to understand and for making quick code edits. We talk about style sheets in detail in Chapter 9.

If you're a complete HTML newbie, consider adding a good HTML reference to your computer book library. One of our favorites is *HTML 4 For Dummies*, 5th Edition, by Ed Tittel and Mary Burmeister (Wiley). You can also find plenty of online tutorials. Here are a few to get you started: www.w3schools.com/html and www.htmlgoodies.com/primers/html.

When we use the term *HTML,* we also mean XHTML, the new-and-improved version of HTML. Unless you tell Expression Web otherwise, it writes your pages' code in XHTML.

Understanding Why You Can't Just Ignore the Code

When it comes to Web publishing, a little bit of HTML knowledge goes a long way. You can make a change in the code and — presto! — the result shows up in your browser, giving you almost instant satisfaction. Likewise, if something looks funky in Design view (or in your browser) and you can't tell what's wrong, a peek at the code often reveals the culprit (which can be as simple as a broken tag or a line break where it shouldn't be). A couple of keystrokes get you back on track.

Expression Web knows how to take care of just about any Web-design problem with its toolbars, task panes, or dialog boxes. But the simple fact remains: Some details are just easier to fix in the code. When you know how to navigate your page's code, you can efficiently make piecemeal changes to your pages. If you want to get serious about Web publishing, HTML fluency has no substitute.

Introducing the HTML Basics

You don't need programming experience to learn to use HTML, because HTML isn't a programming language; it's a *markup language*. The difference is that a programming language gives your computer direct instructions; HTML, by contrast, is a series of codes that signal your Web browser to display content in certain ways. These codes, or *tags*, surround the different elements on your HTML page. Some tags tell the Web browser what to display in the browser window, and some tags tell the browser information about the page and how it's written. Most tags open (<tag>) and close (</tag>), working in layers like Russian nesting dolls. Here's an example:

```
<body><p><em>Content goes here</em></p></body>
```

In this example, think of the <em> tag pair as the littlest doll. The <p> tag is the middle doll with the <em> doll inside it, and the <body> tag is the big doll with both the middle doll and little doll inside it.

The content that the tag displays on the page appears between the opening and closing tag. Here's some content added to the same HTML tags:

```
<body><p>This is a paragraph. The word <em>italic</em> is
          displayed in the browser in italics.</p></body>
```

Figure 14-1 shows this sentence in Expression Web, in both Code view and Design view:

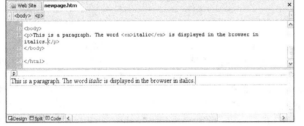

Figure 14-1:
Nesting
HTML tags
in Design
view and
Code view.

Looking at the essential Web page parts

Every HTML page has the same structure and set of tags, regardless of the page's content. When you create a new HTML page in Expression Web, it sets up the basic structure for you and adds the required coding to the page. Table 14-1 lists the different parts and describes their functions. See *HTML 4 for Dummies*, 5th Edition, by Ed Tittel and Mary Burmeister (Wiley) for a more in-depth discussion of these parts.

Table 14-1	The Parts of an HTML Page
Part Name	*Purpose*
doctype	The doctype, or *document type declaration,* tells the Web browser which version of HTML or XHTML code the page is written in so that it knows how to display it correctly. The doctype appears at the top of the page. See the nearby sidebar "What's up, doctype?" for more information.
<html>	Tells the Web browser where the HTML code starts (<html>) and ends (</html>; this closing tag is always the last tag on the page).

(continued)

Table 14-1 *(continued)*

Part Name	Purpose
`<head>`	Tells the Web browser how to display information that doesn't appear inside the main body of the page, such as the title (displayed on the Web browser's title bar) and which language the page is coded for. It can also contain other noncontent stuff, such as embedded styles or links to external style sheets or scripts that control dynamic behaviors on the page. The `</head>` tag closes the page's `<head>` section.
`<body>`	Tells the Web browser where the page's content — the stuff that's shown on the page inside the browser window itself — begins (`<body>`) and ends (`</body>`).

Because HTML coding is basically just text, you can create an HTML page in any text editor. If you were to create a Web page from scratch, you would have to manually add all the tags and information listed in Table 14-1. Fortunately, Expression Web handles all that for you. Create a blank page (we show you how in Chapter 2), and the basic code gets added automatically to the page's code. Figure 14-2 shows a new, blank page with its code revealed.

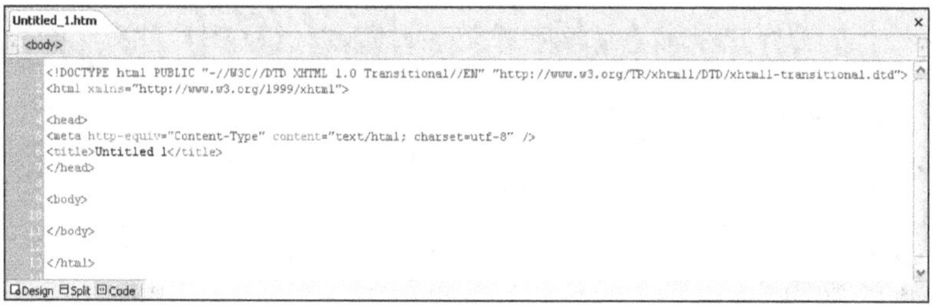

Figure 14-2:
Code view
for a new,
blank page.

When you specify a title for the page (we tell you how in Chapter 2), your title replaces `<title>Untitled 1</title>` in the `<head>` section. When you add content to the page in Design view, the content shows up between the `<body>` and `</body>` tags.

Taking a closer look at HTML elements

An HTML tag plus its content is an *HTML element.* An HTML element begins with the first opening angle bracket (<) and ends with the last closing angle bracket (>). The sidebar "Anatomy of an HTML element" dissects and explains an HTML element's essential parts and shows you their proper names.

What's up, doctype?

You look at the top of your new, "blank" page, and this is what you see:

```
<!DOCTYPE html PUBLIC "-//W3C
    //DTD XHTML 1.0
    Transitional//EN" "http://
    www.w3.org/TR/xhtml1/DTD/
    xhtml1-transitional.dtd">
<html xmlns="http://www.w3.
    org/1999/xhtml">
```

This perplexing-looking mumbo jumbo is a *document type declaration,* or *doctype.* It introduces the Web browser to the page and tells it which version of HTML the page speaks so that the Web browser can display it properly. (It also tells Expression Web which code format to expect so it can alert you if something isn't up to snuff.) The example shown here is the default setting for new pages created in Expression Web: XHTML 1.0 Transitional. Web designers use this standard as the default because it's the most compatible with the greatest percentage of Web browsers now in use and also complies fully with current standards set by the World Wide Web Consortium (the folks who set the road rules for traffic on the Web). For most (perhaps even for all) Web sites you create, the Expression Web default doctype is ideal. If not, someone on your design team is highly likely to know more about HTML and doctype declarations and can let you know which one to pick. You can change the doctype by choosing Tools⇨Page Editor Options; click the Authoring tab and then select an option from the Document Type Declaration list box (in the Doctype and Secondary Schema section). Expression Web displays a page's doctype in the lower-right section of the status bar.

If you want to find out more about doctype declarations, read up in your HTML reference. Or just type **doctype** into your favorite search engine to get more information than you could possibly ever read.

An HTML element can be either *block-level* or *inline.* Here's the difference:

- ✔ **Block-level elements:** If the HTML tag starts a new line with its opening tag and starts another new line after its closing tag, it's a block-level element. Paragraphs (`<p>`) and headings (`<h1>`–`<h6>`) are all block-level elements. An easy way to understand block-level HTML elements is to picture them as separate paragraphs on a page. Each paragraph starts on a new line. When the paragraph ends, a break occurs and then the next paragraph comes along. Block-level elements can contain inline elements and other block-level elements.

- ✔ **Inline elements:** An inline element goes with the flow without interrupting anything. An inline element inserted into a block-level element changes just the part that its tags surround, but leaves everything else the same. Using our paragraph analogy, an inline element is a word or phrase within a paragraph that has been made bold or italic. (In fact, `<em>` and `<strong>` are the inline HTML elements that make the text they surround italic and bold, respectively). Inline elements cannot exist outside block-level elements; they must be nested inside a block-level element (like words within a paragraph). An inline element *can* contain other inline elements, however.

Anatomy of an HTML element

An HTML *element* describes what appears on the page and its content. Here's an HTML element that displays a first-level heading on a Web page:

```
<h1>Piano Tuners of Portland<
/h1>
```

The content — what's displayed on the page — appears between the opening <h1> tag and the closing </h1> tag.

Some HTML elements contain *attribute* and *value* pairs that describe something about the element. The following diagram shows two HTML elements with their attribute/value pairs identified. The first one contains all the information for displaying a picture on the page: the name of the picture file, its width and height, and its alt text (refer to Chapter 5). The second one contains a class attribute/value pair so that a class-based style rule (refer to Chapter 7) can be applied to it:

An HTML element always has this format:

```
<tag attribute="value"
    attribute="value"
    >content</tag>
```

A few HTML elements combine their opening and closing tags into one set of angle brackets. An example of this is the <img> element.

By the way, XHTML, the latest version of HTML (and the version that Expression Web writes by default) is picky about exact syntax. If you have older Web pages that you want to bring up to current XHTML code standards, you have to do some code housecleaning. See Bonus Chapter 18 for tips on how to update old pages. To find this chapter, go to www.dummies.com, use the search box to navigate to this book's Web page, and then click the Bonus Chapters link.

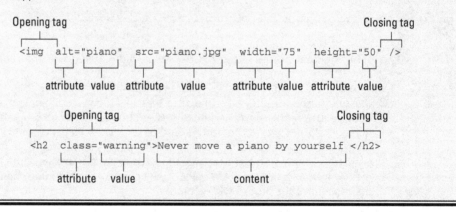

Table 14-2 describes some of the most commonly used HTML elements for building your Web pages.

Table 14-2	Quickie HTML Tag Reference
Block-Level HTML Tag	***HTML Element That It Defines***
`<body>`	Defines the Web-page content itself; all content that appears inside the browser window falls between the `<body>` and `</body>` tags.
`<h1>-<h6>`	Used to indicate first- through sixth-level headings; the content of the heading appears between `<hx>` and `</hx>`.
`<p>`	Specifies a paragraph; the content of the paragraph appears between `<p>` and `</p>`.
`<ol>`	Defines a numbered list (ordered list); these tags indicate the beginning (`<ol>`) and the end (`</ol>`) of the numbered list.
`<ul>`	Defines a bulleted list (unordered list); these tags indicate the beginning (`<ul>`) and the end (`</ul>`) of the bulleted list.
`<li>`	Defines each item within a list (either ordered or unordered); each list item appears between an opening `<li>` tag and a closing `</li>` tag. If you want to get technical, a list item has its own category — called, surprisingly, *list-item* HTML element.
`<div>`	Specifies a container that surrounds other HTML elements, enclosing them between `<div>` and `</div>`; use div tags to define the different parts of your Web page's content, such as navigation, page banner, footer, content area. In HTML alone, they're not much use, but combined with CSS, they give you all sorts of control over layout and styling. We talk about the `<div>` tag and how to use it in Chapter 8.
Inline-Level HTML Tags	
`<a>`	Specifies an anchor (hyperlink); the attribute/value pair `<a href="destination">` in the opening tag defines the hyperlink's destination; the hyperlink source (the thing on the page that gets clicked) appears between the opening tag and the closing `</a>` tag.
`<strong>`	Makes all text between the `<strong>` and `</strong>` bold by default; you can change the appearance by selecting this element and creating a style rule.

(continued)

Table 14-2 *(continued)*

Inline-Level HTML Tags	HTML Element That It Defines
<em>	Makes all text between <em> and </em> italic by default; you can change the appearance by selecting this element and creating a style rule.
<span>	Allows you to define a chunk of content within a block-level element or within another inline element (such as a word in a sentence) in order to apply a style to it. The <span> tag is the inline equivalent of a <div> tag.
<img>	Specifies an image (picture); because this tag has no closing tag, all information about the image is inside the tag (<img src="*imagefilename*" />).

Structuring HTML content

Web-standards experts often banter about the term *well-formed,* or *well-struc-tured,* documents. They're not talking about whether the content is worth reading (you can write anything you want), nor are they talking about whether the page has been checked for spelling errors and typos (although we suggest that you do that). The experts aren't even talking about whether the page has an attractive layout. They're talking about structuring a document so that it follows a logical order and makes sense by using the right HTML elements for the right parts. Just like your composition teacher harped on the importance of having good essay structure — with a topic sentence, supporting paragraphs, and a conclusion — your Web page's content should follow a logical structure.

Figure 14-3 shows an example of well-structured HTML content in Design view. Figure 14-4 shows the code for the content in Figure 14-3.

Using a logical structure like this one can help you create and organize content for your Web pages more quickly by breaking information into chunks. A well-structured content page makes it a snap to prepare the page's content for viewing on different devices (such as mobile phones, PDAs, or printers) just by applying a different style sheet. It also ensures that the content makes sense with no styles at all, in case your style sheet isn't accessible to your page's content.

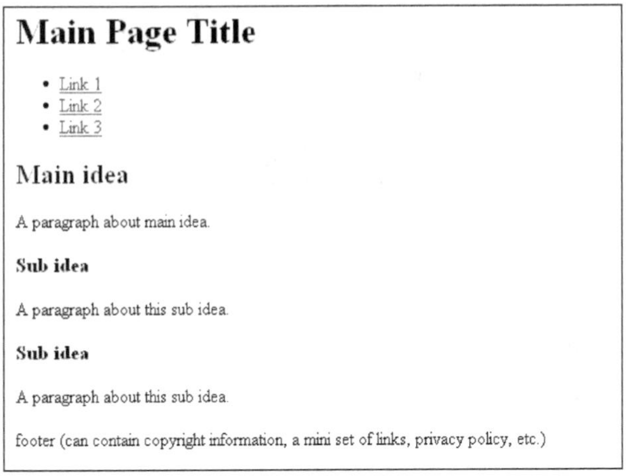

Main Page Title

- Link 1
- Link 2
- Link 3

Main idea

A paragraph about main idea.

Sub idea

A paragraph about this sub idea.

Sub idea

A paragraph about this sub idea.

footer (can contain copyright information, a mini set of links, privacy policy, etc.)

Figure 14-3: Structure your page's content so that it makes logical sense.

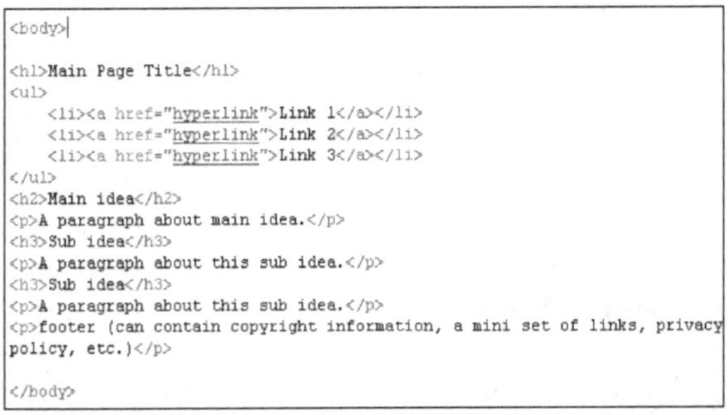

```
<body>

<h1>Main Page Title</h1>
<ul>
    <li><a href="hyperlink">Link 1</a></li>
    <li><a href="hyperlink">Link 2</a></li>
    <li><a href="hyperlink">Link 3</a></li>
</ul>
<h2>Main idea</h2>
<p>A paragraph about main idea.</p>
<h3>Sub idea</h3>
<p>A paragraph about this sub idea.</p>
<h3>Sub idea</h3>
<p>A paragraph about this sub idea.</p>
<p>footer (can contain copyright information, a mini set of links, privacy
policy, etc.)</p>

</body>
```

Figure 14-4: Code view of the page shown in Figure 14-3.

Checking Out the Cool Code Tools

Expression Web figures that most designers will spend time flipping between Code view and Design view. You can work in both views easily by choosing Split view (click the Split button in the lower-left corner of the editing window). To make working with code easy, the folks at Microsoft built in a lot of code tools, some of which, like the Quick Tag Selector bar, give you access to the code directly in Design view.

Code view

If you're comfortable working with HTML, the easiest way to access and edit your page's code is to switch to Code view. Click the Code button in the lower-left corner of the editing window. There you find the HTML, nicely laid out, numbered by line, and color-coded so that it's easier to read (see Figure 14-5).

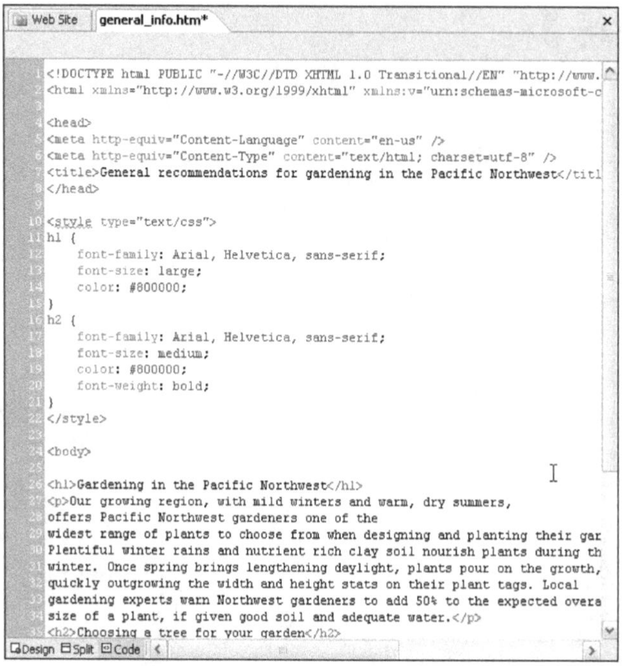

Figure 14-5:
Code view
shows only
the code for
the page.

Quick Tag Selector bar

As you add text and formatting to your page, notice the line of HTML tags growing near the top of the editing window (see Figure 14-6; although you can't see the flashing cursor in the figure, it's inside the italic text *overall size*). This tool is named the *Quick Tag Selector bar* because it gives you instant access to the page's HTML without having to switch to Code view. (If you don't see the Quick Tag Selector bar, choose View⇨Quick Tag Selector.)

To watch the Quick Tag Selector bar in action, click anywhere inside the page. Click a word, a picture, a list — anything. The HTML tags that appear inside the Quick Tag Selector bar are the tags, in order, that affect whatever you just clicked.

If you already know how to use HTML, the contents of the Quick Tag Selector bar probably make sense to you. If you don't know how to use HTML, or if you're just beginning to learn, the Quick Tag Selector bar is an excellent tutor — because when you click a tag on the Quick Tag Selector bar, Expression Web highlights the tag's contents in Design view and Code view. In this way, you can begin to see how HTML operates.

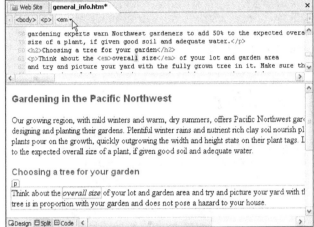

Figure 14-6:
The Quick
Tag Selector
bar.

When you hover your cursor over a tag on the Quick Tag Selector bar, a little down-arrow button also appears next to the tag. To edit that HTML tag, click the button to display a menu of options:

- ✔ **Select Tag:** Select the opening and closing tags and their contents.

- ✔ **Select Tag Contents:** Select only the contents of the tag.

- ✔ **Edit Tag:** Add attributes to the tag by using the Quick Tag Editor (see the next section).

- ✔ **Remove Tag:** Remove the opening and closing tags, but leave the tag contents alone.

- ✔ **Insert HTML:** Insert HTML at the location of the cursor by using the Quick Tag Editor (see the next section).

- ✔ **Wrap Tag:** Insert HTML that surrounds (or *wraps around*) the selected tag by using the Quick Tag Editor (see the next section).

- ✔ **Tag Properties:** Open the Properties dialog box pertaining to the selected tag. Or open the Tag Properties task pane, which shows the tag's attributes.

The Quick Tag Selector bar is a useful tool for precisely selecting elements in Design view. For example, if you want to replace heading text with something else but you don't want to delete the heading tags, click in the heading tag and, click the heading tag's drop-down arrow on the Quick Tag Selector bar. From the drop-down list that appears, choose Select Tag Contents. Then replace the selected text by typing new text. Or use the Quick Tag Selector bar to delete a whole paragraph that you no longer need by clicking in the paragraph, clicking the paragraph tag's drop-down arrow, and choosing the Select Tag option. Press the Delete key and the paragraph departs to cyber-heaven, taking its tags along with it.

Quick Tag Editor

Like the Quick Tag Selector bar, the *Quick Tag Editor* gives you easy access to your HTML code so that you can edit a selected tag, insert new HTML tags, or wrap a tag around one or more existing tags. Use the Quick Tag Editor in either Design view or Code view of your Web page.

To edit an HTML tag by using the Quick Tag Editor, follow these steps:

1. **In either Design view or Code view, select the tag you want to edit.**

   You can either place your cursor somewhere inside the tag (such as somewhere in a paragraph, if you want to edit the paragraph's tag) or use the Quick Tag Selector bar to select the tag you want to edit.

2. **Choose Edit⇨Quick Tag Editor and then, from the drop-down list box in the left-hand portion of the Quick Tag Editor, select Edit Tag.**

   If you're working in Design view, in the Quick Tag Selector bar, click the down-arrow button next to the tag you want to edit and then select Edit Tag.

   The Quick Tag Editor appears with the contents of the selected tag, as shown in Figure 14-7.

Figure 14-7:
The Quick
Tag Editor.

3. **Make any necessary changes to the tag and click the Enter button (the green check mark) to close the Quick Tag Editor and apply the changes to the tag.**

   For example, in Figure 14-6, we could change the `<strong>` tag (bold) to `<em>` (italic) by selecting the word `strong` and typing `em` in its place.

If necessary, the Quick Tag Editor changes the closing tag to match. (Using our example, the Quick Tag Editor automatically changesthe </strong> tag to </em>.)

To close the Quick Tag Editor without making any changes, click the Cancel button (the red X).

To wrap an HTML tag around existing content or other tag, follow these steps:

1. **Select the content, tag, or tags around which you want to wrap another HTML tag.**

   You can do this in a variety of ways. Here are some examples:

   - *Wrap a <span> tag around some text in a paragraph:* In Design view or Code view, select the text.

   - *Wrap a tag around a single tag:* In either Design view or Code view, place your cursor anywhere inside the tag; when you select Wrap Tag, the whole tag gets selected.

   - *Wrap a <div> tag around several other tags, such as an unordered list (the <ul>, each <li></li> pair, and the closing </ul> tag):* To make sure that you select all the tags for the various list parts, in the Quick Tag Selector bar, click the <ul> tag. You can also click the down-arrow button next to the tag and select Wrap Tag directly from the Quick Tag Selector bar (and then skip ahead to Step 3).

2. **Choose Edit⇨Quick Tag Editor and then, from the drop-down list box in the left-hand portion of the Quick Tag Editor, select Wrap Tag.**

3. **In the text entry area of the Quick Tag Editor, type the tag you want to wrap around the selected tags or content and then click the Enter button (or press the Enter key on your keyboard).**

   For example, to wrap a <span> tag with a class attribute around the selected content, type <span class="classvalue">. Notice that, as you type, the Expression Web IntelliSense feature helps you along the way with drop-down menus of suggestions. We tell you how to use IntelliSense later in this chapter.

Using the Quick Tag Editor to insert HTML is most useful in Code view. To do so, follow these steps:

1. **Place your cursor in the location where you want to insert HTML.**

2. **Choose Edit⇨Quick Tag Editor (or press Ctrl+Q).**

3. **From the drop-down menu, choose Insert HTML and type the HTML in the text entry area.**

4. **Click the Enter button (or press the Enter key).**

If you use this method to insert an HTML tag, IntelliSense assumes that you want to add the closing tag along with it, which it does, right after the opening tag (for example, `<span></span>`). In Code view, you can simply click between the tags and add the content.

IntelliSense

As you type HTML tags, Expression Web helps you format your code correctly by automatically closing tags and by popping open menus of tags that are valid for where you are in the HTML code. Expression Web also highlights errors so that they're easy to spot. This code watchdog, named *IntelliSense*, is like a Code view spell checker combined with an autocomplete function.

To insert code from a pop-up code menu, use the up- and down-arrow keys on your keyboard to highlight the code you want to insert (or type the couple of letters of the tag you want to add), and then do one of the following:

✔ Press the Tab or Enter key on your keyboard.

✔ Double-click the item.

 ✔ On the Code View toolbar, click the Complete Word button. (We talk about the Code View toolbar later in this chapter.)

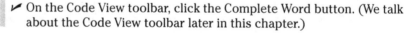 If you don't like the way IntelliSense works, or you *do* like it but wish that it did something a little differently, you can change it. Choose Tools⇨Page Editor Options and then click the IntelliSense tab to change the Expression Web IntelliSense settings.

Code View toolbar

After you switch to Code view (or if you're working in the code portion of Split view), pop open the Code View toolbar by choosing View⇨Toolbars⇨ Code View. The Code View toolbar gives you quick access to many useful code goodies. Table 14-3 lists the buttons and describes what they do. Like most other toolbar buttons, most of their capabilities are also available as commands and keyboard shortcuts. Choose Edit⇨Code View and then choose from the menu.

Table 14-3	Code View Toolbar Buttons	
Button	*Button Name*	*What It Does*
	List Members, Parameter Info, Complete Word	Depending on where you are in your code, displays shortcut menus for inserting code.
	List Code Snippet	Displays a shortcut menu for inserting a code snippet. (We explain code snippets later in this chapter.)
	Follow Hyperlink	When the cursor is in a hyperlink, goes to and opens the hyperlink destination.
	Previous Code Hyperlink, Next Code Hyperlink	Works like the Back and Next buttons in a browser, allowing you to scroll through hyperlink destinations you've followed.
	Toggle Bookmarks	Toggles on and off temporary code bookmarks. (We talk about code bookmarks later in this chapter.)
	Next Bookmark, Previous Bookmark	Goes to the next or previous code bookmark.
	Clear Bookmarks	Removes all code bookmarks from the page.
	Select Tag	Selects the opening and closing tag and all the contents of an HTML element.
	Find Matching Tag	Finds the other tag (either opening or closing) in a tag pair when you put your cursor inside a tag and click to select it; click again to find the other tag in the tag pair.

(continued)

Table 14-3 (continued)

Button	Button Name	What It Does
	Select Block	Selects all the style declarations inside the CSS style rule in which your cursor is located.
	Find Matching Brace	Finds the curly brace that either ends or begins a style rule when the cursor is located next to one of a CSS style rule's curly brace.
	Insert Start Tag, Insert End Tag	Inserts the angle brackets for an opening or closing tag.
	Insert Comment	Inserts the opening and closing characters for a comment. (We talk about using comments later in this chapter.)
	Script Editor	Launches the Microsoft Script Editor, which allows you to add programming scripts (VBScript or JScript) to your code. (See the Microsoft Script Editor Help for instructions.)
	Function Lookup	If you have scripts in your page, jumps to the code containing the function you select from the drop-down list.
	Options	Lets you choose different options for how code is displayed in Code view.

Code snippets

Expression Web can also save frequently used bits of code as *snippets* so that you don't have to type them over and over. To create your own code snippet, follow these steps:

1. **Choose Tools⇨Page Editor Options, and from the dialog box that appears, click the Code Snippets tab.**

2. **Click the Add button.**

   The Add Code Snippet dialog box appears.

3. **In the Keyword text field, type a unique word for the code snippet.**

   When you want to insert your code snippet, you type this word, so use one that describes the code snippet's function to you.

4. **In the Description text field, type a description of the code snippet.**

5. **In the Text Entry field, type the code that will be inserted when you select the code snippet.**

6. **Click OK to save the code snippet.**

To edit a code snippet, choose one from the list and click the Modify button. Make any necessary changes and click OK. Delete a code snippet by selecting it and clicking the Remove button.

To insert a code snippet in your page's HTML code, place your cursor where you want the code snippet to appear, press Ctrl+Enter to display a list of saved snippets, and then double-click the snippet you want to use.

Find and Replace in Code view

While in Code view, you can use the Expression Web Find and Replace function to automatically update HTML tags throughout the page (or even your entire site). If you're a frequent HTML user, you know that this feature is a major timesaver. To access HTML Find and Replace, choose Edit⇨Find (or Edit⇨Replace), and from the dialog box that appears, click the HTML Tags tab.

Code bookmarks

You can use code bookmarks to mark a line of code so that you can find it more easily later on. Code bookmarks don't show up in your Web page's content, and Expression Web deletes all code bookmarks when you close a page. These bookmarks work only in Code view (or in the code portion of Split view).

To insert a code bookmark, follow these steps:

1. **Place your cursor in the line of code you want to mark with a code bookmark.**

2. **On the Code View toolbar, click the Toggle Bookmarks button.**

   Or choose Edit ⇨Code View⇨Toggle Bookmarks.

   A teal rectangle appears in the left margin, next to the code line.

To remove a code bookmark, place your cursor in the line of code containing the bookmark and, on the Code View toolbar, click the Toggle Bookmarks button. (Refer to Table 14-3, earlier in this chapter, for other code bookmark buttons.)

Controlling How Expression Web-Created Code Looks

Does it matter how the code looks? If the page looks good when viewed with a Web browser, what does it matter if the HTML code is a little sloppy?

Although the formatting and layout of the HTML don't affect the look of the finished Web page (unless the HTML contains errors, of course), you're still wise to pay attention to the tidiness of your code. Neatly written HTML is easier to update, especially if the site eventually ends up in the hands of a different administrator (who may or may not use Expression Web to update the site).

And then there's the impression your code makes. Believe it or not, a number of your visitors don't just browse your site — they peruse your code as well. A site's HTML is visible to any visitor who chooses to look. (Every browser can display a page's underlying HTML; check out your browser's Help system to find out how to do it.) Many people teach themselves to use HTML by looking at others' finished pages. Others are simply part of the "under the hood" crowd and are curious how you built your site. Either way, messy code reflects badly on its author, so it pays to keep yours clean.

Expression Web helps by generating tidy lines of code to begin with. Even so, you may want to tinker with the way Expression Web formats your code.

The Page Editor Options dialog box (available by choosing Tools⇨Page Editor Options) contains settings that control how Expression Web outputs HTML and how Expression Web displays HTML and CSS code inside Code view. Here's a quick rundown of how you use the tabs inside this dialog box that deal with HTML and CSS output and formatting (for detailed information, turn to the Expression Web Help system):

- ✔ **General:** Choose how Expression Web generates particular bits of HTML in addition to the basic setup of Code view.

- ✔ **Code Formatting:** Control how the finished HTML and CSS looks by choosing upper- or lowercase tags and attributes, line breaks, indentation, margins, and formatting details for individual tags.

- ✔ **Color Coding:** Tell Expression Web how to color-code the HTML inside Code view. (Click the Code View Settings button in the upper-left corner of the dialog box.) Choose a color scheme that makes the code easiest for you to read as you work with Expression Web. The colors you choose have no effect on the finished look of the page — only how code looks inside Code view.

- ✔ **IntelliSense:** Set options for the Expression Web automatic HTML features.

Finally, Expression Web does last-minute code cleanup when you choose Tools➪Optimize HTML. You use the Optimize HTML dialog box to select redundant or useless HTML that does little more than muddle your code. After you click OK, Expression Web erases the selected items.

Using Comments in HTML

You can pepper your pages with explanatory text and reminders to yourself (or to other members of your Web-building team) in the form of HTML comments. *Comments* are notes that appear only inside the page's code, but not to visitors viewing the finished page with a Web browser. To insert a comment, follow these steps:

1. **With the Web page open, click in Code view wherever you want to insert the comment.**

   Make sure that your insertion location isn't inside an HTML tag.

2. **On the Code View toolbar (choose View➪Toolbars➪Code View), click the Insert Comment button.**

   Or, choose Edit➪Code View➪Insert Comment.

   The opening and closing tags for comments appear in the code, like this:

   ```
   <!-- -->
   ```

3. **Type your comment between the opening and closing comment tags.**

   A comment looks like this in the code:

   ```
   <!-- this is a comment -->
   ```

To edit a comment, select the comment text (without selecting the opening and closing tags) and type the new comment text.

To delete a comment, follow these steps:

1. **In Code view, click anywhere inside the comment.**

2. **On the Code View toolbar, click the Select Tag button.**

   The comment and its opening and closing tags are selected, indicated by gray shading.

3. **Press the Delete key.**

Comments aren't *completely* invisible; your visitors can see the comments if they look at your page's underlying HTML tags. If you want to keep your comments completely private, you can tell Expression Web to strip out the comments before you publish your site. We explain how in Chapter 12.

You can also add comments to your CSS style sheets, but the syntax is a bit different from that of regular HTML comments. We show you how to create CSS comments in Chapter 9.

Part V
The Part of Tens

The 5th Wave   By Rich Tennant

Cleopatra
Carpet Cleaners

"So far our web presence has been pretty good. We've gotten some orders, a few inquiries, and nine guys who want to date our logo."

In this part . . .

In this part, we show you some gizmos you can add to your site to increase its usefulness and cool factor. We also offer a list of resources we think you'll turn to again and again as you use Expression Web and continue to grow as a Web designer.

For tips on designing a Web site from the get-go and fixing one that's horribly outdated, download the two bonus chapters located on the Web. Go to www.dummies.com, use the search box to navigate to this book's Web page, and then click the Bonus Chapters link.

Chapter 15

Ten Cool Gizmos for Your Web Site

*1*f you're ready to take your Web site beyond the ordinary to include some of the cool stuff you see on the Web, this chapter is for you. Here are ten great gizmos that increase your site's utility and "wow" factor. Many of these tools are free, and the rest are relatively cheap. We also give you a rundown on ways to replace the functionality of the most popular FrontPage Web components, or *bots.* Former FrontPage users loved how easy bots were to use, but they didn't make it into Expression Web because the code they generated wasn't up to standards muster.

Some gizmos mentioned in this chapter work by simply linking to a file or URL. Others provide ready-to-go-code that you *embed,* or plop into your page's HTML to make them work. For example, YouTube allows you to link to a video on the YouTube Web site or embed the video in your site so that it plays in a box right on your page. (We tell you more about YouTube later in this chapter.) To create a link, use any of the techniques we outline in Chapter 4. To embed code in your page's HTML, in Design view, place your cursor in the location you want the gizmo to appear. Then look in Code view (or in the code portion of Split view) for the blinking cursor. That's the location in your code that matches the spot on your page. You place the gizmo code right in that spot.

Search Locally or Worldwide-Web-ly

Give your Web visitors the option of searching both the World Wide Web and your Web site by including Google Free WebSearch and SiteSearch on your home page. You can add a miniature Google search box similar to the one on the Google home page, or you can customize the box to blend with your site's color scheme.

Adding Google searching to your site is a simple matter of dropping a chunk of code into your page's HTML in the location you want the search box to appear on the page.

Visit `www.google.com/searchcode.html` for details.

Search Only the Sites You Trust

"Googling" for information has become second nature for most of us. Yet searching the entire Web isn't always the best way to go. Rollyo allows you to create *searchrolls,* or collections of trusted go-to sites on topics you specify. You then search only those sites and increase the probability that the search results are useful.

Rollyo makes it easy to create searchrolls and add search bars to your site (which you can customize). You can also use Rollyo to create single-site or Web-wide searches, similar to Google.

Go to `www.rollyo.com` to get started.

Include a Map on Your Site

How did we ever find our way from one place to another before the Internet? Oh, yeah — maps. You can more easily fold an origami crane than refold one of those oversized hunks of paper.

When your visitors are ready to pay you a visit in the flesh, make it easy for them by putting a map right on your site. You have several options for including maps on your site, but we think MapQuest is the easiest, in part because of its easy-to-follow, step-by-step instructions.

Visit `www.mapquest.com/features/main.adp?page=1f_main` for complete information.

Share Your Favorite Places

Maps are good for more than just driving directions. The innovative map-maniacs at Platial have created the MapKit tool, which you use to place a collaborative map on your site to which your visitors can add their favorite places, along with comments, pictures, and video. MapKit is the brainchild of expatriate Americans living in Amsterdam who created oodles of paper maps for their out-of-town guests; the expats created a way to do the same thing online. Placing a Platial-powered map on your site is easy, and no programming knowledge is required. Take a look at www.platial.com/mapkit.

Share Video

For your visitors' viewing pleasure, YouTube makes it easy to upload short videos and either link to them from your site or embed the video right in your page. (See www.youtube.com/sharing.) You can even include a scrollable list of videos and let your visitors pick which ones they want to watch.

Google Video also provides a great method for making your video content available to visitors. (See https://upload.video.google.com.) For other options, check out David Crowder's *Building a Web Site For Dummies,* 2nd Edition (Wiley), for complete information about including video on your site.

Linking to videos that *someone else* has uploaded to YouTube or Google Video gets a little more complicated due to copyright issues. Know your rights in case the person who uploaded the content stepped on someone's copyright toes. If you're located in the U.S., bone up on the laws of fair use at the U.S. Copyright Office (www.copyright.gov).

Add Flash

One benefit of building a Web site now is that if it's possible to do something easily, someone has probably done it and made it available for everyone. This is the case with adding Flash animation to a Web site. Thanks to Geoff Stearns, you have an easy way to add Flash to a Web page by using JavaScript. This task requires some basic code knowledge, but he steps you through the process and provides the code you need to insert in your page. See blog.deconcept.com/swfobject.

Accept Payments on Your Site

For basic financial transactions, nothing beats PayPal for quick-and-easy. Whether you want to collect donations, sell stuff, or gather subscription payments, PayPal has taken the pain out of getting paid. See www.paypal.com for the scoop.

If you're ready to launch full force into putting up stuff for sale on your site, you want to get informed about the ins and outs of e-commerce. A professional Web designer we know recommends this site for information minus the hype: www.practicalecommerce.com.

Place Ads by Google

Who doesn't want free money? With little effort? Consider embellishing your Web pages with Google AdSense text-based ads. Google "reads" your Web page, compares its content to its vast database of advertisers, and then picks ads targeted to the specific content of the page and places them in the spot you specify. When visitors click (and in some cases even look at) the ad, you get paid.

Visit www.adsense.google.com to find out more.

Create Drop-Down Menus

Maybe you have a large Web site that needs a multilevel navigation system to help visitors find their way around and you don't have the scripting skills to build it yourself. Check out Ultimate Drop Down Menu, by Brothercake, at www.brothercake.com/site/products/menu. The menus created with this program comply fully with Web standards for code and accessibility. That means they work with both Web browsers and screen readers (devices that make Web sites accessible to disabled visitors).

Replace Your Favorite FrontPage Bots

If you're a former user of Microsoft FrontPage, you may be missing some of your buddies from the Web Components menu. Table 15-1 lists a few of the most popular bots along with solutions for finding replacements.

You can open, edit, and publish your FrontPage-created site by using Expression Web. Any Web components already in place and working continue to work as they did in FrontPage. However, you cannot add new Web components by using Expression Web, because the FrontPage Web components produce less-than-standard-compliant code.

Table 15-1	Some FrontPage Web Components and Ideas for Replacing Them
Web Component	*How to Replace It*
Web search	Google Free WebSearch and SiteSearch (explained in this chapter) are good substitutes and put the power of the Google search engine into your site.
Hit counter or Top 10 list	Hit counters are passé, and Top 10 lists are more useful for you than for your visitors. Ask your Web host for detailed log files that provide you with valuable information about your visitors' browsing habits.
Photo gallery	Plenty of good photo gallery options are available on the Web. See the sidebar about photo galleries in Chapter 5.
Link bars	Expression Web doesn't give you the option of automatically generating and customizing link bars. See the sidebar about link bars in Chapter 4. Chapter 8 covers ideas for creating navigation bars with CSS. Another option: drop-down navigation menus; see the section "Create Drop-Down Menus," earlier in this chapter.
Included content	This component (affectionately referred to as *includes*) provided a way to reuse page content without creating a template. Microsoft has agreed to bring back includes soon. See the Expression Web development team Weblog for news about this and other features: `http://blogs.msdn.com/xweb`.

Chapter 16

Ten Essential Resources for Web Designers

In This Chapter

▸ Build your Web knowledge base

▸ Get help with Expression Web and find add-ins

▸ Consult the experts

▸ Find fonts, photos, style sheets, and much more

▸ Get inspired

*W*e asked professional Web designers to share their favorite resources with us, and they obliged with more than enough links, books, and gadgets to keep you out of trouble and in the know. Some of these sites (especially the ones farther down the list) edge into the realm of intermediate knowledge. You may find them more useful after your skills with Web design and CSS have grown a bit.

Expression Web Help and Online Tutorials

The creators of the following Web sites have gone out of their way to help new Expression Web users discover how to build well-structured Web sites easily. The sites are packed with topic-specific tutorials, downloadable CSS templates, and helpful tips. The creators are also long-standing FrontPage experts, so these resources are especially helpful if you're switching to Expression Web from FrontPage.

```
www.expression-web-designer-help.com
http://by-expression.com
http://any-expression.com
```

At the home page for Microsoft Expression Web, check out the training tutorials and links to user communities, and find out all the latest Expression Web news:

```
www.microsoft.com/products/expression/en/expression-web/default.mspx
```

Knowledge Base Builders

W3schools has beginning, step-by-step online tutorials for the complete novice to HTML and CSS.

```
www.w3schools.com
```

This excellent online CSS tutorial gets you up to speed on all aspects of CSS:

```
www.westciv.com/style_master/academy/css_tutorial
```

At the following site, you can find tutorials for various aspects of CSS design, such as floating page elements, creating navigation bar lists, and understanding selectors:

```
http://css.maxdesign.com.au
```

Webmonkey has how-to guides, articles, and reference material. It's a good general Web resource:

```
www.webmonkey.com
```

Consult the Web Powers That Be

W3C is the home of the governing body of Web experts, the folks who make all the rules and think big thoughts about the future of the Web:

```
www.w3.org
```

The Web Standards Project (WaSP) is "a grassroots coalition fighting for standards which ensure simple, affordable access to web technologies for all." Read up about the organization's work with browser manufacturers and standards, and find out why it matters:

```
www.webstandards.org
```

CSS and Web Design Expertise

The following uberlist provides links to Web sites, articles, and tools as well as lists of books and other goodies for all types of CSS and accessibility issues.

```
www.dezwozhere.com/links.html
```

Eric Meyer is an expert speaker, writer, and thinker on All Things CSS. Visit his CSS-related site to check up on what he's up to, look at demos, read articles, and find out where the next generation of CSS is headed:

```
www.meyerweb.com/eric/css
```

Visit this useful, subscription-based user forum to ask questions of experts on mastering Web site building in all its forms and technical nitpickiness:

```
www.webmasterworld.com
```

A List Apart is an online magazine for Web designers, focused on promoting standards and best practices. Packed with articles about Web-related material — if you need to know about it, you find information about it here. For example, read `www.alistapart/stories/goingtoprint.com` to find out how to prepare a style sheet to optimize your page for printers. Browse to the following address for the main page:

```
www.alistapart.com
```

CSS Play demonstrates numerous ways to use CSS to accomplish different design techniques and describes problems in particular browsers.

```
www.cssplay.co.uk
```

Third-Party Extensions and Add-Ins

XAKT Media has added Expression Web support for many components of its InstantFX SE software. Add Flash navigation buttons, Flash MP3 players, slide shows, and more to your Expression Web pages. You can find its site here:

```
www.instantfx.net/
```

Themed Web site templates help you build and launch a Web site faster. The templates are designed for Expression Web and provide themed, prebuilt sites complete with dummy pages and valid style sheets:

www.i3dthemes.com

More extensions and add-ins for Expression Web will likely be popping up. Type **Microsoft Expression Web extensions** in your search engine to hunt for new goodies.

Code Validation

Check your HTML code with the W3C free Markup Validation Service. You can point the validator at a published page or upload a file for checking.

http://validator.w3.org

Validate your CSS style sheets to see whether they conform to W3C recommendations.

http://jigsaw.w3.org/css-validator

Design-Related Goodies

MyFonts is a useful resource for all sorts of fonts, including a What the Font? tool that distinguishes a font from an image, or at least identifies the closest match:

www.myfonts.com

Check out this helpful grab bag of resources, such as GIF images in different sizes to use for mocking up page headers and menus, as well as a Lorem Ipsum generator for creating dummy copy to use as placeholder text:

www.designerstoolbox.com

Analyze your color choices for contrast with this nifty tool. Type in your text and background colors to see whether you provided enough contrast to comply with accessibility standards:

```
http://juicystudio.com/services/colourcontrast.php
```

Pick colors using this online color wheel, which gives you the hexadecimal number of every color along with the closest Web-safe color match:

```
www.febooti.com/products/iezoom/online-help/online-color-
              chart-picker.html
```

iStockphoto is an inexpensive source to find photos, background textures, design elements, and line art.

```
www.istockphoto.com
```

This free stock-photo site also contains tutorials, blogs, and articles about types of photo-related issues:

```
www.sxc.hu
```

Treasure Trove of Downloads

At CSS Vault, you can download style sheets for all sorts of purposes.

```
http://cssvault.com
```

Download.com is a great place to download software, including different versions of popular browsers:

```
www.download.com
```

If you want to include a script (in JavaScript or another language) in your Web page, but you don't know how or want to write it yourself, look to this site for a collection of stock scripts to use on Web pages:

```
www.hotscripts.com
```

Inspiration

Create a Favorite Web Sites folder in your Web browser, and drop a bookmark to Web sites that inspire you and that you want to take a closer look at.

Stroll through CSS Zen Garden, and play with changing the look of a single Web page just by changing the style sheet attached to it. This site challenges designers to master CSS and push the envelope on what's possible. Check out the luscious, full-color book *The Zen of CSS Design: Visual Enlightenment for the Web (Voices That Matter)*, by Dave Shea and Molly E. Holzschlag (Peachpit Press).

```
www.csszengarden.com
```

Figure out *what* to do, while looking at what *not* to do!

```
www.webpagesthatsuck.com
```

Last, but Certainly Not Least. . . .

Whip out your calculator! Get the math right when figuring out dimensions on your Web pages.

Also, get some good chocolate. We can't write without a bite or two. Is the creative process even possible without it?

Index

• G •

• H •

BUSINESS, CAREERS & PERSONAL FINANCE

0-7645-9847-3   0-7645-2431-3

Also available:
- Business Plans Kit For Dummies
  0-7645-9794-9
- Economics For Dummies
  0-7645-5726-2
- Grant Writing For Dummies
  0-7645-8416-2
- Home Buying For Dummies
  0-7645-5331-3
- Managing For Dummies
  0-7645-1771-6
- Marketing For Dummies
  0-7645-5600-2

- Personal Finance For Dummies
  0-7645-2590-5*
- Resumes For Dummies
  0-7645-5471-9
- Selling For Dummies
  0-7645-5363-1
- Six Sigma For Dummies
  0-7645-6798-5
- Small Business Kit For Dummies
  0-7645-5984-2
- Starting an eBay Business For Dummies
  0-7645-6924-4
- Your Dream Career For Dummies
  0-7645-9795-7

HOME & BUSINESS COMPUTER BASICS

0-470-05432-8   0-471-75421-8

Also available:
- Cleaning Windows Vista For Dummies
  0-471-78293-9
- Excel 2007 For Dummies
  0-470-03737-7
- Mac OS X Tiger For Dummies
  0-7645-7675-5
- MacBook For Dummies
  0-470-04859-X
- Macs For Dummies
  0-470-04849-2
- Office 2007 For Dummies
  0-470-00923-3

- Outlook 2007 For Dummies
  0-470-03830-6
- PCs For Dummies
  0-7645-8958-X
- Salesforce.com For Dummies
  0-470-04893-X
- Upgrading & Fixing Laptops For Dummies
  0-7645-8959-8
- Word 2007 For Dummies
  0-470-03658-3
- Quicken 2007 For Dummies
  0-470-04600-7

FOOD, HOME, GARDEN, HOBBIES, MUSIC & PETS

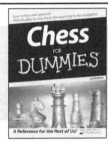

0-7645-8404-9   0-7645-9904-6

Also available:
- Candy Making For Dummies
  0-7645-9734-5
- Card Games For Dummies
  0-7645-9910-0
- Crocheting For Dummies
  0-7645-4151-X
- Dog Training For Dummies
  0-7645-8418-9
- Healthy Carb Cookbook For Dummies
  0-7645-8476-6
- Home Maintenance For Dummies
  0-7645-5215-5

- Horses For Dummies
  0-7645-9797-3
- Jewelry Making & Beading For Dummies
  0-7645-2571-9
- Orchids For Dummies
  0-7645-6759-4
- Puppies For Dummies
  0-7645-5255-4
- Rock Guitar For Dummies
  0-7645-5356-9
- Sewing For Dummies
  0-7645-6847-7
- Singing For Dummies
  0-7645-2475-5

INTERNET & DIGITAL MEDIA

0-470-04529-9   0-470-04894-8

Also available:
- Blogging For Dummies
  0-471-77084-1
- Digital Photography For Dummies
  0-7645-9802-3
- Digital Photography All-in-One Desk Reference For Dummies
  0-470-03743-1
- Digital SLR Cameras and Photography For Dummies
  0-7645-9803-1
- eBay Business All-in-One Desk Reference For Dummies
  0-7645-8438-3
- HDTV For Dummies
  0-470-09673-X

- Home Entertainment PCs For Dummies
  0-470-05523-5
- MySpace For Dummies
  0-470-09529-6
- Search Engine Optimization For Dummies
  0-471-97998-8
- Skype For Dummies
  0-470-04891-3
- The Internet For Dummies
  0-7645-8996-2
- Wiring Your Digital Home For Dummies
  0-471-91830-X

* Separate Canadian edition also available
† Separate U.K. edition also available

Available wherever books are sold. For more information or to order direct: U.S. customers visit www.dummies.com or call 1-877-762-2974.
U.K. customers visit www.wileyeurope.com or call 0800 243407. Canadian customers visit www.wiley.ca or call 1-800-567-4797.

 WILEY

SPORTS, FITNESS, PARENTING, RELIGION & SPIRITUALITY

0-471-76871-5

0-7645-7841-3

Also available:
- Catholicism For Dummies
  0-7645-5391-7
- Exercise Balls For Dummies
  0-7645-5623-1
- Fitness For Dummies
  0-7645-7851-0
- Football For Dummies
  0-7645-3936-1
- Judaism For Dummies
  0-7645-5299-6
- Potty Training For Dummies
  0-7645-5417-4
- Buddhism For Dummies
  0-7645-5359-3

- Pregnancy For Dummies
  0-7645-4483-7 †
- Ten Minute Tone-Ups For Dummies
  0-7645-7207-5
- NASCAR For Dummies
  0-7645-7681-X
- Religion For Dummies
  0-7645-5264-3
- Soccer For Dummies
  0-7645-5229-5
- Women in the Bible For Dummies
  0-7645-8475-8

TRAVEL

0-7645-7749-2

0-7645-6945-7

Also available:
- Alaska For Dummies
  0-7645-7746-8
- Cruise Vacations For Dummies
  0-7645-6941-4
- England For Dummies
  0-7645-4276-1
- Europe For Dummies
  0-7645-7529-5
- Germany For Dummies
  0-7645-7823-5
- Hawaii For Dummies
  0-7645-7402-7

- Italy For Dummies
  0-7645-7386-1
- Las Vegas For Dummies
  0-7645-7382-9
- London For Dummies
  0-7645-4277-X
- Paris For Dummies
  0-7645-7630-5
- RV Vacations For Dummies
  0-7645-4442-X
- Walt Disney World & Orlando
  For Dummies
  0-7645-9660-8

GRAPHICS, DESIGN & WEB DEVELOPMENT

0-7645-8815-X

0-7645-9571-7

Also available:
- 3D Game Animation For Dummies
  0-7645-8789-7
- AutoCAD 2006 For Dummies
  0-7645-8925-3
- Building a Web Site For Dummies
  0-7645-7144-3
- Creating Web Pages For Dummies
  0-470-08030-2
- Creating Web Pages All-in-One Desk
  Reference For Dummies
  0-7645-4345-8
- Dreamweaver 8 For Dummies
  0-7645-9649-7

- InDesign CS2 For Dummies
  0-7645-9572-5
- Macromedia Flash 8 For Dummies
  0-7645-9691-8
- Photoshop CS2 and Digital
  Photography For Dummies
  0-7645-9580-6
- Photoshop Elements 4 For Dummies
  0-471-77483-9
- Syndicating Web Sites with RSS Feeds
  For Dummies
  0-7645-8848-6
- Yahoo! SiteBuilder For Dummies
  0-7645-9800-7

NETWORKING, SECURITY, PROGRAMMING & DATABASES

0-7645-7728-X

0-471-74940-0

Also available:
- Access 2007 For Dummies
  0-470-04612-0
- ASP.NET 2 For Dummies
  0-7645-7907-X
- C# 2005 For Dummies
  0-7645-9704-3
- Hacking For Dummies
  0-470-05235-X
- Hacking Wireless Networks
  For Dummies
  0-7645-9730-2
- Java For Dummies
  0-470-08716-1

- Microsoft SQL Server 2005 For Dummies
  0-7645-7755-7
- Networking All-in-One Desk Reference
  For Dummies
  0-7645-9939-9
- Preventing Identity Theft For Dummies
  0-7645-7336-5
- Telecom For Dummies
  0-471-77085-X
- Visual Studio 2005 All-in-One Desk
  Reference For Dummies
  0-7645-9775-2
- XML For Dummies
  0-7645-8845-1

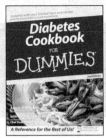
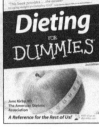

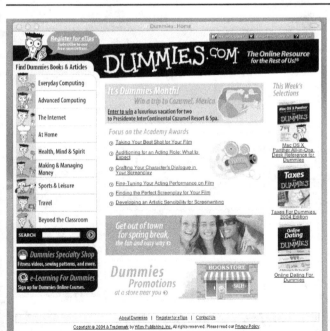

Microsoft® Expression Web For Dummies®

Cheat Sheet

Common CSS Properties

You specify which properties to use in Expression Web in the New/Modify Style dialog box and the CSS Properties task pane. This table lists many CSS properties available in Expression Web.

Font

Property	How or Where to Select It	What It Modifies or Determines
font-family	Choose from list box (`Arial`, `Helvetica`, `sans-serif`)	Font (typeface) of an element's text
font-size	Choose relative size (`xx-small`, `medium`, `x-large`), `larger`, `smaller`, or enter value	Size of an element's text
font-weight	`normal`, `bold`, `lighter`, `bolder` or a numeric value	Weight of an element's text characters
font-style	`italic`, `normal`, `oblique`	Italic or oblique (slanted) characters for an element's text characters
font-variant	`normal`, `small-caps`	Text element's characters to small capitals (or normal)
text-transform	`capitalize`, `lowercase`, `none`, `uppercase`	Text element's capitalization
Color	Enter color value	Color of an element's foreground (usually text)
text-decoration	`underline`, `overline`, `line-through`, `blink`, `none`	Character decoration for an element's text

Block

Property	How or Where to Select It	What It Modifies or Determines
line-height	`normal` or enter value	Amount of space between lines of text within an element
vertical-align	Pick position or enter value	Vertical alignment of text within lines of text or table cell
text-align	`center`, `justify`, `left`, `right`	How text aligns within a block-level element
text-indent	Enter value	Indentation for first line of text in an element
word-spacing	`normal` or enter value	Amount of space between words within an element
letter-spacing	`normal` or enter value	Amount of space between text characters within an element

Background

Property	How or Where to Select It	What It Modifies or Determines
background-color	Enter color value	Solid color of an element's background
background-image	Enter image file URL	Image to use for the element's background
background-repeat	`no-repeat`, `repeat`, `repeat-x`, `repeat-y`	Background image repeat and direction (x horizontal, y vertical)
background-attachment	`fixed`, `scroll`	Background image scrolling in browser window
background-position	`center`, `left`, `right` (x)/`bottom`, `center`, `top` (y), or enter value	Horizontal (x) and vertical (y) position from which repeated background image starts

For Dummies: Bestselling Book Series for Beginners

Microsoft® Expression Web For Dummies®

Cheat Sheet

Border

Property	How or Where to Select It	What It Modifies or Determines
border-style	Choose line style	Line style for a box's borders or individual border side
border-width	thin, medium, thick, or enter value	Width for a box's borders or individual border side
border-color	Enter color value	Color for a box's borders or individual border side

Box

Property	How or Where to Select It	What It Modifies or Determines
Padding	Enter value	CSS box padding values for element or for each side of an element (space between content and border)
Margin	Enter value	CSS box margin values for element or for each side of an element (space between border and surrounding elements)

Position

Property	How or Where to Select It	What It Modifies or Determines
Position	absolute, fixed, relative, static	How element is positioned in relation to document flow
Top	Enter value	Offset between top outer margin edge and top edge of containing block (absolute positioned element)
Right	Enter value	Offset between right outer margin edge and right edge of containing block (absolute positioned element)
Bottom	Enter value	Offset between bottom outer margin edge and bottom edge of containing block (absolute positioned element)
Left	Enter value	Offset between left outer margin edge and left edge of containing block (absolute positioned element)
Width	auto, enter value	Width of element's content area
Height	auto, enter value	Height of element's content area
z-index	auto, enter number	Position of stacked elements; higher number values stacked on top of lower numbers

Layout

Property	How or Where to Select It	What It Modifies or Determines
Float	left, right, none	Direction an element moves so that other elements can flow around it
Clear	left, right, both, none	On which side of element no floated elements can appear
Display	Choose value	Display box of an element; commonly used to change a block-level element to inline and vice versa

List

Property	How or Where to Select It	What It Modifies or Determines
list-style-type	none, choose value	Bullet or counting number/letter style for list items
list-style-image	Enter image file URL	Image file to use as list bullet
list-style-position	inside, outside	Position of list item bullets/characters in relation to left text edge

For Dummies: Bestselling Book Series for Beginners

CPSIA information can be obtained
at www.ICGtesting.com
Printed in the USA
LVHW062303250119
605364LV00019B/245/P